Lecture Notes in Computer Science 11373

Commenced Publication in 1973
Founding and Former Series Editors:
Gerhard Goos, Juris Hartmanis, and Jan van Leeuwen

More information about this series at http://www.springer.com/series/7409

Meikang Qiu (Ed.)

Smart Blockchain

First International Conference, SmartBlock 2018
Tokyo, Japan, December 10–12, 2018
Proceedings

 Springer

Editor
Meikang Qiu (iD)
Columbia University
New York, NY, USA

ISSN 0302-9743   ISSN 1611-3349 (electronic)
Lecture Notes in Computer Science
ISBN 978-3-030-05763-3   ISBN 978-3-030-05764-0 (eBook)
https://doi.org/10.1007/978-3-030-05764-0

Library of Congress Control Number: 2018963971

LNCS Sublibrary: SL3 – Information Systems and Applications, incl. Internet/Web, and HCI

This Springer imprint is published by the registered company Springer Nature Switzerland AG
The registered company address is: Gewerbestrasse 11, 6330 Cham, Switzerland

Preface

This volume contains the papers presented at SmartBlock 2018: the International Conference on Smart Blockchain 2018 held during December 10–12, 2018 in Tokyo.

There were 105 submissions. Each submission was reviewed by at least three, and on average four, Program Committee members. The committee decided to accept 18 papers.

The recent rapid development of blockchain has attracted major attention by both academia and industry. Migrating a centralized computing to decentralized computing seems to be a main stream to establish a trust and secure a storage and trading environment. However, it is too early to make a solid statement about the adoption of blockchain technology, since there are many unsolved problems in the field. The success of blockchain technique in Bitcoin does not mean the technique can be successfully deployed in all domains. This international conference aims to gather the most up-to-date papers in the field of blockchain and provides a platform for both scholars and practitioners.

The scope of SmartBlock covers a broad range of topics related to blockchain realms, from privacy-preserving solutions to designing advanced blockchain mechanism, from empirical studies to practical manuuals. All high-quality current work is highly welcomed!

SmartBlock 2018 was organized by the SmartBlock 2018 Committees. We warmly thank the conference sponsors: Springer LNCS, Waseda University, Columbia University, Beijing Institute of Technology, UINP Global Community, Birmingham City University, LD Research Inc., North America Chinese Talents Association, and Longxiang High Tech Group Inc.

November 2018   Meikang Qiu

Organization

General Chairs

Liehuang Zhu	Beijing Institute of Technology, China
Mak Sharma	Birmingham City University, UK
Meikang Qiu	Columbia University, USA

Program Chairs

Keke Gai	Beijing Institute of Technology, China
Paul Kearney	Birmingham City University, UK

Industry Chairs

Yonghao Wang	Birmingham City University, UK
Wei Hu	Wuhan University of Science and Technology, China

Local Chairs

Cheng Zhang	Waseda University, Japan
Celimuge Wu	University of Electro-Communications, Japan

Publicity Chairs

Peng Li	Aizu University, Japan
Suhua Tang	University of Electro-Communications, Japan

Host Chair

Zhi Liu	Shizuoka University, Japan

Technical Program Committee

Vitor Jesus	Birmingham City University, UK
Xin Li	Duke University, USA
Sang-Yoon Chang	Advanced Digital Sciences Center, Singapore
Jinjun Xiong	IBM Research, USA
Emmanuel Bernardez	IBM Research, USA
Yan Zhang	University of Oslo, Norway
Haibo Zhang	University of Otago, New Zealand
Suman Kumar	Troy University, USA
Bharat Rawal	Pennsylvania State University, USA

Contents

Hiding Bitcoin Transaction Information Based on HEVC

Si Liu, Yunxia Liu$^{(\boxtimes)}$, Guoning Lv, Cong Feng, and Hongguo Zhao

College of Information Science and Technology, Zhengzhou Normal University,
Zhengzhou, China
liuyunxia0110@hust.edu.cn

Abstract. Blockchain technology in Bitcoin is a decentralized, de-trusted, open and transparent distributed data storage technology that can reduce trust costs and achieve secure and reliable data interaction. However, an attacker can easily obtain all the Bitcoin transaction information from a public global ledger and use big-data analysis techniques to mine private information such as user transaction laws. Therefore, it is necessary to hide some of the transaction information in the public data. This paper presents a Bitcoin transaction information hiding algorithm based on HEVC without intra-frame distortion drift. We embed the specified transaction data into the three-tuple of the 4×4 luminance DST blocks which meet our conditions to avert the distortion drift. With the cross using of multiple three-tuple, the visual quality of the embedded video had a better promotion than using single three-tuple. The experimental results show that this new data hiding algorithm can effectively avert intra-frame distortion drift and get good visual quality.

Keywords: Bitcoin · HEVC · Data hiding · Blockchain
Intra-frame distortion drift

1 Introduction

In the digital currency world, security issues have always been a concern. Since the birth of Bitcoin, the originator of digital currency, many stolen incidents have occurred, causing major losses. Moreover, in the event of a bitcoin theft, the loss is not only the property of the direct victim, but also the impact on the entire bitcoin market, leading to significant fluctuations in the price of the bitcoin [1]. Each Bitcoin node maintains an exact copy of a distributed ledger called blockchain. The blockchain is a database used to store the transactions. Several transactions that are sent into the network in a period of time are grouped into a block. The newly created block is then chained to the preceded block as such that all of the created blocks create a chain-like logical structure.

However, the global ledger that records Bitcoin transaction information in the blockchain is public in the network, and any attacker can obtain all transaction information, leaving the trader's privacy risk of disclosure. By analyzing and arranging the data in the ledger, the attacker can obtain all the transactions corresponding to any account, and can also analyze the trading relationship map between different accounts.

M. Qiu (Ed.): SmartBlock 2018, LNCS 11373, pp. 1–11, 2018.
https://doi.org/10.1007/978-3-030-05764-0_1

Even if users use different accounts for transactions, attackers can use address clustering techniques to analyze different accounts belonging to the same user. And since every Bitcoin transaction made by the user will be permanently recorded in the blockchain, once a historical transaction is real-named (for example, a bitcoin transaction is hacked, resulting in user account information leakage), then relevant trader identification information in all transaction records will be disclosed [2]. In addition, as blockchain transactions are increasingly applied to the daily payments field, attackers can use the extra-chain information to infer the identity of accounts in the blockchain. For example, the user's shopping record and the Bitcoin account payment record are compared, and the identity information of the account is analyzed.

For privacy stealing methods based on data analysis, some privacy protection mechanisms have emerged. The main idea is to hide some of the information in the public data without affecting the normal operation of the blockchain system, and to increase the difficulty of data analysis. HEVC is the latest and most advanced standard for video compression with high compression efficiency [3]. It is well adapted for network transmission. [4]. In order to protect the privacy and security of Bitcoin transactions, this paper uses HEVC video to hide transaction information.

However, intra-frame distortion drift is a big problem of data hiding in HEVC video streams. From the beginning of the H.264/AVC period, some researchers have proposed methods for without intra-frame distortion drift data hiding algorithm [5–9]. The method proposed in [5] employed the paired-coefficients of a 4×4 DCT block for embedding data to compensate the intra-frame distortion, which is readable and covert. The method proposed in [6], which improve the algorithm [5], employed the paired-coefficients and the directions of intra-frame prediction to avert the distortion drift. However, these algorithms developed based on H.264/AVC cannot be applied to HEVC [10–13]. Especially for the 4×4 luminance blocks in HEVC, where the DST (discrete sine transform) is used instead of DCT. To solve the DST coefficient distortion drift problem in HEVC, [14, 15] proposed a group of three-tuple which had a similar effect to the paired-coefficients used in [6]. But this single three-tuple will cause some obvious image hot pixels that greatly affects the visual quality of the video.

In this paper, a Bitcoin transaction information hiding algorithm based on HEVC is proposed. We find out a coefficient compensation rule and some other three-tuple whose coefficients meeting this rule would applicable to 4×4 luminance DST blocks for embedding transaction information to compensate the intra-frame distortion, and the random embedding strategy is applied to these three-tuple in order to improve the visual quality of the video.

The rest of the paper is organized as follows. Section 2 describes the theoretical framework of the proposed algorithm. Section 3 describes the proposed algorithm. Experimental results are presented in Sect. 4 and conclusions are in Sect. 5.

2 Theoretical Framework

2.1 Bitcoin Transaction Information

A Bitcoin transaction is constructed by series of mathematical puzzle which will be evaluated by the system. The mathematical puzzle is built by using Bitcoin Operation Codes (OpCodes) to determine what the system should do with the data. A bitcoin transaction consists of two parts: ScriptSig and ScriptPubKey. The ScriptSig is a requirement that needs to be fulfilled by the redeem transaction, while ScriptPubKey is the answer to the requirement of the referenced transaction.

Several types of Bitcoin transactions are: Pay To Address (P2A), Pay To Script Hash (P2SH), and Null Data [1]. P2A is a transaction that pays to a Bitcoin Address, P2SH is a transaction that pays to a predetermined script, while Null Data does not actually pay but rather a mechanism to embed a metadata to the transaction. The user can choose which part of the Bitcoin transaction data to be embedded into the HEVC video.

2.2 Intra-frame Prediction

A prediction block of HEVC intra prediction method is formed based on previously encoded adjacent blocks. The sixteen pixels in the 4 × 4 block are predicted by using the boundary pixels of the upper and left blocks which are previously obtained, which use a prediction formula corresponding to the selected optimal prediction mode, as shown in Fig. 1.

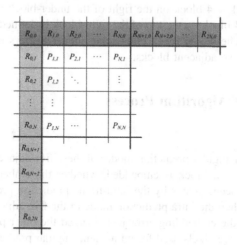

Fig. 1. Labeling of prediction samples

2.3 Intra-frame Distortion Drift

The intra-frame distortion drift emerges because we embed bits into I frames. As illustrated in Fig. 2, we assume that current prediction block is $B_{i,j}$, then each sample of

$B_{i,j}$ is the sum of the predicted value and the residual value. Since the predicted value is calculated by using the samples which are gray in Fig. 2. The embedding induced errors in blocks $B_{i-1,j-1}$, $B_{i,j-1}$, $B_{i-1,j}$, and $B_{i-1,j+1}$would propagate to $B_{i,j}$ because of using intra-frame prediction. This visual distortion that accumulates from the upper left to the lower right is defined as intra-frame distortion drift.

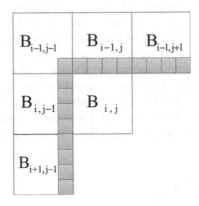

Fig. 2. The prediction block $B_{i,j}$ and the adjacent encoded blocks

For convenience, we give several definitions, the 4×4 block on the right of the current block is defined as right-block; the 4×4 block under the current block is defined as under-block; the 4×4 block on the left of the under-block is defined as under-left-block; the 4×4 block on the right of the under-block is defined as under-right-block; the 4×4 block on the top of the right-block is defined as top-right-block, as shown in Fig. 3. The 4×4 block embedding induced errors transfer through the edge pixels to these five adjacent blocks.

3   Description of Algorithm Process

3.1   Embedding

According to the intra angular prediction modes of these five adjacent blocks, it can be judged that if the current block is embedded, whether the embedding error will be transmitted to the adjacent blocks by the intra-frame prediction process.

In other words, when the intra prediction mode of the five adjacent blocks satisfies certain conditions, if the embedding error just changed the other pixels of the current block instead of the edge pixels used for intra-frame angular prediction reference, then the distortion drift can be avoided. We proposed two conditions to prevent the distortion drift specifically.

Condition1:   Right-mode $\in \{2\text{–}25\}$,   under-right-mode $\in \{11\text{–}25\}$,   top-right-mode $\in \{2\text{–}9\}$

Condition2: under-left-mode $\in \{27\text{–}34\}$, under-mode $\in \{11\text{–}34\}$.

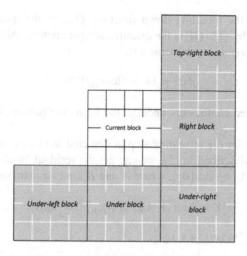

Fig. 3. Definition of adjacent blocks

If the current block meets Condition1, the pixel values of the last column should not be changed in the following intra-frame prediction. If the current block meets Condition 2, the pixel values of the last row should not be changed in the following intra-frame prediction. If the current block meets the Condition 1 and 2 at the same time, the current block should not be embedded. If both the Condition 1 and 2 cannot be satisfied, the current block can be arbitrarily embedded where the induced errors won't transfer through the edge pixels to the five adjacent blocks, that means the distortion drift won't happen, but in this paper we don't discuss this situation, the current block should also not be embedded.

The integer discrete sine transform (IST) which is developed from the DST is used in HEVC standard. The transform based on 4×4 blocks is shown in (1). $D_{4\times4}$ is the matrix of unscaled DST coefficients corresponding to the residual block $R_{4\times4}$. The "core" IST transform between D and R can be expressed in a matrix form (1):

$$D = C_f R C_f^T /(128 * 128) \tag{1}$$

Where

$$C_f = \begin{pmatrix} 29 & 55 & 74 & 84 \\ 74 & 74 & 0 & -74 \\ 84 & -29 & -74 & 55 \\ 55 & -84 & 74 & -29 \end{pmatrix}$$

Then the post-scaling and quantization process is shown in (2):

$$\tilde{Y} = \text{floor}\left(D \cdot \frac{2^{qbits}}{Q_{step}}\right) \gg shift \tag{2}$$

Where floor() is the rounding down function, Q_{step} is the quantization step size which is determined by QP (QP is the quantization parameter), *shift* is the offset, *qbits* is an intermediate variable as shown in (3):

$$qbits = 14 + \text{floor}(QP/6) \tag{3}$$

Then the quantized coefficients undergo the following process in encoder such as entropy encoding.

At the decoder, after the re-scaling step as depicted in (4), the inverse IST and the post-scaling step as described in (5), we can get the residual block R'. (In this paper, $A = \text{floor}[B]$ means $A_{ij} = \text{floor}[B_{ij}]$, where A and B are two matrixes.)

$$Y = \text{floor}\left(\tilde{Y} \times 2^6 \times Q_{step}\right) \gg shift \tag{4}$$

$$
\begin{aligned}
R' &= C_f^T Y C_f / (128 * 128) \\
&= \text{floor}\left[\left(C_f^T \tilde{Y} C_f \times 2^6 \times Q_{step}\right) \gg shift\right] / (128 * 128)
\end{aligned}
\tag{5}
$$

In data hiding algorithm, the encoded information is embedded into the quantized luminance DST coefficients as shown in (6):

$$\tilde{Y}' = \tilde{Y} + \Delta \tag{6}$$

Where Δ is the error matrix added to the quantized DST coefficient matrix $Y_{4\times4}$ by data hiding, $\Delta = (a_{ij})_{4\times4}$.

After the re-scaling step as depicted in (7), the inverse IST and the post-scaling step as described in (8) of the decoder, we can get the residual block R'' after embedding Δ.

$$
\begin{aligned}
Y &= \text{floor}\left(\tilde{Y}' \times 2^6 \times Q_{step}\right) \gg shift \\
&= \text{floor}\left(\tilde{Y} \times 2^6 \times Q_{step}\right) \gg shift \\
&\quad + \text{floor}\left(\Delta \times 2^6 \times Q_{step}\right) \gg shift
\end{aligned}
\tag{7}
$$

$$
\begin{aligned}
R'' &= C_f^T Y C_f / (128 * 128) \\
&= \text{floor}\left[\left(C_f^T \tilde{Y} C_f \times 2^6 \times Q_{step}\right) \gg shift\right] / (128 * 128) \\
&\quad + \text{floor}\left[\left(C_f^T \Delta C_f \times 2^6 \times Q_{step}\right) \gg shift\right] / (128 * 128)
\end{aligned}
\tag{8}
$$

The deviation of the pixel luminance value between the original block and the one after embedding is $E_{4\times4}$, where $E_{4\times4} = (e_{ij})_{4\times4}$, which can be calculated according to (9).

$$
\begin{aligned}
E &= R'' - R' \\
&= \text{floor}\left[\left(C_f^T \Delta C_f \times 2^6 \times Q_{step}\right) \gg shift\right] / (128 * 128)
\end{aligned}
\tag{9}
$$

Using $B (B = (b_{ij})_{4 \times 4})$ to express $C_f^T \Delta C_f$ when the Δ meets the conditions as making $b_{i3} = 0 (i = 0, 1, 2, 3)$ or $b_{3j} = 0 (j = 0, 1, 2, 3)$, the distortion drift can be prevented as mentioned above. We proposed some three-tuple can meet the above conditions when embedded in.

The three-tuple can be defined as a three-coefficient combination (C_1, C_2, C_3), C_1 is used for bit embedding, and C_2, C_3 are used for distortion compensation. There are two group three-tuple we used in this paper that applicable to 4×4 luminance DST blocks, we can define them as follow:

VS(Vertical Set) = $(a_{i0} = 1, a_{i1} = -2, a_{i3} = 8)$, $(a_{i0} = 1, a_{i2} = -1, a_{i3} = 1)$ $(i = 0, 1, 2, 3)$

HS(Horizontal Set) = $(a_{0j} = 1, a_{1j} = -2, a_{3j} = 8)$, $(a_{0j} = 1, a_{2j} = -1, a_{3j} = 1)$ $(j = 0, 1, 2, 3)$

In fact, we found a coefficient compensation rule can create more usable three-tuple. We can define it as follow:

Vertical Rule

If the embedding coefficients of any row in a 4×4 DST block meet

$$84a_{i0} - 74a_{i1} + 55_{i2} - 29a_{i3} = 0 \, (i = 0, 1, 2, 3)$$

Then the pixel values of the last column in the 4×4 luminance block would not be changed by the embedding.

Horizontal Rule

If the embedding coefficients of any column in a 4×4 DST block meet

$$84a_{0j} - 74a_{1j} + 55a_{2j} - 29a_{3j} = 0 \, (j = 0, 1, 2, 3)$$

Then the pixel values of the last row in the 4×4 luminance block would not be changed by the embedding.

As we can see, the three-tuple $(a_{i0} = 1, a_{i1} = -2, a_{i3} = 8)$, $(a_{i0} = 1, a_{i2} = -1, a_{i3} = 1)$ $(i = 0, 1, 2, 3)$ meet the Vertical Rule, the three-tuple $(a_{0j} = 1, a_{1j} = -2, a_{3j} = 8)$, $(a_{0j} = 1, a_{2j} = -1, a_{3j} = 1)$ $(j = 0, 1, 2, 3)$ meet the Horizontal Rule. According to the coefficient compensation rule, we can even create some four-tuple to prevent the intra-frame distortion, but relatively speaking, these two three-tuple we used have better PSNR performance.

After the original video is entropy decoded, we get the intra-frame prediction modes and quantized DST coefficients. We embed the hiding data by the three-tuple into the 4×4 luminance DST blocks of the selected frames which meet the conditions. Finally, all the quantized DST coefficients are entropy encoded to get the target embedded video.

We can select $(a_{i0} = 1, a_{i1} = -2, a_{i3} = 8)$, $(a_{i0} = 1, a_{i2} = -1, a_{i3} = 1)$ $(i = 0, 1, 2, 3)$ to embed one bit in a row when current block meets Condition 1, we also can select $(a_{0j} = 1, a_{1j} = -2, a_{3j} = 8)$, $(a_{0j} = 1, a_{2j} = -1, a_{3j} = 1)$ $(j = 0, 1, 2, 3)$ to embed one bit in a column when current block meets Condition 2. Since only using single three-tuple mode like $(1, -1, 1)$ in [15] to embed will easily lead to significant visual hot pixels, in this paper we randomly cross-use the $(1, -1, 1)$ and $(1, -2, 8)$ modes in order to solve this problem.

Assume (a_1, a_2, a_3) is the selected quantized DST coefficients to be embedded, where a_1 is used to hide information, a_2, a_3 are used to compensate the intra-frame distortion. We take the three-tuple $(1, -1, 1)$ as an example.

(1) If the embedded bit is 1, a_1, a_2, a_3 are modified as follows:
    If a_1 **mod2** $= 0$, then $a_1 = a_1 + 1$, $a_2 = a_2 - 1$, $a_3 = a_3 + 1$. If a_1 **mod2** $\neq 0$, then $a_1 = a_1$, $a_2 = a_2$, $a_3 = a_3$.
(2) If the embedded *bit* is 0, a_1, a_2, a_3 are modified as follows:
    If a_1 **mod2** $\neq 0$, then $a_1 = a_1 + 1$, $a_2 = a_2 - 1$, $a_3 = a_3 + 1$. If a_1 **mod2** $= 0$, then $a_1 = a_1$, $a_2 = a_2$, $a_3 = a_3$.

3.2 Data Extraction and Restoration

After entropy decoding of the HEVC, we choose the embeddable blocks of one frame and decode the embedded Bitcoin transaction information. Then, we extract the hidden data M as follows, $(i = 0, 1, 2, 3)$:

$$M = \begin{cases} 1 & \text{if } \tilde{Y}_{i0} \text{mod2} = 1 \quad \text{and} \quad \text{current} \quad \text{block} \quad \text{meet} \quad \text{condition} \quad 1 \\ 0 & \text{if } \tilde{Y}_{i0} \text{mod2} = 0 \quad \text{and} \quad \text{current} \quad \text{block} \quad \text{meet} \quad \text{condition} \quad 1 \end{cases}$$

$$M = \begin{cases} 1 & \text{if } \tilde{Y}_{0i} \text{mod2} = 1 \quad \text{and} \quad \text{current} \quad \text{block} \quad \text{meet} \quad \text{condition} \quad 2 \\ 0 & \text{if } \tilde{Y}_{0i} \text{mod2} = 0 \quad \text{and} \quad \text{current} \quad \text{block} \quad \text{meet} \quad \text{condition} \quad 2 \end{cases}$$

4 Case Study

The proposed method has been implemented in the HEVC reference software version HM16.0. In this paper we take "Keiba" (416 * 240), "Basketball" (416 * 240) and "Akiyo" (176 * 144) as test video. The GOP size is set to 1 and the values of QP are set to be 16, 24, 32 and 40. Since we can embed 4 bits Bitcoin transaction information in one 4×4 luminance DST block with randomly use $(1, -1, 1)$ or $(1, -2, 8)$ mode, in this paper we set the using probability of $(1, -1, 1)$ mode is 0.75, the using probability of $(1, -2, 8)$ mode is 0.25. Because the $(1, -1, 1)$ mode have a better PSNR than $(1, -2, 8)$ mode, but only using single triple-coefficients mode will easily lead to significant visual hot pixels. The method in [15] only using $(1, -1, 1)$ mode is used for performance comparisons.

As shown in Table 1, the PSNR of the method used in [15] is slightly lower than the method proposed in our paper. Also its visual effect is worse than our method, as we can see in Fig. 5, there are some significant visual hot pixels on the pictures.

Table 1. PSNR (dB) of embedded frame in each video sequences

Sequences	Method	QP = 16	QP = 24	QP = 32	QP = 40
Keiba	In this paper	47.12	40.38	36.94	31.16
	In [15]	46.62	39.16	35.13	30.48
Basketball	In this paper	48.31	41.25	37.13	32.45
	In [15]	46.98	40.23	35.86	31.79
Akiyo	In this paper	48.41	40.88	36.42	31.78
	In [15]	47.19	40.10	35.56	31.23

Fig. 4. Method in this paper (QP = 24)

Fig. 5. Method in [15] (QP = 24)

With the increase of QP value, the quality of the decoded image and the embedded image are reduced. Because the single using of the three-tuple $(1, -1, 1)$ sometimes will greatly change several fixed pixels in 4×4 luminance DST blocks, which is easy to cause significant hot pixels when the QP value is big. However, adding another set of three-tuple can significantly improve this visual problem, as shown in Fig. 4.

5   Conclusion

This paper proposed a Bitcoin transaction information hiding algorithm based on HEVC. Coefficient compensation rule and the hybrid three-tuple are utilized to prevent the intra-frame distortion drift. With the cross using of multiple three-tuple, this method can get better visual effects than only using single three-tuple. Experimental results demonstrate the feasibility and superiority of the proposed method.

Acknowledgment. This paper is sponsored by the National Natural Science Foundation of China (NSFC, Grant 61572447).

References

1. Wijaya, D.A., Suwarsono, D.A.: Securing digital evidence information in bitcoin. Technical report, Monash University Melbourne, Australia (2016)
2. Androulaki, E., Karame, G.O.: Hiding transaction amounts and balances in bitcoin. In: Holz, T., Ioannidis, S. (eds.) Trust 2014. LNCS, vol. 8564, pp. 161–178. Springer, Cham (2014). https://doi.org/10.1007/978-3-319-08593-7_11
3. Shaikh, S., Sayyad, S.: Data hiding in encrypted HEVC/AVC video streams. Int. J. Adv. Res. Comput. Commun. Eng. **5**(8), 60–65 (2016)
4. Kim, I., Min, J., Lee, T., Han, W., Park, J.: Block partitioning structure in the HEVC standard. IEEE Trans. Circ. Syst. Video Technol. **22**(12), 1697–1706 (2012)
5. Ma, X.J., Li, Z.T., Lv, J., Wang, W.D.: Data hiding in H.264/AVC streams with limited intra-frame distortion drift. In: Computer Network and Multimedia Technology, CNMT (2009)
6. Ma, X.J., Li, Z.T., Tu, H., Zhang, B.: A data hiding algorithm for H.264/AVC video streams without intra frame distortion drift. IEEE Trans. Circ. Syst. Video Technol. **20**(10), 1320–1330 (2010)
7. Liu, Y.X., Li, Z.T., Ma, X.J.: Reversible data hiding scheme based on H.264/AVC without distortion drift. J. Syst. Softw. **7**(5), 1059–1065 (2012)
8. Liu, Y.X., Li, Z.T., Ma, X.J., Liu, J.: A robust without intra-frame distortion drift data hiding algorithm based on H.264/AVC. Multimed. Tools Appl. **72**(1), 613–636 (2014)
9. Liu, Y.X., Li, Z.T., Ma, X.J., Liu, J.: A robust data hiding algorithm for H.264/AVC video streams. J. Syst. Softw. **86**(8), 2174–2183 (2013)
10. Liu, Y.X., Hu, M.S., Ma, X.J., Zhao, H.G.: A new robust data hiding method for H.264/AVC without intra-frame distortion drift. Neurocomputing **151**, 1076–1085 (2015)
11. Liu, Y.X., Ju, L.M., Hu, M.S., Ma, X.J., Zhao, H.G.: A robust reversible data hiding scheme for H.264 without distortion drift. Neurocomputing **151**, 1053–1062 (2015)
12. Liu, Y., Jia, S., Hu, M., Jia, Z., Chen, L., Zhao, H.: A robust reversible data hiding scheme for H.264 based on secret sharing. In: Huang, D.-S., Bevilacqua, V., Premaratne, P. (eds.) ICIC 2014. LNCS, vol. 8588, pp. 553–559. Springer, Cham (2014). https://doi.org/10.1007/978-3-319-09333-8_61
13. Liu, Y.X., Jia, S.M., Hu, M.S., Jia, Z.J., Chen, L., Zhao, H.G.: A reversible data hiding method for H.264 with Shamir's (t, n)-threshold secret sharing. Neurocomputing **188**, 63–70 (2016)

14. Chang, P.-C., Chung, K.-L., Chen, J.-J., Lin, C.-H., et al.: A DCT/DST-based error propagation-free data hiding algorithm for HEVC intra-coded frames. J. Vis. Commun. Image Represent. **25**(2), 239–253 (2013)
15. Chang, P.-C., Chung, K.-L., Chen, J.-J., Lin, C.-H.: An error propagation free data hiding algorithm in HEVC intra-coded frames. In: Signal & Information Processing Association Summit & Conference, pp. 1–9 (2013)

A New Sustainable Interchain Design on Transport Layer for Blockchain

Jing Wu[1,2]($\boxtimes$), Xin Cui[3], Wei Hu[1,2], Keke Gai[4], Xing Liu[1], Kai Zhang[1], and Kai Xu[4]

[1] College of Computer Science, Wuhan University of Science and Technology, Wuhan, Hubei, China
1633270529@qq.com, {huwei,liuxing1975,zhangkai}@wust.edu.cn
[2] Hubei Province Key Laboratory of Intelligent Information Processing and Real-Time Industrial System, Wuhan, China
[3] UINP Lab, Hangzhou, Zhejiang, China
scofield@uinp.io
[4] School of Computer Science and Technology, Beijing Institute of Technology, Beijing, China
{gaikeke,3220180758}@bit.edu.cn

Abstract. Blockchain is the technology architecture to provide reliable and trustworthy services for the transactions on Internet. Blockchain can remove the middleman or the third parties from the chain of the transactions, which will make the sellers and buyers complete the transactions directly without the help from the other parties. When blockchains are widely used in different areas, a problem is emerging: how to exchange the information among different blockchains. Traditionally, a public blockchain is used to link to the two blockchains which need to exchange their information. Such design can provide a solution to the cross-chain problem. However, there will be three blockchains involved in the data exchange. In this article, a cross-chain protocol is proposed to solve the cross-chain problem. This cross-chain protocol is called Unitary Interchain Network Protocol on Transport Layer (UINP), which supports cross-chain mechanism from the transport-layer. UINP is used in Unitary Blockchain network, and it can give the low latency convenience to blockchain networks that built on the application-layer.

Keywords: Blockchain · Network protocol-transport layer
UINP application-layer protocol · UINP transport-layer protocol

1 Introduction

With the development of network technology, online payment has become an important means of trading, especially for financial institutions. At the same

This work is partially supported by the Basic and Frontier Technology Research of Henan Province Science and Technology Department (No. 162300410198), and is partially supported by the National Science Foundation of China under Grant 61472293.

© Springer Nature Switzerland AG 2018
M. Qiu (Ed.): SmartBlock 2018, LNCS 11373, pp. 12–21, 2018.
https://doi.org/10.1007/978-3-030-05764-0_2

time, more efficient payment methods are still required to enhance the performance of the transactions. Most of the existing payment methods are based on
the trust of financial institutions and related third-party software. Although most
transactions are secured, there are still certain trading risks. Paying in Bitcoin is
an effective way to reduce this threat [1]. New design should be provided to deal
with the risks and improve the efficiency of the transactions. Bitcoin first introduced by Nakamoto [2], which uses the P2P network structure to enable mutual
communication between the two parties of the transaction [3], and can eliminate
the need for a series of liquidation processes by intermediate third-party trading
institutions [4]. Meanwhile, Bitcoin can also prevent double-flowering problems
[5]by using digital signatures, block such transactions without issuers, and avoid
the manipulation of currency by third-party institutions [6].

However, due to the advantages of Bitcoin in online transactions, the research
on the storage mode blockchain of Bitcoin has not stopped because of the decline
of Bitcoin [7]. On the basis of Bitcoin, it has expanded such as Bitcoin-NG [8].
The new blockchain agreement and the blockchain application market is also
constantly expanding. As a bitcoin-originated technology, blockchain is a distributed, reliable, secure, and continuously growing distributed ledger [9], which
is the underlying fabric for various cryptocurrencies to record transactions in a
verifiable and permanent way acrossing a peer-to-peer network of participants
[10]. Blockchain leverages cryptographic protocols and distributed consensus
algorithms to provide key characteristics, such as decentralization, anonymity,
auditability, data immutability, and non-repudiation [11].

Blockchain is recognized to be able to solve complex technical or socio-
economic problems [12]. There is a great interest in applying Blockchains
approaches to other use cases [13–18]. The popularity and rapid development
of Blockchain also bring many technical challenges for research communities
[19,20]. The urgent one is how to solve the cross-chain problem. This is also the
focus of this paper.

2   Related Work

Recently, cryptocurrencies and various blockchain systems have received significant attention in both academia and industry. The blockchain is becoming a
hot area of technology research as virtual currencies such as bitcoin skyrocket.
It is believed that the blockchain that creates the bitcoin phenomenon is with a
much broader application prospect [11]. The rapid development of Bitcoin in the
past few years has in turn verified that the blockchain technology can achieve
trusted peer-to-peer value transmission without relying on third-party trusted
intermediary structures. Ethereum is proposed as the blockchain platform [21],
which is used to sign the smart contracts [22].

Although there are still various doubts, a common view is that blockchain
technology is the prototype of the next generation of cloud computing, and it is
expected to completely reshape human social activities like the Internet and realize the Internet from the current information Internet to the value Internet [23].

Although there is no well-established definition of blockchain, the blockchain technology usually refers to distributed storage, consensus mechanism, encryption algorithm, point-to-point transmission and so on [11].

From a technical point of view, the core elements of the blockchain contain three aspects: first,blockchain structure, that is, each block has a timestamp, and each block uses the hash encryption information of the previous block to verify each transaction; Multiple independent copy storage, that is, each node stores the same information, enjoys the same rights, operates independently, mutual suspicion, and mutual supervision; 3 Byzantine fault tolerance, that is, tolerate less than 1/3 of nodes maliciously cheated or hacked to ensure that the system remains working normally [24]. The blockchain is developed rapidly in the industrial sectors such as virtual currency, financial technology and initial coin offering, however, the research on underlying technology and basic theory is still relatively backward [23]. The business scope of the blockchain has expanded from simple virtual currency transactions to government management and food security. In the future, whether it is instant messaging, social networking, media, banking, e-commerce, public services, etc., will be reconstructed by blockchain thinking, and a new era of blockchain application is coming [25]. Each blockchain virtual reality world can be combined to provide a unified service to the real world through Dapp Ecologies [26]. Therefore, a unified interchain protocol and network blockchain network (the world's first Internet) was born [27].

However, many of the transport layer problems encountered by modern network applications, the main functions of the transport layer are transport connection management and processing transmission errors, and transport connection management provides the function of establishing, maintaining and tearing down transport connections. The transport layer provides "connection-oriented" and "non-connected" services to the upper layers on the basis of the network layer. Handling transmission errors provides reliable "connection-oriented" and less reliable "connectionless" data transmission services, error control and flow control [3].

When a "connection-oriented" service is provided, the data transmitted through this layer will be acknowledged by the target device, and if the confirmation message is not received within the specified time, the data will be resent [28]. The interactive network protocol suite supports the cross-chain mechanism of the transport layer. Solving many transport layer problems encountered in modern network applications, the transport layer protocol with inter-chain network protocol set can provide low-latency convenience for blockchain networks built on the application layer.

3   Unitary Interchain Network

The blockchain network has broken the Douglas middleman's trust model for the business world and everyone's daily life. This will inevitably lead to business models and societies built outside the virtual economy Internet (including the mobile Internet) that have dominated other economic forms over the past 20 years. A new generation of comprehensive economic digital transformation is taking shape. From the connection between people on the Internet, the era to people, the complete P2P link between people and machines, and the machines and machines in the blockchain era, the value era-based on the digital economy is coming. Replacing connections with links has become an inevitable requirement for the traditional sharing economy driven by information networks and the sustainable development of machine-driven intelligent economy.

On the one hand, at present, the blockchain technology has reached the 3.0 era, but it is undeniable that the blockchain is still in its infancy. Many industry access and technical issues have led developers to encounter bottlenecks in creating Dapps that connect the real world to the real world, and virtual worlds become reality through blockchains. Especially in some specific industries, the application mechanism is too complicated and demanding, and the concurrency is very strong. Those who need a targeted and custom blockchain operating system to meet their business loan needs. Anyone can connect from anywhere, create value for others and pay for it. There really is no middleman built on the engine through a peer-to-peer token economy engine and Dapps. Therefore, the Ultra Blockchain Engine is a high performance blockchain, and a general-purpose business engine was born. On the other hand, there are countless blockchain infrastructures on the market, many of which may die, and some will survive. Since Dapps and the blockchain network are closely linked to the infrastructure in business. If the blockchain dies, all Dapps are built on the blockchain and the infrastructure is sacrificed forever. Therefore, the emergence of a unity.

Dapp can be transferred to any blockchain network where the blockchain network is an urgent need for many communities and organizations. Each blockchain virtual reality world can be combined to provide a unified service to the real world through Dapp Ecologies. Therefore, a unified interchain protocol and network blockchain network (the world's first Internet) was born.

Unitary Interchain Network is a set of protocols (UINP) formed by a switched network, including an application layer and a transport layer protocol. UNIP forms a single node of a network consisting of a single plug-in (the observation chain in the application layer and The router chain in the transport layer) and the single node itself selected from the parliament, commissioned monitoring and other functional states (Byzantine nodes, erroneous network status, computational power statistics, etc.), prediction requirements, and adjustment parameters.

4   Network Protocol-Transport Layer

The Transport Layer is the fourth layer of the OSI model. Therefore, this layer is the interface and bridge of the communication subnet and the resource subnet, which plays a role of linking up and down. The main task of this layer is to provide users with reliable end-to-end error and flow control to ensure the correct transmission of packets. The role of the transport layer is to mask the details of the underlying data communication to the upper layer, i.e. to transparently transmit messages to the user. Common protocols at this level are the

TCP protocol in TCP/IP, the SPX protocol in Novell networks, and Microsoft's NetBIOS/NetBEUI protocol.

The transport layer provides transport services between the session layer and the network layer, which obtains data from the session layer and, if necessary, splits the data. The transport layer then passes the data to the network layer and ensures that the data is delivered to the network layer correctly. Therefore, the transport layer is responsible for providing reliable transmission of data between the two nodes. When the connection between the two nodes is determined, the transport layer is responsible for supervising the work. In summary, the main functions of the transport layer are as follows:

1. Transport Connection Management: Provides the ability to establish, maintain, and tear down transport connections. The transport layer provides "connection-oriented" and "non-connected" services to the upper layers on the basis of the network layer.
2. Handling Transmission Errors: Provides reliable "connection-oriented" and less reliable "connectionless" data transmission services, error control and flow control. When a "connection-oriented" service is provided, the data transmitted through this layer will be acknowledged by the target device, and if the confirmation message is not received within the specified time, the data will be resent which improved monitoring service quality.

4.1   Overview of Unitary Interchain Network Protocol-Transport

UDP is the abbreviation of User Datagram Protocol. The Chinese name is User Datagram Protocol. It is a [connectionless] transport layer protocol in the OSI (Open System Interconnection) reference model. It provides transaction-oriented simple unreliable information delivery service.

These characteristics are as follows:

1. No connection.
2. Safety and reliability are not high.
3. High efficiency.
4. UDP is suitable for application environments that transmit only a small amount of data (64K) at a time and have low reliability requirements.

Unlike other cross-chain protocols, the interactive network protocol suite supports the cross-chain mechanism of the transport layer. In addition, by solving many of the transport layer problems encountered in modern network applications, the transport layer protocol with an interchain network protocol set can provide low latency convenience for a blockchain network built on the application layer.

The main advantages of the UINP application layer protocol are:

1. Crossing different consensus algorithm chains and different types of "chains" from atomic transactions, such as DAG and other blockchains that are suitable for generalized blockchain models in the future.

2. Low connection establishment delay to improve congestion control.
3. Perceptual hash entanglement network to network routing algorithm.
4. Multiple multiplex without wire header blocking.
5. Forward error correction.
6. Connection migration.

4.2 Zero RTT Time

RTT (Round-Trip Time) round-trip time is an important performance indicator in computer networks. It indicates the time elapsed from the time when the sender sends data, and the sender receives the acknowledgment from the receiver (the acknowledgment is sent immediately after the receiver receives the data, and the data transmission time is not included).

The RTT is determined by three parts: the propagation time of the link, the processing time of the end system, the queuing and processing time in the router's cache. The values of the first two parts are relatively fixed as a TCP connection, and the queuing and processing time in the router's cache will change with the degree of congestion of the entire network. Therefore, the change of RTT reflects the change of network congestion degree to some extent. Simply put, it is the time elapsed since the sender sent the data and received the confirmation message from the recipient.

This value is an important indicator in RPC. If the RTT is 1 ms, this means that only 1000 RPC round-trip responses can be completed in 1 s. Each Put operation in HBase is an RPC. If the user can submit the modified data to the server in batches, the number of RPCs can be reduced, and the performance will be improved accordingly. The concept of a write buffer is proposed in HBase. Save the Put instance in the client process first, and submit it to the server in batches when certain conditions are met or when the refresh method is called.

UINP is a new blockchain interconnect and traditional Internet transport protocol. The UINP transport layer protocol solves many application layer problems encountered by transport layer and blockchain networks and traditional Internet, while requiring little or no need to change blockchain protocol applications. A separate protocol allows existing protocols to be an impossible innovation because they are hindered by legacy clients and intermediate boxes.

See UINP Yellow Paper for a complete description of connection establishment. In short, in short, a single handshake often requires zero round trips before sending a payload compared to 1–3 round trips and TLS for TCP. When the first peer 1 node is connected to a single peer 2 node for the first time, the peer 1 must perform one round-trip handshake to obtain the information needed to complete the handshake. Peer 1 sends an early (empty) client request (REQ), and peer 2 sends a reject (REJ) with the information needed by peer 1 to advance the progress, including the source address token and the signature of the target. Next time peer 1 sends a REQ, it can use the previous cached credentials. Connect to immediately send an encrypted request to the server.

4.3   Congestion Control

Congestion control refers to techniques and mechanisms to prevent congestion before congestion occurs or to eliminate congestion after congestion occurs.Congestion control improves network utilization, reduces packet loss rate, and ensures network resources are fair to each data stream.

UINP transport-layer protocol has pluggable congestion control and provides richer information to the congestion control algorithm than TCP. One example of richer information is that each packet, both original and retransmitted, carries a new sequence hash number. This allows a Unitary sender to distinguish ACKs for retransmissions from ACKs for originals and avoids TCP's retransmission ambiguity problem. UINP transport-layer protocol's ACKs also explicitly carry the delay between the receipt of a packet and its acknowledgment being sent, and together with the monotonically-increasing sequence numbers. This allows for precise roundtrip-time calculation.

4.4   Security Consideration

At UINP, we have been working hard to make blockchain application layer transfers faster. However, despite the increasing bandwidth, the time around the trip (RTT)-ultimately limited by the speed of light, the number of mobile networks has not decreased for the foreseeable future. In order to continue to improve network performance, we need to reduce the number of surrounding trips, which is difficult for protocols that currently rely on Transmission Control Protocol (TCP).

The UINP transport layer protocol (a form of fast UDP Internet connection and Blockchain Cross-chain Route) is an early network protocol, and we are experimenting with running a new Transport Layer Security (TLS) style on top of UDP instead of TCP. Stream multiplexing protocol.

The UINP transport layer protocol combines a carefully selected collection of technologies to reduce the number of trips we need to go online. Here are some highlights:

1. High security similar to TLS.
2. fast (usually 0-RTT) connection.
3. Packet pacing to reduce packet loss.
4. Packet error correction to reduce retransmission delay.
5. UDP transmission to avoid TCP line header blocking.
6. Pluggable congestion control mechanism.

Early testing of UDP connections has been promising, but we have learned from past experience that real-world network conditions often vary widely. We hope to work with other members to develop the features and technologies of the UINP transport layer protocol into the web standards.

5   Discussions and Conclusions

Technical geeks have used the unique technical characteristics of blockchain to create software miracles such as Bitcoin and Ethereum since 2009. With the popularization of technical principles and the decline of technical thresholds, the blockchain that once belonged to the geek world will become a software infrastructure and become an important basic component of various applications. At present, the research on the basic theory and application of blockchain technology is still in its infancy. The efficiency of the blockchain consensus is inefficient compared to the centralized system. The disclosure of the consensus book makes the information transmission between the participants have the possibility of leaking. The smart contract also has various types of vulnerabilities that can be attacked. This kind of application development is far better than the theoretical research, which leads to the existence of many application products.

Fatal weakness is not conducive to the long-term development of the blockchain. I hope more researchers will participate in the research of blockchain related principles, algorithms, architecture and other fields. In short, although there are still many problems to be solved in the blockchain, it does not affect its development and application in the fields of value Internet, financial technology, digital currency, etc. It will still be studied for a long time in the future. In order to solve many of the transport layer problems encountered in modern network applications, the blockchain provides a single interchain network protocol transport (UINP) in a cross-link protocol. Blockchain provides the importance of Unitary Interchain Network Protocol-Transport (UINP) in cross-chain protocols. This paper proposes zero RTT time, congestion control and security considerations in the UINP application layer protocol and UINP transport layer protocol, which have many advantages.

Blockchain technology still has some serious problems, such as scalability issues. Today's blockchain is slow and takes a lot of effort. Converging blockchains with AL technology will increase efficiency and delivery, and blockchain is one of the drivers for Web 3 development. At this point the blockchain is an experimental technique and the field is open. The operation of the blockchain requires more information, such as educational background. Case studies will involve a variety of technologies in which curriculums are most inspiring for their potential and relevance. The most credible model is the Open University's Smart Contract, which is used to store Microcredentials and MIT/Learning Machine Blockcerts. It is not possible to combine functions at this time, because the technology still develops but develops rapidly. We will continue to study the various issues of the blockchain, find a better solution, and continue to optimize the UINP application layer protocol.

References

1. Juan, F., Galvez, J., Me, J.: Future challenges on the use of blockchain for food traceability analysis. J. Comput. Sci. Technol. **33**(3), 527–537 (2018)
2. Fu, L., Wu, X., Hu, Z., Fu, X., Wang, X.: De-anonymizing social networks with overlapping community structure. CoRR, abs/1712.04282 (2017)
3. Zheng, B., Zhu, L., Shen, M.: Scalable and privacy-preserving data sharing based on blockchain. J. Comput. Sci. Technol. **33**(3), 557–567 (2018)
4. Yuan, R., Xia, Y., Chen, H.: Private smart contract on public blockchain. J. Comput. Sci. Technol. **33**(3), 542–556 (2018)
5. Dorr, A., Steger, M., Kanhe, S., Jurdak, R.: A distributed solution to automotive security and privacy. IEEE Commun. Mag. **55**(12), 119–125 (2017)
6. Huckle, S., Bhattacharya, R., White, M., Beloff, N.: Internet of things, blockchain and shared economy applications. In: The 7th International Conference on Emerging Ubiquitous Systems and Pervasive Networks (EUSPN 2016)/The 6th International Conference on Current and Future Trends of Information and Communication Technologies in Healthcare (ICTH-2016)/Affiliated Workshops, 19–22 September 2016, London, United Kingdom, pp. 461–466 (2016)
7. Münsing, E., Mather, J., Moura, S.: Blockchains for decentralized optimization of energy resources in microgrid networks. In: 2017 IEEE Conference on Control Technology and Applications (CCTA), pp. 2164–2171 (2017)
8. Ma, Z.: Digital rights management: model, technology and application. China Commun. **14**(6), 156–167 (2017)
9. Mettler, M.: Blockchain technology in healthcare: The revolution starts here. In: 18th IEEE International Conference on e-Health Networking, Applications and Services, Healthcom 2016, Munich, Germany, 14–16 September 2016, pp. 1–3 (2016)
10. Mylrea, M., Gourisetti, S.: Blockchain for smart grid resilience: exchanging distributed energy at speed, scale and security. In: 2017 Resilience Week (RWS), Wilmington, USA, pp. 18–23 (2017)
11. Kosba, A.E., Miller, A., Shi, E., Wen, Z., Papamanthou, C.: Hawk: the blockchain model of cryptography and privacy-preserving smart contracts. In: IEEE Symposium on Security and Privacy, SP 2016, San Jose, CA, USA, 22–26 May 2016, pp. 839–858 (2016)
12. Meidan, A., García-García, J.A., Cuaresma, M.J.E., Ramos, I.M.: A survey on business processes management suites. Comput. Stan. Interfaces **51**, 71–86 (2017)
13. Käll, J.: Blockchain control. Law Critique **29**(2), 133–140 (2018)
14. Zhang, A., Lin, X.: Towards secure and privacy-preserving data sharing in e-health systems via consortium blockchain. J. Med. Syst. **42**(8), 140 (2018)
15. Gai, K., Qiu, M., Zhao, H.: Energy-aware task assignment for mobile cyber-enabled applications in heterogeneous cloud computing. J. Parallel Distrib. Comput. **111**, 126–135 (2018)
16. Gai, K., Qiu, M., Ming, Z., Zhao, H., Qiu, L.: Spoofing-jamming attack strategy using optimal power distributions in wireless smart grid networks. IEEE Trans. Smart Grid **8**(5), 2431–2439 (2017)
17. Gai, K., Choo, K.R., Qiu, M., Zhu, L.: Privacy-preserving content-oriented wireless communication in internet-of-things. IEEE Internet Things J. **5**(4), 3059–3067 (2018)
18. Gai, K., Qiu, M., Xiong, Z., Liu, M.: Privacy-preserving multi-channel communication in edge-of-things. Future Gener. Comput. Syst. **85**, 190–200 (2018)

19. Pappalardo, G., Di Matteo, T., Caldarelli, G., Aste, T.: Blockchain inefficiency in the bitcoin peers network. EPJ Data Sci. **7**(1), 30 (2018)
20. Valenta, L., Rowan, B.: Blindcoin: blinded, accountable mixes for bitcoin. In: Brenner, M., Christin, N., Johnson, B., Rohloff, K. (eds.) FC 2015. LNCS, vol. 8976, pp. 112–126. Springer, Heidelberg (2015). https://doi.org/10.1007/978-3-662-48051-9_9
21. Kim, H.W., Jeong, Y.S.: Secure authentication-management human-centric scheme for trusting personal resource information on mobile cloud computing with blockchain. Hum.-Centric Comput. Inf. Sci. **8**(1), 11 (2018)
22. Gai, K., Qiu, M.: Blend arithmetic operations on tensor-based fully homomorphic encryption over real numbers. IEEE Trans. Ind. Inf. **14**(8), 3590–3598 (2017)
23. Herian, R.: Taking blockchain seriously. Law Critique **29**(2), 163–171 (2018)
24. Griggs, K.N., Ossipova, O., Kohlios, C.P., Baccarini, A.N., Howson, E.A., Hayajneh, T.: Healthcare blockchain system using smart contracts for secure automated remote patient monitoring. J. Med. Syst. **42**(7), 130 (2018)
25. Wang, H., Song, Y.: Secure cloud-based EHR system using attribute-based cryptosystem and blockchain. J. Med. Syst. **42**(8), 152 (2018)
26. Eyal, I., Gencer, A.E., Sirer, E.G., Renesse, R.: Bitcoin-NG: a scalable blockchain protocol. In: 13th USENIX Symposium on Networked Systems Design and Implementation, NSDI 2016, Santa Clara, CA, USA, 16–18 March 2016, pp. 45–59 (2016)
27. Zhu, L., Yulu, W., Gai, K., Choo, K.-K.R.: Controllable and trustworthy blockchain-based cloud data management. Future Gener. Comput. Syst. **91**, 527–535 (2019)
28. Gai, K., Qiu, M., Zhao, H., Tao, L., Zong, Z.: Dynamic energy-aware cloudlet-based mobile cloud computing model for green computing. J. Netw. Comput. Appl. **59**(C), 46–54 (2016)

Design and Implementation of a Loan System Based on Smart Contract

Qi Yang[1,2(✉)], Fangfang Xu[1,2], Yu Zhang[3], Fang Liu[4], Wei Hu[1,2], and Qinghan Liao[1,2]

[1] College of Computer Science, Wuhan University of Science and Technology, Wuhan, Hubei, China
kidandkite@163.com
[2] Hubei Province Key Laboratory of Intelligent Information Processing and Real-time Industrial System, Wuhan, China
[3] College of Computer Science, Huazhong University of Science and Technology, Wuhan, Hubei, China
[4] Department of Information Engineering, City College, Wuhan University of Science and Technology, Wuhan, Hubei, China

Abstract. With the continuous development of the economy, the problems of complicated procedures, mutual distrust, and transaction amount limitation in the traditional lending model can no longer meet the needs of the market. This paper proposes a smart contract-based loan system which uses the decentralized and non-tamperable features of the blockchain to join the loan system through an auto-signing loan treaty. In our system, there is no need to establish any trust base between users, nor does it require the participation of any third-party intermediate trust medium. Users can conduct peer-to-peer transactions with any user in the loan system. The actual test proves that the system can intelligently realize the process of borrowing, loan and repayment. The distributed application is robust, easy to operate and practical.

Keywords: Blockchain · Smart contract · Loan system Ethereum private network

1 Introduction

In real life, the process of signing a contract has many problems such as the lack of trust between the two parties and the breach of contract during the execution of the contract. Therefore, in the process of signing the contract, a third-party intermediate trust medium is required as a guarantee for contracting [1]. It directly led to the tedious process of traditional lending. In the process of lending, both lenders and borrowers need to carry out a series of complicated and strict signing procedures.

In recent years, the rise of P2P network lending has made the operation of the market more efficient. The State Banking Regulatory Commission and the Ministry of Industry and Information Technology have jointly issued the Interim Measures for the Management of Business Activities of Internet Lending Information Intermediaries,

© Springer Nature Switzerland AG 2018
M. Qiu (Ed.): SmartBlock 2018, LNCS 11373, pp. 22–31, 2018.
https://doi.org/10.1007/978-3-030-05764-0_3

which clarified the legal status of the P2P network lending platform. But so far, the market management of traditional P2P lending platform is still confusing.

This paper designs and implements a smart contract-based loan system for real-life lending behavior. Combining blockchain and smart contracts not only makes the P2P lending market have a new development direction, but also creates a perfect foundation for the construction of multiple loan trust platforms [2]. The smart contract-based loan system has the following advantages: (1) automatic contracting; (2) no restrictions on transactions between borrowers and lenders; (3) achieve personal assessment risk liberalization; (4) achieve decentralized trust mechanism; (5) transactions cannot be tampered.

2   Related Technology

2.1   Blockchain Definition

A blockchain is essentially a cryptographically based distributed database. In 2008, "Bitcoin: a peer-to-peer electronic cash system" published by Nakamoto brought blockchain into the public eye [3]. The blockchain forms transactional data into blocks within a certain period of time, and then connects these blocks to form a chain structure. Based on P2P network and cryptography the blockchain will construct a set of decentralized absolutely real distributed ledgers. There is no need to establish any trust relationship between nodes on the blockchain, as long as the nodes in the blockchain can copy, download, and maintain data records on the chain [4]. Depending on the environment and the type of node, the blockchain can be divided into three types: open chain, federated chain and private chain. The blockchain consists of six parts: data layer, network layer, consensus layer, incentive layer, contract layer and application layer. The basic architecture model is shown in Fig. 1:

2.2   Smart Contract

A smart contract is essentially a program that runs on a computer after digitizing the contract [5]. In 1994, Nick Szabo first proposed the innovative concept of smart contract. Since there is no platform for the development of smart contracts, smart contracts have always been in a state of concept. Smart contracts can be performed unsupervised after digitizing traditional contracts, and no trust base is required between the parties [6].

Smart contracts can not only define the rules that are acceptable to both parties as traditional contracts, but they can automatically enforce the regulations in the contract without any third-party supervision. The enforceability of the code eliminates the occurrence of breach of contract. After programming and decentralizing, the contract can intelligently and automatically executes the protocol that needs to be manually completed before [7].

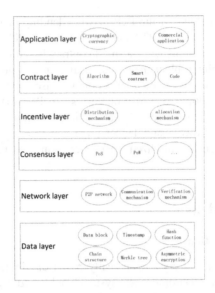

Fig. 1. Blockchain basic architecture model

2.3 Ethereum

Ethereum is a blockchain platform that uses decentralized virtual machines to handle point-to-point smart contracts, using specialized Ethereum for all types of transactions. Applications developed based on Ethereum will not be attacked by third parties. Ethereum can be seen as a combination of blockchain and smart contracts [8]. It has the following four design principles: (1) succinct principle. Ensure that the application of Ethereum is for the general public, not the traditional use of special organizations; (2) general principle. All types of users in Ethereum can define and publish their own smart contracts; (3) modular principle. The modularization of the various parts of Ethereum is beneficial to the development of a complete system; (4) non-discrimination principle. All users and applications are equal. Smart contracts cannot create discriminatory provisions for specific users or applications [9].

3 Design of Loan System

The blockchain bank loan system uses digital ownership management to propose a peer-to-peer lending platform that supports digital mortgages [10]. The blockchain bank built on Ethereum technology is a network lending platform that links borrowing institutions and lending institutions. The main features of the loan system are as follows:

(1) Decentralization based on smart contracts. In this system, the integrity of the lending process is guaranteed by smart contracts and does not require the participation of any third party intermediary. The system realizes complete point-to-point lending, which can realize untrusted loan between the borrower and the lender, and

can also directly interact with the official organization through the reserved interface.

(2) The loan interest rate is liberalized without the limitation of the loan amount. Since there is no third-party intermediary institution, the lender can freely define the loan interest rate according to the loan certificate of the borrower provided by the official institution, and the interest generated by the loan will be fully obtained by the lender.

(3) The total risk of loans is decentralized. The system realizes the liberalization of loan risk assessment. The losses and benefits of both parties are randomly distributed and do not need to rely on a single decision made by any third-party intermediary institution. This also avoids the high risk of concentrating risk on third parties.

(4) Strong security performance of the system. The system uses blockchain and smart contract technology. The security of the system is guaranteed by the highly transparent and non-tamperable nature of transactional information in the blockchain and the enforcement of smart contracts.

3.1 System Architecture Design

Traditional centralized applications typically use a server-centric C/S architecture. The user interacts with the web application through the client. Different from the traditional application architecture, this system uses the Ethereum decentralized application architecture. The smart contract is executed on the Ethereum virtual machine EVM. The client only needs to perform RPC calls through the web browser to interact with the instance without requesting access to the centralized server [11]. The architecture of the entire system is shown in Fig. 2:

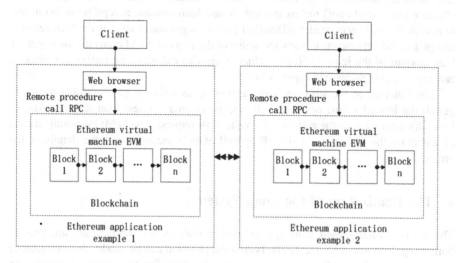

Fig. 2. System architecture design

3.2   Design of Smart Contracts

The smart contracts in this system are mainly loan contracts. The loan content mainly includes the loan information and the status of the loan. The loan information is defined in the form of a structure, including the borrower, the loan amount, the repayment date, and the number of borrowings accepted. The loan status is defined by the enumeration type, including waiting for acceptance and latching, successful borrowing and failure of borrowing. The definition of the loan content for lender is similar to the loan content for borrower which is shown in Figs. 3 and 4.

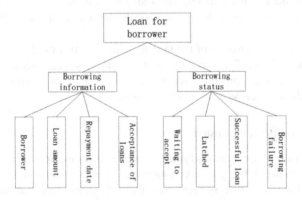

Fig. 3. Borrowing content

The definition of the loan contract function is shown in Fig. 5. The function of the loan contract function is as follows: hasActiveLoan() means to view the existing effective loan, newLoan() means to create a new loan request, acceptProposal() means to accept the loan item, getLoanDetails() means to get the details of the loan request, and getLoanState() means to view the status of the request, lockLoan() means to get the loan amount of the loan, getRepayValue() means to calculate the repayment amount, and repayLoan() means the repayment.

The function of the loan contract function is as follows: getProposal() means to get all the loaned items, newProposal() means to create a new loan item, getActive-LoanId() means to get the address of a valid loan request, revokeMyProposal() means to withdraw the loan item, and getProposalDetails() means to get the details of the project.

4   The Realization of the Loan System

The smart contract-based loan system mainly realizes the three main functions of borrowing, loan and repayment. The borrowing function can be subdivided into issuing loan requests and accepting corresponding borrowings. The loan function realizes the acceptance of borrowing requests, and the repayment function is divided into due repayments and overdue payments.

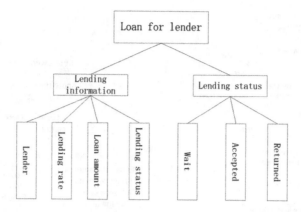

Fig. 4. Leading content

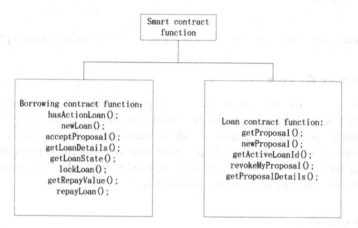

Fig. 5. Loan contract function

4.1 Loan Request

The loan request is initiated by the borrower. In the loan request, the loan amount and the repayment date are stated. The loan request is broadcast on the whole network through the loan contract, and each loan account can receive the loan request. An account that is interested in a loan request can conduct a risk assessment based on the proof of the borrower's loan collateral provided by the government's public trust institution, and then give the appropriate loan amount and loan interest. After the lender accepts the loan request, the corresponding loan amount in the lender's account will be temporarily deducted through the smart contract. The loan information issued by the lender will be broadcasted throughout the network [11]. The proof of loan collateral requires the participation of official agencies, and an interface is reserved in the system for future implementation. The process of issuing loans is shown in Fig. 6.

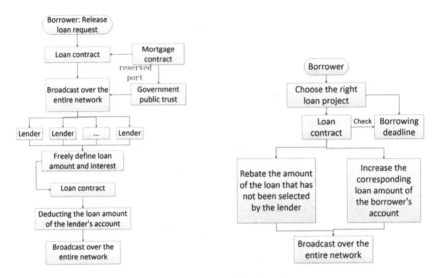

Fig. 6. Releases the loan request process   **Fig. 7.** Accepts the loan request process

4.2 Accepting the Loan

Borrowers can choose the most beneficial loan program from the loans provided by many lenders according to the amount of interest generated. After the borrower selects the appropriate plan, the loan amount will be increased to the borrower's account balance through the loan contract. At the same time, the loan funds provided by the lenders not selected by the borrower will be refunded to the lender's account balance. The process of accepting the loan is shown in Fig. 7.

4.3 Repayment

After the loan transaction is generated, it will be published in the entire network and recorded in the corresponding block. The loan smart contract will continuously monitor the borrowing conditions generated in the loan transaction, such as the repayment date. After the loan expires, the smart contract is executed to implement the repayment regulations. The borrower can also freely initiate the repayment request in advance. During the repayment process, the loan amount and interest are increased to the lender's account through the loan contract. At the same time, the loan amount and corresponding interest are deducted from the borrower's account. The process of repayment due is shown in Fig. 8.

4.4 Overdue Repayment

If the borrower has not repaid the loan due to the repayment date, either party to the loan can make a request for seizing the borrower's collateral to trigger the loan contract. After the loan contract passes the request, the collateral contract is triggered. The value of the collateral is transmitted back to the loan contract after the relevant government department processes the collateral. The loan contract distributes the value of the collateral to the corresponding lender's account according to the proportion of the loan amount of the lender, and then broadcasts the results of the processing in the entire network. The process of overdue repayment is shown in Fig. 9.

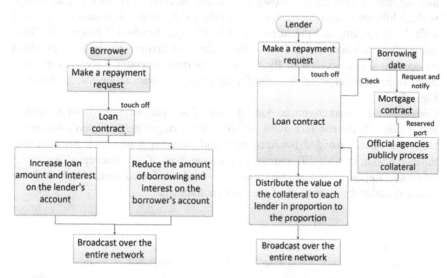

Fig. 8. Due repayment process   **Fig. 9.** Overdue repayment process

5   System Testing and Analysis

The development environment used in this system is based on the Ubuntu-16.04 version of the operating system under Linux. The system uses the Truffle application development framework, Node.js runtime environment, Testrpc local simulation of Ethereum environment and MetaMask Ethereum wallet.

Use the Testrpc command on the terminal to directly launch the local Ethereum test environment built by Testrpc. Use the Truffle deploys command to deploy the smart contract to Testrpc and then add the test account in Testrpc to the MetaMask Ethereum wallet. After the system is deployed and started successfully, performing functional tests on each module of the system to verify the feasibility of the system design. The system test uses four accounts and tests from the following two aspects:

(1)   The feasibility of issuing a loan request, generating a loan project and selecting a suitable loan project. Account 2 issues a loan request. The loan request is for the borrowing of 30 Ethereum and the repayment date is June 30, 2018. Account 2 broadcasts its own loan request through the smart contract on the entire network, and each account in the system can receive the loan request from account 2, as shown in Fig. 10. After receiving the loan request from Account 2, Account 3 can

conduct a free evaluation of the loan risk after viewing the loan certificate of Account 2 provided by the official institution through the reserved interface. If Account 3 initiates a transaction that agrees to the loan request and pays the transaction, the transaction information is broadcasted on the entire network through the smart contract, as shown in Fig. 11. Similar to Account 3, Account 4 and Account 5 give corresponding loan items. Account 4 is loaned to account 2 with 20 Ethereum, and the interest rate is 10% pa. Account 5 is loaned to account 2 with 10 Ethereum, and the interest rate is 10% pa. Account 2 receives the loan items from each account, and then selects the most favorable loan items provided by account 4 and account 5. By the smart contract, Account 2 receives the loan items from Account 4 and Account 5 after paying the transaction fee, as shown in Fig. 12.

(2) Consistency of smart contracts. After Account 2 accepts loan items from Account 4 and Account 5, the contract status automatically changes to 'Accepted'. Account 2 locks the funds provided by Account 4 and Account 5 into their own account through a loan contract. The status of the loan item of the unaccepted account 3 becomes 'Repaid'. At the same time, the funds deducted from Account 3 are returned under the execution of the loan contract.

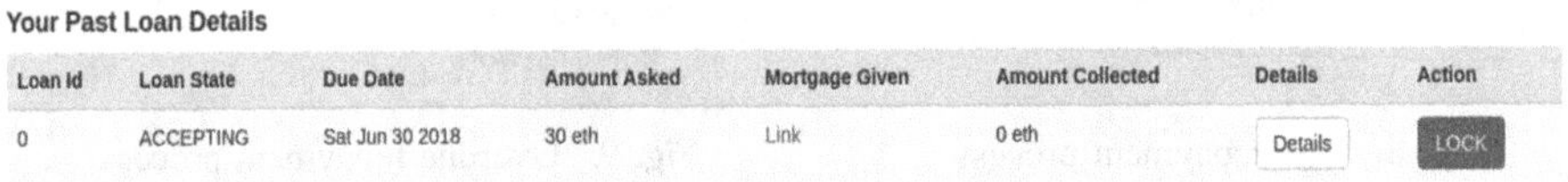

Your Past Loan Details

Loan Id	Loan State	Due Date	Amount Asked	Mortgage Given	Amount Collected	Details	Action
0	ACCEPTING	Sat Jun 30 2018	30 eth	Link	0 eth	Details	LOCK

Fig. 10. Account 2 loan request

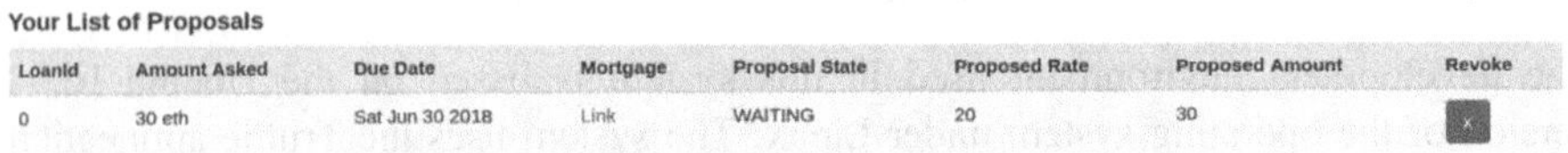

Your List of Proposals

LoanId	Amount Asked	Due Date	Mortgage	Proposal State	Proposed Rate	Proposed Amount	Revoke
0	30 eth	Sat Jun 30 2018	Link	WAITING	20	30	x

Fig. 11. Account 3 loan information

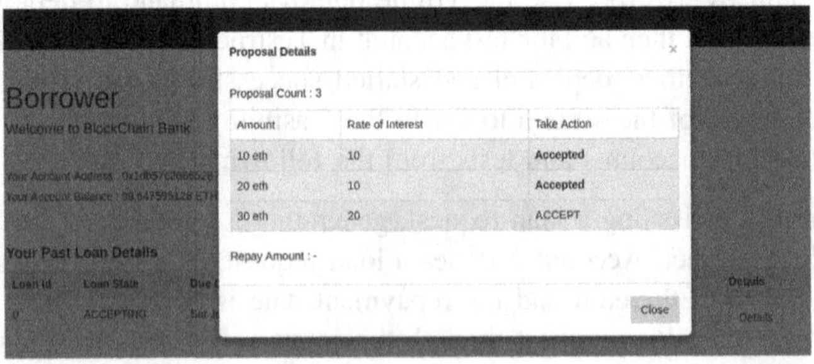

Fig. 12. Account 2 receives account 4 and account 5 lending

6   Conclusion

This paper proposes a loan platform based on smart contracts and blockchain, which digitizes traditional lending contracts and then deploys them into the blockchain environment. It achieves absolute honest lending behavior between users using the enforceability of programmatic contracts as well as decentralization and non-tamperable transaction of blockchain. The simulation results prove the feasibility of the method, and the smart contract-based loan system implemented does not require high design and development costs. It is simple in operation, simple in page, powerful and stable, and has great practical value.

Acknowledgment. This paper was sponsored by Key Project of Hubei Provincial Department of Education under Granted No. D20181103.

References

1. Gazali, H.M., Hassan, R., Nor, R.M., et al.: Re-inventing PTPTN study loan with blockchain and smart contracts. In: International Conference on Information Technology, pp. 751–754 (2017)
2. Croman, K., et al.: On scaling decentralized blockchains. In: Clark, J., Meiklejohn, S., Ryan, P.Y.A., Wallach, D., Brenner, M., Rohloff, K. (eds.) FC 2016. LNCS, vol. 9604, pp. 106–125. Springer, Heidelberg (2016). https://doi.org/10.1007/978-3-662-53357-4_8
3. Nakamoto, S.: Bitcoin: A peer-to-peer electronic cash system. Consulted 1–2 (2008)
4. Ron, D., Shamir, A.: Quantitative analysis of the full bitcoin transaction graph. In: Sadeghi, A.-R. (ed.) FC 2013. LNCS, vol. 7859, pp. 6–24. Springer, Heidelberg (2013). https://doi.org/10.1007/978-3-642-39884-1_2
5. Surhone, L.M., Timpledon, M.T., Marseken, S.F.: Smart contract, pp. 3–4. Betascript Publishing (2010)
6. Bragagnolo, S., Rocha, H., Denker, M., et al.: SmartInspect: solidity smart contract inspector. In: International Workshop on Blockchain Oriented Software Engineering, pp. 9–18 (2018)
7. Norta, A.: Designing a smart-contract application layer for transacting decentralized autonomous organizations. In: Singh, M., Gupta, P.K., Tyagi, V., Sharma, A., Ören, T., Grosky, W. (eds.) ICACDS 2016. CCIS, vol. 721, pp. 595–604. Springer, Singapore (2017). https://doi.org/10.1007/978-981-10-5427-3_61
8. Kosba, A., Miller, A., Shi, E., et al.: Hawk: the blockchain model of cryptography and privacy-preserving smart contracts. In: Security and Privacy, pp. 839–858. IEEE (2016)
9. Bhargavan, K., Swamy, N., Zanella-Béguelin, S., et al.: Formal verification of smart contracts: short paper. In: ACM Workshop, pp. 91–96. ACM (2016)
10. Zhang, F., Cecchetti, E., Croman, K., et al.: Town Crier: an authenticated data feed for smart contracts. In: ACM Conference on Computer and Communications Security, pp. 270–282. ACM (2016)
11. Hirai, Y.: Defining the ethereum virtual machine for interactive theorem provers. In: Brenner, M., et al. (eds.) FC 2017. LNCS, vol. 10323, pp. 520–535. Springer, Cham (2017). https://doi.org/10.1007/978-3-319-70278-0_33

Formal Verification of Smart Contracts from the Perspective of Concurrency

Meixun Qu[1], Xin Huang[1(✉)], Xu Chen[2], Yi Wang[3], Xiaofeng Ma[3], and Dawei Liu[1]

[1] Xi'an Jiaotong-Liverpool University, Suzhou, China
Meixun.Qu16@student.xjtlu.edu.cn, {Xin.Huang,Dawei.Liu}@xjtlu.edu.cn
[2] Tongji Blockchain Research Institute, Suzhou, China
chenxu@tj-fintech.com
[3] Tongji University, Shanghai, China
{xiaofengma,1631665}@tongji.edu.cn

Abstract. Blockchain is an emerging technology with broad applications. As an important application of the blockchain, smart contracts can formulate trading rules to manage thousands of virtual currencies. Nowadays, the IoT (Internet of Things) combined with blockchain has become a new trend and smart contract can implement different transaction demands for IoT-blockchain systems. Once there exits vulnerability in the smart contract program, the security of the virtual currency will not be guaranteed. However, ensuring the security of smart contracts is never an easy task. On the one hand, existing smart contracts cannot identify fake users or malicious programs, which is difficult to be regulated at present; on the other hand, smart contracts involving in multiple trading users are very similar to shared-memory concurrent programs. To deal with these problems, this study uses formal verification methods, adopting the Communicating Sequence Processes (CSP) theory to formally model concurrent programs. Then the FDR (Failure Divergence Refinement), a refinement checker or model checker for CSP, is utilized to successfully detect the vulnerability regarding concurrency in one smart contract public in Ethereum. The results show the potential advantage of using CSP and FDR tool to check the vulnerability in smart contracts especially from the perspective of concurrency.

Keywords: Blockchain · Smart contracts · Concurrency
CSP theory · FDR

1 Introduction

The security of smart contracts is a prerequisite for ensuring the normal operation of the blockchain system. However, this characterization may not live up to people's expectation due to the frequent reveal of vulnerabilities in smart contracts recently. The reasons behind these incidents are various, but there is one perspective that people tend to overlook, which is the analogy between smart

© Springer Nature Switzerland AG 2018
M. Qiu (Ed.): SmartBlock 2018, LNCS 11373, pp. 32–43, 2018.
https://doi.org/10.1007/978-3-030-05764-0_4

contracts and conventional concurrency programs [1]. And adversaries often utilize this kind of vulnerability to obtain virtual currencies, thus causing huge losses. One prominent example is the DAO contract [1], which suffered the loss of 60 million dollars due to its vulnerability in a concurrency environment. Therefore, it is significantly important to analyze the logic design of smart contracts.

In order to detect the vulnerabilities of smart contracts, many formal verification methods are proposed. Several verification tools such as Why3 [2], F* [3] and Oyente [4] are developed to detect problems in programming languages like array overflow, poor handling of return value and etc. However, these tools rarely test the design logic of the smart contract itself [5]. If the programs have concurrency features, the vulnerabilities are most likely caused by the unreasonable design logic itself.

Given the above analysis, this study will focus on concurrency-related vulnerabilities in smart contracts and use the formal method to check it. In order to model the smart contracts in a formal way, we adopt Communicating Sequential Processes (CSP) theory. Proposed by Hoare as an algebraic language, it specially describes the interactions of entities in a concurrent system [6]. We then use FDR, a model checking tool based on CSP to do automated verification [7]. The past decades have witnessed many successful industrial applications of CSP theory, like modelling the control flow of in European train control system [8]. And FDR is well-known for its successful detection of attack in concurrent security protocol [9]. Therefore, the scientific nature of CSP theory and the convenience of FDR can provide strong support for the detection of concurrent vulnerabilities in smart contracts.

In the following sections, Part 1 will introduce basics of CSP theory used for modelling and present the workflow of formal verification of smart contract. One classic smart contract will be analyzed in Part 2. Part 3 serves as discussion. At last, Part 4 concludes this study.

Preliminaries

1.1   Basics of CSP Theory

This part introduces some basics of CSP that will be used in this study. The details can be referred to [6].

Process. Process is the abstraction of a series of behaviors of an object. The behaviors of the object can be illustrated by a finite set of events called *alphabet*. In this study, the name of a process begins with a capital and the name of an event begins with a lowercase letter. For example, the following formula describes the behaviors of a ticket vending machine.

$$\alpha TVM = \{in1d, single\}$$

The ticket vending machine is a process and can be represented as TVM. αTVM means the alphabet. It includes 2 events, which are *in1d* (input 1 dollar), *single* (buy a single ticket). Among all the processes, *STOP* is the simplest one which means "doing nothing at all".

Prefix. Process $(x \to P)$ is called prefix. It first executes event x and follows the instructions of process P for subsequent actions. Combining process and prefix will derive the basic model of interactions between processes. For example,

$$Bob\_morning = getup \to shower \to breakfast \to Work$$

$$Work = programming \to lunch \to STOP$$

In this example, process *Bob_morning* characterizes the actions of Bob in the morning, which begins with getting up. After taking a shower, he will have breakfast. This event is followed by another process named *Work*. In the *Work* process, he programs. Then he has lunch, which finally ends the morning with *STOP*.

Input and Output

$$c?x : T \to P(x)$$

$$c!y : T \to P(y)$$

As a whole, the two formulae are prefix notations. Both $c?x{:}T$ and $c!y{:}T$ are events and c is a channel like a buffer. $c?x{:}T$ means x is chosen from event set T by the environment and then is put into a channel c. $c!y{:}T$ means y is chosen from event set T by the environment and then is pushed out of a channel c. $P(x)$ and $P(y)$ are processes which contain event x and y, respectively.

Traces and Interleaving. The trace is a finite sequence of events that processes execute until a certain moment. $\langle x, y \rangle$ is a trace with event y happening closely after event x. The concept of traces is of great significance to this study. The main purpose of using CSP to model smart contracts is to generate a set of traces that includes possible behaviors of smart contracts under any condition. The attacker model is also a trace which depicts the sequence of malicious events under specific circumstances. If the attack sequence exists in the trace set mentioned above, the smart contract is vulnerable. And this vulnerability may be exploited by the attacker to become a real attack point to steal digital assets in the contract. If the attack sequence does not exist in the trace set, it means that the contract is able to defend this kind of attack.

If we take the smart contract as a whole process, then it can be divided into several child processes. The trace set of the smart contract is composed of all possible behaviors generated by interleaving child processes. In a concurrent circumstance, the interleaving among process X, Y can be formally defined as $X|||Y$. And their trace set can be described as

$$traces(X|||Y) = \{t | \exists u \in traces(X),\ \exists v \in traces(Y),\ t\ interleaves(u, v)\}\}$$

In this formula, t *interleaves(u, v)* means trace alternatively extracts the sequences of u and v while preserves their partial order. For example, if

$$u = \langle a, b, c, d, e \rangle \in traces(X),$$
$$v = \langle f, a, g \rangle \in traces(Y)$$

then one element of $traces\,(X|||Y)$ can be described as

$$\langle a, b, f, a, c, g, d, e \rangle \in traces\,(X|||Y)\,.$$

1.2   Workflow of Verification

In this study, the procedure for formal verification of smart contracts can be generally divided into four steps as shown in Fig. 1. Part III will illustrate these steps in detail.

(1) Analyze the given smart contract from the code level;
(2) Model the contract program by translating its codes into formal language with CSP theory;
(3) Design attacker model;
(4) Convert the modelling results into the FDR-supported CSP_M language and use FDR for verification.

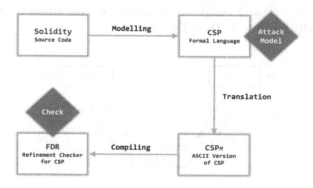

Fig. 1. Workflow of formal verification in this study.

2   The Safe Remote Purchase

This part will demonstrate how to use CSP and FDR to check the vulnerability of one smart contract case public in Ethereum. The programming language for it is Solidity.

2.1   Code Analysis

Published on [10], the Safe Remote Purchase smart contract contains 99 lines of source codes and aims to support safe and reliable transaction operation of untrusted buyers and sellers on the decentralized e-commerce platform.

For convenience to analyze, in this smart contract we assume that there are only three accounts including the buyer, the seller and the contract where the contract is the third party.

We firstly represent *value* as the price of the item involved in a single order. Then the contract is expected to work as follows. In the constructor function served for initialization, the account who sends the required ethers (2*value as the guaranty) to the contract is considered as the seller. If the constructor function executes successfully, the state of the order becomes *created*. Then the seller waits for the purchase confirmation from buyer. Before the buyer confirms to purchase, the seller has the opportunity to call the **abort()** function to abort the order, then the guaranty will return to the seller's account after the state of the order becomes *inactive*.

The account who invokes the **confirmPurchase()** function is the buyer. As stated in **confirmPurchase()** function, only if the buyer successfully sends the deposit (2*value) to the contract can the state of the order become *locked*, which finishes the confirmation procedure. The transaction will proceed smoothly until the buyer receives the item.

At last, the buyer calls the **confirmReceived()** function. In this function, the state of the order becomes *inactive*, then 1*value ethers are transferred back to the buyer account, and finally the remaining 3*value ethers in the contract account are fully returned to the seller account.

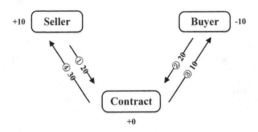

Fig. 2. Flowchart of normal transaction (value = 10 ethers).

Figure 2 shows the flowchart of normal transaction described above. From the perspective of sequential programs, the above content is conformed to the expected design purpose of Safe Remote Purchase contract. However, for a concurrent program, the problems of data race may bring about undesired behaviors that can be exploited by adversaries, which is exactly the motivation of this study. As shown in Fig. 3, the vulnerability we have discovered lies in the line order of line 72, which sends Ethers to the contract account, and line 77, which changes the order state into *locked*. In the course of the executed line 72 and non-executed line 77, the order state is still created. Hence, in this specified period, the seller is allowed to call the **abort()** function. Once **abort()** is invoked, the state of the order becomes aborted and the total balance of the contract's account, containing the guaranty from the seller and the deposit from the buyer, will be transferred to the seller's account.

```
13  constructor() public payable {                                     71      inState(State.Created)
14      seller = msg.sender;                                           72      condition(msg.value == (2 * value))
15      value = msg.value / 2;                                         73      payable
16      require((2 * value) == msg.value, "Value has to be even.");    74  {
17  }                                                                  75      emit PurchaseConfirmed();
    ......                                                             76      buyer = msg.sender;
55  function abort()                                                   77      state = State.Locked;
56      public                                                         78  }
57      onlySeller                                                         ......
58      inState(State.Created)                                         82  function confirmReceived()
59  {                                                                  83      public
60      emit Aborted();                                                84      onlyBuyer
61      state = State.Inactive;                                        85      inState(State.Locked)
62      seller.transfer(address(this).balance);                        86  {
63  }                                                                  87      emit ItemReceived();
    ......                                                                 ......
66  /// Transaction has to include `2 * value` ether.                  91      state = State.Inactive;
67  /// The ether will be locked until confirmReceived                     ......
68  /// is called.                                                     96      buyer.transfer(value);
69  function confirmPurchase()                                         97      seller.transfer(address(this).balance);
70      public                                                         98  }
```

Fig. 3. Safe remote purchase code fragments.

2.2   CSP Modelling on the Safe Remote Purchase

This section mainly discusses how CSP is employed to model the Safe Remote Purchase smart contract. CSP can model systems that is decomposed into multiple concurrent sub-components. In this study, we model the smart contract mainly by defining CSP processes corresponding to public-type functions in the program. And all these processes constitute a system with interleaving mode. CSP can also describe the attack sequence which is termed as the undesired trace hidden in the program. Then, FDR is used to test whether the attack sequence exits theoretically. Considering the properties of smart contract, the modelling process will focus on formal definition for five types of objects: variable, event, process, concurrent model and attacker model.

Variable. Variables in the Safe Remote Purchase are split into two types: global variables (GVs) and key variables. Analogous to the shared variable in conventional concurrent programs, multiple accounts may read or write the GVs in smart contracts in an inappropriate way, which potentially causes the concurrent vulnerabilities. Therefore, precise modelling on GVs is virtually required. In the case of Safe Remote Purchase, the global variable is the state of the order and we define it as

$$State := \{created, locked, inactive\}$$

State is a set containing three elements representing three different states of the order. We use *state* (beginning with a lowercase letter) to represent any element in *State*, namely $state := created \mid locked \mid inactive \in State$. In this formula, $"\mid"$ meansselection.

The key variable is also abstracted from the contract. Here we list two groups of variables that are often used in this contract. The first group is

$$Object := \{seller, buyer, eth\}$$

In this group, *seller,buyer* and *eth* mean the account of the seller, buyer and the smart contract, respectively. And we also have $object := seller \mid buyer \mid eth \in Object$.

The second group represents the extra information with the behavior of money transfers and it is described as

$$MoneyInfo := \{guaranty, deposit, balance, trans\}$$

In this group, *guaranty* indicates the money transferred is paid as guaranty; *deposit* means the money transferred is used to pay the deposit; *balance* indicates that all the balance of a particular account is transferred to other accounts; and *trans* means ordinary money transfer behavior without any special information. Still, we can define $moneyInfo := guaranty \mid deposit \mid balance \mid trans \in MoneyInfo$.

Event. The part of actions in the contract can generally be abstracted into events such as initialization of the constructor function, money transfer, changing the value of certain variables and so on. In addition, the judging course of the certain condition in the program can also be considered as events although there may not be any real actions occurring. Since there can be more than one scenarios involved in an event, a set is generally used to describe a type of events. To avoid name confusion, the definition of event names generally ends with "msg".

The following shows the event in which the seller initializes the constructor function:

$$INITmsg \triangleq \{init.Int\}$$

This event contains only one element which only represents the initialization action semantically. "." indicates the information carried with the event. If there are more than one types of information, this symbol can be used repeatedly. *Int* is an integer by default. Therefore, *init.Int* can be specified as the event in which the seller initializes the transaction and an order valued *Int* ethers gets generated.

Then we define the money transfer event shown as below:

$$MTmsg \triangleq \{ object.moneyInfo.object.Int \mid object \in Object,$$
$$moneyInfo \in MoneyInfo\}$$

This formula describes a series of money transfer events in which *object. moneyInfo.object:Int* represents that one object transfers a certain amount of ethers to another object in a certain way. If *moneyInfo=balance*, then *Int* is automatically marked as all balances of the first *object* and *Int* is denoted by *"overall"*. The following three types of events model the conditional statements in this contract.

$$RImsg\wedge = \{access?object|\ object \in Object\}$$

$$RSmsg\wedge = \{state'\ ?\ state|state \in State\}$$

$$RDmsg\wedge = \{buyer\ ?\ Int\}$$

In order to verify the given condition, the first formula depicts events in which the identity of the function caller is input into channel *access*. The second one means the current state of the order is input into channel *state'*. The last one represents that the deposit paid by the buyer is put into channel *buyer*. The formula below defines the event in which the state of the order gets changed.

$$WSmsg\wedge = \{state'\ !state|state \in State\}$$

In this event, the renewed state gets written and is pushed out of channel *state'*. There are some statements in smart contracts that indicate some information is sent to all participants during transaction. In Solidity, such information is modified with the keyword *emit*. When modelling, we only assign a name to these events. In the case contract, these events are

$$abort,\ purchaseConfirmed,\ itemReceived,\ warning.$$

Process. We model four functions (shown in Fig. 3), namely **constructor()**, **abort()**, **confirmPurchase()** and **itemReceived()** into four processes - *INIT*, *ABORT(x)*, *ConfirmPurchased(x)* and *itemReceived(x)*, respectively.

INIT $=$ $init?msg\_value : Int \rightarrow$ **if** $(msg\_value\ \%\ 2 == 0)$
    then$(seller.guaranty.eth.msg\_value \rightarrow state'!state = created \rightarrow$
    $PURCHASE\,(state)$ **else**$(warning \rightarrow INIT)$

ABORT$(x) =$ $access?object : Object \rightarrow$ **if** $(object\ ==\ seller)$
    then$(state'?x \rightarrow$ **if** $(x\ ==\ created)$ **then**$(abort \rightarrow state!inactive \rightarrow$
    $eth.balance.seller.overall \rightarrow STOP)$
        else$(warning \rightarrow STOP))$
        else$(warning \rightarrow STOP)$

ConfirmPurchased$(x) =$ $access?object : Object \rightarrow state'?x \rightarrow$ **if** $(\ x\ ==\ created\ )$
        then$(buyer?value : Int \rightarrow$ **if** $(value\ ==\ msg\_value)$
            then$(purchaseConfirmed \rightarrow state'!locked \rightarrow STOP)$
            else$(warning \rightarrow STOP))$
        else$(warning \rightarrow STOP)$

$$ItemReceived\,(x) = access?object\,:\,Object \rightarrow \textbf{if}\,(object\,==\,buyer)$$
$$\textbf{then}(state'?x \rightarrow \textbf{if}\,(x\,==\,locked)\,\textbf{then}(itemReceived$$
$$\rightarrow state'!inactive \rightarrow eth.trans.buyer.\,(msg\_value/2)$$
$$\rightarrow eth.balance.seller.overall \rightarrow STOP)$$
$$\textbf{else}\,(warning\,!\,STOP))$$
$$\textbf{else}\,(warning\,!\,STOP)$$

Concurrent Model. As we have detailed before, except for the *INIT* process, it is not hard to see the order of occurrence of *ABORT(x)*, *ConfirmPurchased(x)* and *ItemReceived(x)* is non-deterministic. Owing to the existence of GV, the proceeding of each process is largely related to the changing value of the element of GV, *state*. Therefore, we use interleaving as the concurrent mode to model all possible sequences happening in theory. The parameter x represents any element of the GV and will be synchronously transmitted to each process. Then, the PURCHASE(x) is defined as

$$\textbf{PURCHASE(x)}\,=(ABORT(x)|||ConfirmPurchased(x)|||ConfirmReceived(x))\,.$$

traces(PURCHASE(x))

$$=\begin{cases} s\,|\,\exists t \in traces\,(ABORT(x)), \\ \quad \exists u \in traces\,(ConfirmPurchased(x)), \\ \quad \exists w \in traces(ConfirmReceived(x)), \\ \quad\quad s\;interleaves(t,u,w) \end{cases}$$

The definition of *traces(PURCHASE(x))* shows that PURCHASE(x) can engage in any possible sequences when the trace of the specific three processes gets interleaved.

As for *traces(SYS)*, it represents a set including all possible traces as well as state transitions for the Safe Remote Purchase contract, which essentially equals to *trace(INIT)*.

$$traces(SYS) = \{s\,|\,s \in traces(INIT)\}$$

Attacker Model. Attacker model is a trace where the vulnerability resides in. And formal definition of this model is shown as follows.

$$attack = \begin{cases} init.msg\_value, seller.guarantee.eth.msg\_value, state'!created, \\ access?\,buyer, state'?\,created, buyer?\,msg\_value, access?\,seller, \\ state'!?\,created, abort, state'!inactive, eth.balance.seller.overall, \\ purchaseConfirmed, state'!locked, STOP \end{cases}$$

2.3   Using FDR to Verify the Contract

The above formal language is translated into CSP_M language for automated verification by FDR. As is shown in the blue rectangular box of Fig. 4, "*Passed*" means the *attack* trace exists in the *traces(SYS)*.

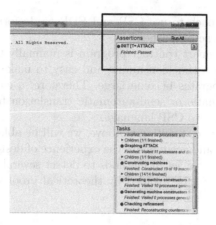

Fig. 4. Screenshot for verification result. (Color figure online)

3   Discussion

From the analysis and verification in part 2, theoretically we can make sure that there is vulnerability in the Safe Remote Purchase smart contract. The vulnerabilities exposed in the former case are very similar to racing problems in traditional concurrent programs. In this case, both **abort()** and **confirm-Purchase()** have the ability to execute writing operation to the global variable named state. The value of this global variable gets tampered by calling **abort()** while **confirmPurchase()** is under execution. Therefore, this kind of concurrent vulnerability can be grouped into the *Tamper by Interference* problems. Regarding this, these problems are probably ubiquitous in smart contracts especially in application of e-commerce. How to efficiently check and repair them is considered to be a future direction in the verification field.

Another point that will be discussed here is the seemingly atomic property of smart contract functions. Many people hold the view that functions in smart contracts will not be interrupted during execution. They believe that the consensus mechanism of the blockchain will guarantee this property. However, it seems logically insufficient for programming languages to rely on third parties like consensus mechanism to avoid the responsibilities of the language itself. And to the best of our knowledge so far, there has not been any evidence in literature to prove this atomic property can be ensured only through consensus mechanism. Hence, it should be admitted that although programming languages like Solidity is flexible to write smart contracts, their support for concurrency is not perfect.

This study only provides a framework of using CSP and FDR to check the vulnerability of smart contracts. And the readers may get puzzled that in the case study part, the vulnerability is known ahead of modelling through CSP. However, if we verify other unfamiliar smart contracts, the vulnerability may not be revealed with ease. And if the program is very complicated itself, it is nearly impossible to find its vulnerability from the code level. In this regard, it is still a good approach to use CSP and FDR to do formal verification but refinements should be accomplished.

In this study, the smart contract program is manually translated into CSP language, which is both time-consuming and easy to make mistakes especially when the scale of programs become large. Therefore, a compiler is needed in order to realize automatic or semi-automatic translation from smart contract programming languages to CSP language.

Through the endeavors mentioned above, we will be able to efficiently verify many smart contracts and accumulate the experience of designing attacker models. Then we can sum up a set of methods to detect several types of concurrent vulnerabilities, which can be avoided by theoretical proof when designing new contracts.

4   Conclusion

In this paper, we analyze the vulnerability of smart contracts especially from the perspective of concurrency. The analogy between smart contracts and concurrency programs is vividly revealed with the illustration of one example contract, in which possible attacks can be implemented by virtue of operating shared variables. Then CSP theory and FDR model checking tool are employed to detect the existing vulnerability. As shown, the example contract and its attack sequences can be modelled in a formal way by CSP theory with the interleaving of processes constituting the state space. Finally, the automated checking of FDR manifests that the attack sequence does exist in the state space, which proves the efficiency of CSP and FDR to check the vulnerability of smart contracts regarding concurrency.

Acknowledgment. This work was supported by the XJTLU research development fund projects under Grant RDF140243 and Grant RDF150246, in part by the National Natural Science Foundation of China under Grant No. 61701418, in part by Innovation Projects of The Next Generation Internet Technology under Grant NGII20170301, in part by the Suzhou Science and Technology Development Plan under Grant SYG201516, and in part by the Jiangsu Province National Science Foundation under Grant BK20150376.

References

1. Sergey, I., Hobor, A.: A concurrent perspective on smart contracts. In: Brenner, M., et al. (eds.) FC 2017. LNCS, vol. 10323, pp. 478–493. Springer, Cham (2017). https://doi.org/10.1007/978-3-319-70278-0_30
2. Filliâtre, J.-C., Paskevich, A.: Why3—where programs meet provers. In: Felleisen, M., Gardner, P. (eds.) ESOP 2013. LNCS, vol. 7792, pp. 125–128. Springer, Heidelberg (2013). https://doi.org/10.1007/978-3-642-37036-6_8
3. Swamy, N., Hriţcu, C., Keller, C., et al.: Dependent types and multi-monadic effects in F. ACM SIGPLAN Notices **51**(1), 256–270 (2016)

4. Luu, L., Chu, D.H., Olickel, H., et al.: Making smart contracts smarter. In: Proceedings of the 2016 ACM SIGSAC Conference on Computer and Communications Security, pp. 254–269. ACM (2016)
5. Atzei, N., Bartoletti, M., Cimoli, T.: A survey of attacks on ethereum smart contracts (SoK). In: Maffei, M., Ryan, M. (eds.) POST 2017. LNCS, vol. 10204, pp. 164–186. Springer, Heidelberg (2017). https://doi.org/10.1007/978-3-662-54455-6_8
6. Hoare, C.A.R.: Communicating sequential processes. Commun. ACM **21**(8), 666–677 (1978)
7. Roscoe, A.W.: Understanding Concurrent Systems. Springer, London (2010). https://doi.org/10.1007/978-1-84882-258-0
8. Faber, J., Jacobs, S., Sofronie-Stokkermans, V.: Verifying CSP-OZ-DC specifications with complex data types and timing parameters. In: Davies, J., Gibbons, J. (eds.) IFM 2007. LNCS, vol. 4591, pp. 233–252. Springer, Heidelberg (2007). https://doi.org/10.1007/978-3-540-73210-5_13
9. Lowe, G.: Breaking and fixing the needham-schroeder public-key protocol using FDR. In: Margaria, T., Steffen, B. (eds.) TACAS 1996. LNCS, vol. 1055, pp. 147–166. Springer, Heidelberg (1996). https://doi.org/10.1007/3-540-61042-1_43
10. Safe Remote Purchase contract. https://solidity.readthedocs.io/en/v0.4.24/solidity-by-example.htmlsafe-remote-purchase

A Blockchain Based Data Management System for Energy Trade

Mengjie Chen[(✉)], Yuexuan Li, Zhuocheng Xu, Xin Huang,
and Wei Wang

Department of Computer Science and Software Engineering,
Xi'an Jiaotong-Liverpool University, Suzhou, People's Republic of China
{Mengjie.Chen15,Yuexuan.Li15,Zhuocheng.Xu15,
Xin.Huang,wei.wang03}@xjtlu.edu.cn

Abstract. A new type of energy trade called the distributed energy resource has emerged in recent years, which can bring several benefits to people. However, trust issue also appeared among governments, users and energy companies. To solve the problem, smart contract and Ethereum are used to develop a system for distributed energy trade. A smart contract is a computer protocol intended to digitally facilitate, verify, or enforce the negotiation or performance of a contract. Ethereum is one of the decentralized platforms that run smart contracts. With the usage of smart contract and Ethereum, the system is reliable and it avoids the risk of using centralized energy management system. Therefore, the purpose of this project is to develop a blockchain based data management IoT system for energy chain transaction by Ethereum and test the smart contract by communicating sequential process (CSP) which is a formal language for describing patterns of interaction in concurrent systems.

Keywords: Blockchain · Smart contract · Energy auction · CSP
Ethereum

1 Introduction

Currently, nearly all the users purchase the electric power for domestic or industry need from the local electric utility. The power plants generate electric power according to beforehand estimation of regional daily power assumption. There is some amount of electricity power remained to be unexploited because the capacity of generated electricity exceeds that of consumed electricity. The extra power will be wasted if not used. In this case, an energy bidding system is proposed to solve this problem, offering an intermediary platform for everyone to bid for the extra energy out of individual usage. However, current centralized bidding system can incur several security issues. The typical vulnerabilities are replay attack and customer collusion which compromise anonymity and privacy [1]. The reliability of a third-party agency cannot be guaranteed since clandestine information can be leaked by the agency itself. Even if the third-party one is worth trusting, such an agency often demands expensive agency fee [2].

To avoid the above risks, the intermediate agency should be replaced or even obviated. Blockchain technology can satisfy this requirement. It is a distributed ledger

M. Qiu (Ed.): SmartBlock 2018, LNCS 11373, pp. 44–54, 2018.
https://doi.org/10.1007/978-3-030-05764-0_5

technology that allows users to remove middleman and decrease transaction cost and time lapse of working through the third parties. Moreover, the immutable and transparent ledger is not owned or controlled by any central authority and can be accessible to everyone [3]. One feature of the newly blockchain technology is the integration with smart contracts which are codes stored on the blockchain and executed automatically without a third-party control [4]. As a decentralized platform for running smart contracts, Ethereum provides a mature environment for contract development and deployment on a custom built blockchain. The developers can adopt smart contract to implement a decentralized energy biding system by Ethereum.

Even though smart contract evades the third-party risky, its concurrency feature can lead to several vulnerabilities which can be exploited by others. Most of those vulnerabilities are caused by the design logic errors of smart contracts. To detect the vulnerabilities of smart contracts for energy auction, communicating sequential process (CSP) is recommended as the verification method. CSP can specify and verify the interactions among concurrent systems [5].

In this paper, a blockchain based data management system for energy auction will be proposed to implement energy auction via Ethereum smart contract. The paper will focus on the feasibility and reliability of a decentralized energy auction system. The proposed smart contract for energy bidding will be evaluated based on CSP.

This paper is organized as follows: Sect. 2 introduces the development of energy auction. Section 3 displays the experiment for testing contract functions. Section 4 analyses CSP model checking process and results for the proposed smart contract. Finally, conclusions are drawn in the Sect. 5.

2 Research Method

The process of the energy auction is divided into several main stages which is shown in Fig. 1, at the first stage the supplier deploys the smart contract and post the bidding information which includes the energy amount, time of auction and address of supplier. Bidders sends the quoted price to bid the energy. After receiving the price, the smart contract compares the given price with the current highest price. If the given price is higher than the current highest price, then the contract will accept the quoted price and change the current highest price with the given price. Otherwise, the quoted price will be rejected. In the next phase, the bidder transfers a deposit to the smart contract and the account of the contract keeps the deposit until bidders require for withdraw or a bidder win the auction. When the bidding time is up, the auction ends and the contract account transfers the winner's deposit to the supplier's account. In the following phase, bidders who lose in the auction can withdraw their deposit. Using the structure of the blockchain, all bidders and suppliers can participate in the auction without a third-party platform such as an auction company.

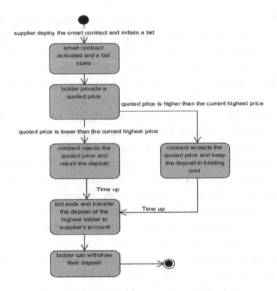

Fig. 1. State diagram of energy auction

The energy auction system must meet the following requirements:

1. The supplier should have the proof to get the money from the successful bidder when the auction is finished.
2. The bidders are able to get the deposit back if their quoted price is transcended.
3. The deposit can be returned only when the bidders start withdraw, which means the smart contract cannot start withdraw on their own.
4. The bidder should post their quoted price during the bidding time; otherwise, the quoted price is invalid.
5. If the bidder post the same price as the current highest price, the system will reject the quoted price.
6. The price of the individual bidder is private unless the quoted price is the highest price currently, which means only the highest is public.

The smart contract is a program deployed on the Ethereum platform. In Ethereum, smart contract cannot be activated by itself but it can be triggered by the external account [6]. The smart contract can be implemented using several languages such as Solidity, Golang and Serpent. In our experiment, we used Solidity to implement the smart contract for energy auction. The smart contract is accessible to the public and users can activate the smart contract using the address of the contract. Users can check the bidding information through several interfaces that is showed below:

1. Bidding time: the last time of the auction.
2. Supplier: the account address of the energy supplier.
3. Energy_for_trade: the amount of the energy supplied by supplier.
4. Highest_bidder: the account address of the bidder who provided the highest price.
5. Highest_bid: the highest quoted price.

6. Return: a mapping used to store the deposit information of bidders. (mapping is a data structure like the map in Java).

In the energy auction smart contract, we defined functions that is showed below:

1. Bid (): This function can be called by any people in public to join in the auction. At the entrance of the function, there are three requirements:
   (a) The bidder cannot be the supplier itself.
   (b) The current time must be in the bidding time.
   (c) The quoted price of this bidder must be higher than the current highest price.

If this bid satisfy the above requirements, the current highest price and highest bidder will change to the message sender's quoted price and address respectively.

2. Return_deposit (): return the deposit of the bidders except the winner of the auction.
3. Auction_End (): At the beginning of the function, it requires the current time should be later than the auction end time. Additionally, it is required that the auction has never been closed. In this function, the variable End is used to record whether the auction has been closed before. When the auction ends, the smart contract transfers the winner's deposit to the energy supplier.
4. In the smart contract, the key words event and emit are used to record the transaction log.

3   Experiment Progress and Functional Test

In the experiment, we deployed the smart contract and did the functional test which is divided into two main parts. The first one is based on JVM. We deployed the smart contract on the JVM to test if the contract satisfy the functional requirements. We used Remix as the Solidity compiler in this test. Remix also provided an interaction interface (which is showed in Figs. 2 and 3) for us to deploy contracts and call functions.

Fig. 2. The interface of remix

Fig. 3. The interface of contract deployment

We do not need to sign up an account when we test the contract on JVM because Remix will provide users with several accounts as showed in Fig. 3. After we deployed the smart contracts, we can implement the unit test via the Remix.

In the testing stage, we set one provided account as the supplier address when we deploy the contract. Then, we change the account and add the new bidding by using Remix.

The second part is based on the test network. In this part, we used Meta-Mask as the Wallet that provides several distinct accounts and we also used a tool Ganache which can establish a local private chain for people to deploy the smart contract. Ganache provides several available accounts and there are 100 ETH in each account for trade. Then we created a test network with Meta-Mask and Ganache. The account information can be synchronized with Remix, which means once we make a transaction via Remix, the account information in Meta-Mask will be updated immediately.

Here is an instance to explain the progress of bidding in a test network.

Step 1: We deploy the smart contract with the supplier account (provided by Ganache): **0xC6**7f6Fb04dfdCbBfA4f2b8BF2A65Fa991A5E3920 and 30 unit energy

Step 2: We create three distinct account as bidders:
0x8487e47c74d059bCEEA05804056Ded5F7C9d0a61
0xAaEAdeF6Ee95B3d773488079472F980d1555bF62
0xC518089037C3FAEf1A3599BD51B3AAba9D7d6664
Now we use the first four characters to represent the account.

Step 3: We starts the bidding:

    i. 0x84 provides the price 0.5 ETH
    ii. 0xAa provides the price 1 ETH
    iii. 0x84 provides the price 2 ETH
    iv. 0x5c provides the price 4 ETH
    v. Auction ends

The final result of the auction is that 0x5c wins the auction and the final price is 4 ETH. In addition, the contract returns 2.5 ETH to 0x84 and 1 ETH to 0xAa.

The transaction information, account information and private chain information can be viewed on Ganache as showed in Figs. 4, 5 and 6 respectively.

Fig. 4. Transaction information on private chain

ADDRESS	BALANCE
0×8487e47c74d059bCEEA05804056Ded5F7C9d0a61	97.50 ETH
0×AaEAdeF6Ee95B3d773488079472F980d1555bF62	99.00 ETH
0×2b3Eda3b071f5A3CAdD7E453b7Ca299b09085D09	100.00 ETH
0×B52185FA6115A3aE5c5cB66D7624897e9b4C298E	100.00 ETH
0×C518089037C3FAEf1A3599BD51B3AAba9D7d6664	96.00 ETH

Fig. 5. Balance of each account

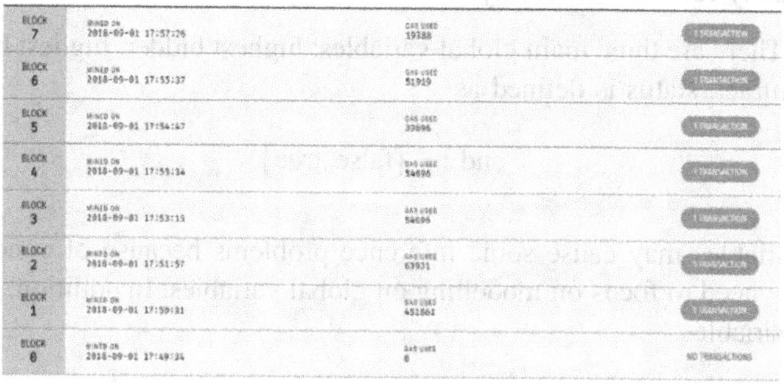

BLOCK	MINED ON	GAS USED	
7	2018-09-01 17:57:26	19388	1 TRANSACTION
6	2018-09-01 17:55:37	51919	1 TRANSACTION
5	2018-09-01 17:54:47	39696	1 TRANSACTION
4	2018-09-01 17:55:34	54496	1 TRANSACTION
3	2018-09-01 17:53:15	54694	1 TRANSACTION
2	2018-09-01 17:51:57	63931	1 TRANSACTION
1	2018-09-01 17:50:31	451861	1 TRANSACTION
0	2018-09-01 17:49:34	0	NO TRANSACTIONS

Fig. 6. Block information on private chain

4   Contract Vulnerability Test

4.1   Progress of Verification

As is showed in Fig. 7, the progress of verification can be divided into three main stages:

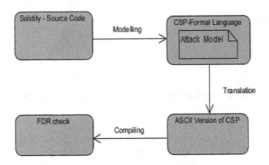

Fig. 7. Work flow of verification

5. Establish the model by translating the contract source code into formal language with CSP theory;
6. Develop an attacker model;
7. Compile the modelling result and use FDR for verification.

4.2   CSP Modelling

In this test, CSP is used to describe the attack sequence which is hidden in the program. Then, we use FDR, which is well-known for its successful detection of attack in concurrent security protocol [7], to test if the attack sequence in theory exits. The modelling mainly focus on three objects: variable, process and attacker model.

8. Variable: There are three main global variables: highest bidder, highest bid and end. In this contract, status is defined as

$$end := \{false, true\}$$

Global variables may cause some inference problems because of concurrent process. Thus, we need to focus on modelling on global variables. In addition, there is one other set of variables:

$$Object := \{supplier, bidder, contract\}$$

Supplier, bidder and contract means the account information of supplier, bidder and contract respectively.

9. Process: In this phase, we developed the contract function model, which contains four main functions: constructor(), bid(), auction_end() and return_deposit() which

is represented by Energy_Trade(x, y, z, u, w), Bid(x, y, z, u, w), Auction_end(x, y, z, u, w) and Return_deposit(x, y, z, u, w) respectively in process modelling

```
Bid(x,y,z,u,w)=bidder?caller:Object->
  if(caller==y)then STOP
   else(now?time:Int ->
         if(time>u) then STOP
         else bid?msg_value:{1,2}->
             if(msg_value>x)
             then(if (msg_value>0)
                   then mapping  ->
                      highest_bidder!caller ->
                      highest_bid!msg_value ->
                      Energy_Trade(msg_value,supplier,
                         energyforTrade,auctionEnd,caller)
                   else STOP)
             else STOP)


Return_deposit(x,y,z,u,w)=highest_bidder?w ->
        highest_bid?x -> return_money?money{0,1} ->
        if(money>0) then (send?result:{true,false} ->
           if(result==false) then successFalse-> STOP
                             else successTrue -> STOP)
        else(successTrue -> STOP)


Auction_End(x,y,z,u,w)=highest_bidder?w -> high-
     est_bid?x -> now?time:Int ->
        if(time<u) then STOP
        else (end?status:{false,true} ->
```

```
        if (status==false) then auctionClosed ->

                          end.true        ->

                          Auction_ended ->

                          Transfer!x!y   ->

                          STOP

    else STOP)


Energy_Trade(x,y,z,u,w)=Bid(x,y,z,u,w) |||

                      Return_deposit(x,y,z,u,w) |||

                      Auction_End(x,y,z,u,w)
```

10. Attacker model: The traces in the CSP model describe all the possible error states a smart contract can generate during conditions such as biding, returning deposit, and ending the auction. They are modeled according to the energy trading scenarios. In this experiment, the model checks the vulnerability about whether the money in the contract is transferred into corresponding suppliers and bidders' addresses and the energy is given to the winner address in the end of auction. The definition of the attack in this model is shown as follows:

$$ATTACK = \left\langle \begin{array}{c} init,\ bidder.msgSender1, \\ highest\_bid.2, \\ return\_money.1, \\ send.false, \\ successFalse,\ STOP \end{array} \right\rangle$$

4.3 Verify the Contract with FDR

The formal model is compiled and automatically verified by FDR and the final result indicate whether the attack trace exists.

4.4 Final Test Result

The final result is failed (showed in Fig. 8) which means the attack trace did not appear in the trace sets of our CSP model. It demonstrates this proposed smart contract does not have the vulnerability that may lead to transaction errors and thus can completely resist such attacking.

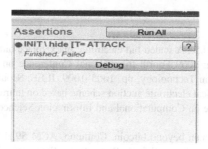

Fig. 8. Check result

5 Contributions

Compared with the traditional energy trade system, our system has the following advantages:

11. In traditional mode of energy trade, users only play the role of consumers, however, users not only play the role of consumers but also are able to play the role of energy suppliers in our system.
12. Our system is a decentralized energy trade system and it makes the trade more transparent and reliable. A decentralized system enables users to participate in the decision of the energy price.   •

In addition, compared with general p2p network, the advantages of blockchain make it more beneficial for our system:

13. Blockchain has its own consensus mechanism which means we do not need to develop protocols to help users establish trust between each other.
14. The trade information is transparent and unchangeable on the blockchain.
15. The users' privacy such as their real name is under protect on the blockchain.

6 Conclusion

In this paper, we provides a data management system based on blockchain for energy auction. The system based on the blockchain ensures that the system is decentralized, confidential and unchangeable. Additionally, we verify the system using Communicating Sequence Process (CSP).

However, the user may make some errors while using the system. For example, the bidders may forget to withdraw their deposit. To solve this problem, we will add a new function that the system will send remind message to the bidder who needs to withdraw their deposit.

References

1. Shi, W., Jang, I., Yoo, H.S.: A sealed-bid electronic marketplace bidding auction protocol by using ring signature. In: 2009 Fourth International Conference on Computer Sciences and Convergence Information Technology, pp. 1005–1009. IEEE, Seoul (2009)
2. Cao, G., Chen, J.: Practical electronic auction scheme based on untrusted third-party. In: Fifth International Conference on Computational and Information Sciences (ICCIS), pp. 493–496. CPS, Hubei (2013)
3. Underwood, S.: Blockchain beyond bitcoin. Commun. ACM **59**, 15–17 (2016)
4. Gatteschi, V., Lamberti, F., Demartini, C., Pranteda, C., Santamaría, V.: To blockchain or not to blockchain: that is the question. IT Prof. **20**, 62–74 (2018)
5. Hoare, C.A.R.: Communicating sequential processes. Commun. ACM **21**, 666–677 (1978)
6. Buterin, V.: A next-generation smart contract and decentralized application platform. White Paper (2014)
7. Lowe, Gavin: Breaking and fixing the Needham-Schroeder Public-Key Protocol using FDR. In: Margaria, Tiziana, Steffen, Bernhard (eds.) TACAS 1996. LNCS, vol. 1055, pp. 147–166. Springer, Heidelberg (1996). https://doi.org/10.1007/3-540-61042-1_43

A Distributed Digital Asset-Trading Platform Based on Permissioned Blockchains

Rong Wang[1(✉)], Wei-Tek Tsai[1,2,3,4,5], Juan He[1], Can Liu[1], and Enyan Deng[3]

[1] Digital Society and Blockchain Laboratory, Beihang University, Beijing, China
wangrong@buaa.edu.cn
[2] Arizona State University, Tempe, AZ, USA
[3] Beijing Tiande Technologies, Beijing, China
[4] Andrew International Sandbox Institute, Qingdao, China
[5] IOB Laboratory, National Big Data Comprehensive Experimental Area, Guizhou, China

Abstract. With the rapid development of cryptocurrencies, digital-asset transaction has become important, and the security and privacy of the centralized asset-trading platform are becoming serious. Distributed digital asset-trading platform has many characteristics such as high security and low transaction cost, thus received significant attention. In this paper, we first introduce distributed digital-asset-trading platforms, and evaluates currently available platforms by showing the strength and weakness of these platforms. Second, based on these analyses, we propose some principles of distributed digital-asset-trading platforms. Third, based on these principles, we put forward a novel exchange blockchain (EBC), which is based on permissioned blockchain (BC). We introduce the EBC system (EBCS), and analyse the performances of EBCS. Finally, we summarize and prospect future work of EBCS.

Keywords: Decentralized digital assets exchanges · Exchange blockchain Permissioned blockchains · Asset-trading platforms

1 Introduction

Ever since the birth of digital currencies such as Bitcoin [1], there has been an endless stream of stolen tokens in trading platforms. Since 2014, due to the explosive growth of digital currencies, many centralized exchanges have been established. Specifically, at least more than 4000 exchanges have been established in the world. Many exchanges have experienced numerous attacks resulted in large capital losses, such as the famous MtGox [2], Bitfinex [3], Shapeshift [4], and Bithumb [5]. While most digital currencies claim to be "decentralized", these tokens are often traded in centralized exchanges.

The characteristic of centralized asset-trading exchange (CDAE) is that all the information of the user is stored in the platform, and all the transaction operations are done on the platform. These CDAEs are efficient, but security is often an issue. More than \$12.5B USD of tokens have been stolen by hacker since the birth of

M. Qiu (Ed.): SmartBlock 2018, LNCS 11373, pp. 55–65, 2018.
https://doi.org/10.1007/978-3-030-05764-0_6

cryptocurrencies, from exchanges or wallet [6]. The tokens are in the custody of the CDAE vulnerable to hacker attacks, and lead to capital loss and theft risk [7]. The comparisons between these systems are shown in Table 1.

Table 1. CDAE and DDAE comparisons

	CDAE	DDAE
Safety	Less safe	Vuinerable to DDoS attacks, more safe
Transaction fee	Higher fees	Lower fees
Transparency	Rather opaque	Transparent
Asset custody	Need	No need
Throughput	High	Low
Delay	Low delay	High delay
Liquidity	Poor liquidity	High liquidity
Privacy	Poor privacy	Good privacy

Permissioned BCs include consortium and private BCs. Each organization runs one or more nodes that store the same data, nodes in the system are allowed to read and write these data, send and record transactions. Permissioned BCs have the characteristics of low-cost operation, high transaction speed, scalability, and security [11]. The permissioned BCs are suitable for transactions, settlement and liquidation between different institutions. For example, payment systems, clearing and settlement systems, interbank transactions can run on permissioned BCs [12, 13]. When more than 2/3 nodes on the network confirm a block, all the transactions in the block will be confirmed at the same time.

2 Distributed Trading Platforms

Currently main DDAEs include: 0x [8], Kyber [9], Airswap [10], Stex [14], Loopring [15], EtherDelta [16]. They can be divided into three modes:

(1) Asset Custody Model (ACM) such as 0x;
(2) Asset Reservoir Model (ARM) such as Kyber;
(3) Asset P2P Mode (APM) such as Airswap.

2.1 ACM

ACM is different from the fully CDAE asset custody in the BC. The 0x asset custody matches transactions under the BC, which can solve some speed and expense issues, but it also brings a certain degree of centrality.

0x is not a trading platform but an open-source decentralized trading protocol [14]. Its goal is to become a shared infrastructure for various Dapps in Ethereum ecosystem. 0x takes better advantages of decentralization than EtherDelta and combines them in a BC. It keeps the clearing function on the BC, and at the same time puts the transaction into the BC. On the one hand, the security of user assets is guaranteed. On the other hand, using the Relayer under the BC enhances the user experience and reduces user transaction costs. In terms of the key three elements, there has been great progress compared to EtherDelta.

0x introduces the concept of Relayer. 0x does not match transactions automatically. Taker (transaction receiver) must sign the order, then return to the smart contract, and the contents of the order (exchange targets, exchange rates) are accurate. Relayer can be understood as any market makers, exchanges or Dapps that implement the 0x protocol and provides BC asset custody services. Relayer's asset custody implementation can be centralized or decentralized. Relayer earns fees from transactions.

2.2 ARM

Asset Reservoir Model (ARM) is different from ACM. There is no asset custody but a reservoir provided by the reserve manager in the ARM. Kyber is a decentralized exchange on the Ethereum, providing users with a variety of applications including building a variety of useful trading APIs and providing them to businesses and users so that they can easily and "without trust" exchange tokens instantly [15]. The user will obtain the exchange rate between various types of tokens before sending the transaction and receive the corresponding number of tokens after the transaction is confirmed. The entire network is based on smart contracts. Kyber smart contracts provide the reasonable price, and settlement can be completed quickly through smart contracts on the BC. Its greatest advantage is its rapid settlement. However, there will also be problems that needs a balance sheet and enough reserve tokens to start it.

There are four entities in the Kyber network: users, reserve managers, reserve contributors, and platform operators. Each role independently interacts with smart contracts in different ways. Users can be personal accounts, smart contract accounts and merchant accounts. Besides, users can query conversion rates and conduct token transactions; reserve managers need to pass KYC certification and lock the exchange rate between different tokens in the contract to ensure the normal operation of the transaction; reserve contributors contribute tokens to the reserve pool and obtain profits from network spreads; Kyber operators are responsible for managing functions that they can control adding or removing pairs of transactions.

In addition, like 0x, it needs people to promote the flow of trading. Kyber allows others to create a reserve pool and collect tokens, and even get support from other exchanges. The ability to provide enough start-up pools and attract enough other reserve pool providers is key to Kyber's network operations. Only enough reserve pools can provide enough competitive prices so that it can have enough trading volume to make a good user experience.

2.3 APM

Asset P2P Mode (APM) is different from ACM and ARM. The transactions are p2p and the user's identity information remains hidden. The Airswap platform is based on the Ethereum BC and uses the ERC20 token [16]. The platform uses smart contracts that allow users to connect and execute transactions. Through smart contracts, users can easily complete transactions around the world. The use of off-of- chain negotiation and on-chain settlement provide p2p transactions and support free-price negotiation, commission orders, and transaction integration, and transaction settlement services.

Airswap's APM does not require strong operational drivers and users can only trust its Indexer and Oracle to provide traders and pricing advice. The APM is mainly for direct P2P price negotiation and provide personal communication. However, because there are steps such as negotiation, finding a counterparty, negotiating price and quantity, problems will arise that the transaction speed will be slowed down and determine the transaction price is hard to determine. Other models of DDAE, including single book hosting mode and reserve pool model, are all references to asset custody prices or reserve pool prices. The premise is that the transaction volume should be sufficient, otherwise it is difficult to have a reference to the optimal transaction price. The APM, in general, will rely on third parties, such as the price of a large CDAE as a reference.

AirSwap consists of seven parts: Maker, Taker, Order Book, Router, Oracle, Indexer and Smart Contract. Maker provides orders, Taker accepts the order, Router provides routing services, Oracle provides pricing information services to Taker and Maker, Indexer is a kind of sub BC transaction matching and summary service to match the transaction parties and Smart Contract is an Ethereum smart contract.

2.4   DDAE Model Comparison

The differences between these models are shown in Table 2.

Table 2. Comparison of DDAE models

	ACM	ARM	APM
On-chain account book	No account book	No account book	No account book
On-chain transaction confirmation	Yes	Yes	Yes
Transaction matching	Relayers match under the BC	Smart contract/reserve pool	Index
Fees	Trade fees	Pool and transaction costs are required	Need to pay index to provide prices service
Asset custody	Host crypto currencies to trading platforms	Host crypto currencies to smart contracts	Host crypto currencies to smart contracts
Transaction speed	High speed	Low sped related Ethereum transaction performance	Transaction matching off the BC high speed

(*continued*)

Table 2. (*continued*)

	ACM	ARM	APM
Settlement	Rely on smart contracts to implement transaction settlement function	Settlement between custody accounts	Settlement between custody accounts
Safety	Safe	Safe	Safe
Delay and throughput	High speed	Rely on Ethereum Protocols	Rely on Ethereum protocols
Scalability	Strong scalability	A certain degree of scalability	A certain degree of scalability
Privacy	A certain degree of privacy	A certain degree of privacy	Strong privacy
Supervision	Difficulty in supervision	Difficulty in supervision	Difficulty in supervision
Delay and throughput	Low delay, high throughput	High delay, low throughput	High delay, low throughput

3 Application Principles of Decentralized Platform

DDAE provides four functionalities: asset custody, transaction integration, transaction settlement, and capital withdrawal. A good DDAE should have the following features:

Security. Security has two aspects. First, it guarantees the security of the DDAEs. It is not vulnerable to common network attacks such as witch attacks and DDoS attacks. It can provide long-lasting and reliable services. Second, it protects user's tokens. Security ensures that the tokens that the user hosts on the DDAE cannot disappear or stolen by hackers. In exchanges, the security reflected in different functions is different. In the custody of tokens, security mainly means that digital assets will not be stolen; security in transaction integration is to ensure the instantaneousness, fairness and correctness of transaction prices; the security of transaction settlement is to ensure the safe transfer of digital assets. The security of asset extraction is that assets can be safely extracted.

Privacy and Supervision. Privacy refers to protect users' personal information such as ID and transactions, and prevent these to be disclosed to third parties. However, the supervisory authority can promptly check the identity of both sides of the transaction and the transaction details. Supervision ability often needs to judge whether the transaction conforms to the rules according to the transaction data, so as to immediately stop illegal transactions and realize the functions of KYC (Know Your Customer), AML (Anti-money Laundering), and Big Data Analysis that implement the supervision system [2]. In this process, the user's ID information is needed. Therefore, it is often difficult to supervise the privacy of a good exchange, and the privacy of an easily monitored exchange is poor.

Low Cost. Expenses include custody fees, matching fees, transaction fees, and settlement fees. In most exchanges, fees are charged once and for all. This fee includes the cost for these four parts. Some exchanges do not charge hosting fees to attract customers. Low costs can attract users to join the trading platform, increase trading volume, and increase the liquidity of digital assets.

Delay and Throughput. Delays include matching, settlement, and extraction delays, respectively. Throughput is used to measure the trading volume of the trading platform, including transaction blending throughput, transaction settlement throughput, and fund withdrawal throughput.

Scalability. Scalability includes the expansion of asset custody, transaction matching, transaction settlement, and asset transfer. The scalability of asset custody and asset extraction is determined by the corresponding mode of custody and the way assets are extracted; the scalability of transaction blending is determined by the blending system used, and the scalability of the transaction settlement is determined by the settlement method.

4 EBCS

4.1 Model Introduction

The EBCS consists of three parts: the ABC (Account BC) [17], the TBC (Trading BC) [17] and EBC (Exchange BC). The overall model is shown in Fig. 1. Each exchange has its own ABC and TBC, and each exchange is also a node of the EBC.

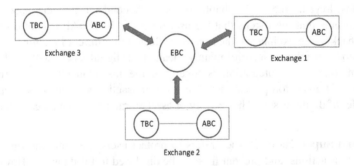

Fig. 1. EBCS system structure

ABC: This is responsible for maintaining the internal account information of the exchange. An exchange can have one or more ABC and ABC to store user information and commissioned orders information. A small exchange could maintain one ABC, while a larger exchange can maintain two or more ABCs to handle the load. Each ABC adopts multi-node BC designed, thus making the records secure from unauthorized modifications. All account modification will be recorded in the BC to prevent tampering.

TBC: This is responsible for orders matching within the exchange. An exchange can have one or more TBC and TBC to store orders matching data. The internal orders of the exchanges can be matched according to a certain orders matching mechanism, such as the principle of price priority, time priority, and etc. The order which completes matching is stored in the TBC and submitted to the EBC for asset transfers.

EBC: This is responsible for executing transactions and transfer assets and is composed of many exchange nodes. When the user needs to conduct an order, the order will send to the TBC for matching. After the completion order matching, the EBC transfers the assets and records the transaction asset transfer record on the EBC. EBC does not keep any account information.

Each exchange may have one or more ABCs and TBCs and each adopts CBFT (Concurrent Byzantine Fault Tolerance) consensus mechanism [18] independently to ensure the consistency of the information between the nodes and the unauthorized modification. Each BC has its own consensus mechanism, each of which maintains its own consistency.

4.2   Trading Process

The transaction process of EBCS digital asset trading platform is as follows:

(1) The user uses the client (including mobile phone APP, computer client, web page) to open an account or login in.

(2) The user fills in the purchase/sale consignment order application and sends a buy/sell consignment order request to the digital asset trading platform which is the fastest response exchange, and at the same time transfers the digital assets in the wallet to the EBC temporary address.

(3) After the exchange receives a request for purchase/sale order from the user,the exchange authenticate the user's signature to verify that the signature is correct and whether the order has not expired. After the exchange confirmation, the exchange put this order into the trading pool and recorded on the ABC of the exchange.

(4) The TBC of the exchange matches the internal orders of the exchanges according to matching rules, such as the principle of price priority, time priority. After order matching, the transactions will be submit to the EBC for asset transfer and the TBC will record these transactions at the same time.

(5) The EBC checks and confirms the order information and transfers the assets through smart contracts. See Sect. 4.3 Asset Transfer Protocol.

(6) After completing the transfer of assets, the EBC will send information to ABC and record the transaction on its BC.

4.3   Asset Transfer Protocol

The asset transfer agreement includes the following four steps, using the example of Alice's 10 BTC transaction with Bob's 100 ETH transaction as an example. As shown in Fig. 2.

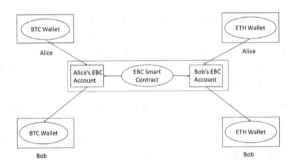

Fig. 2. Asset transfer agreement

(1) Alice and Bob enter the transaction through the exchange and Alice's 10 BTC exchanges with Bob's 100 ETH. At this time, Alice's 10 BTC exists in Alice's temporary account on the EBC, and Bob's 100 ETH exists in Bob's temporary account on the EBC. The EBC generates smart contracts for this asset transfer transaction.

(2) The smart contract verifies the transaction and checks Alice and Bob's digital assets in the EBC's temporary accounts. If the verification is successful, continue the following operations. If the verification fails, mark the transaction as failed. Return the digital assets in Alice's and Bob's temporary accounts on the EBC to Alice and Bob's wallet, and record the failure on the EBC.

(3) The smart contract will generate two transactions Tx1 (EBC to Bob transfer 10BTC) and Tx2 (EBC transfer to Alice 100ETH).

(4) When the transaction Tx1 and the transaction Tx2 are completed at the same time, the EBC complete transfers the transaction assets and records the transaction. Otherwise, EBC will launch the failed transaction again.

4.4   System Performance Analysis

Trading Speed. The EBCS trading platform separates transaction and asset transfers. Trading is performed on the TBC within the exchange. The TBC uses the CBFT consensus mechanism with fast execution. An important advantage of CBFT is its concurrent consensus building. Each block can be voted and built in parallel with other blocks [19], and this greatly increase the speed of consensus.

Trading digital asset transferred is carried out on the EBC. Smart contracts are used to complete transactions. The EBC also uses the CBFT consensus mechanism. The speed of the transfer of digital assets depends on the confirmation rate of other digital assets.

Transaction Costs. The EBCS uses the CBFT consensus mechanism. The capital custody only manage the tokens of the current transaction, and the custody tokens are placed in the temporary account corresponding to the EBC user. In the digital asset transfer phase, transactions are completed through smart contracts. The entire process costs only one transaction fee and costs less than a centralized research institute.

ABC Scalability. ABC provides a method for splitting accounts. When the number of accounts causes ABC to fail to maintain these accounts in time, ABC can be split into two ABCs. Both ABCs keep old books to keep historical accounts. Integrity, while using load-balancing policies between the two ABCs, maintains the books together to meet the scalability requirements. The ABC account is divided as shown in Fig. 3.

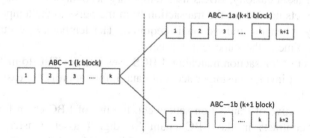

Fig. 3. ABC scalability

TBC Scalability. If the transaction volume increases, the problem of insufficient TBC performance can be solved by increasing the TBC, because all TBCs can run in parallel. Therefore, the processing speed of the system becomes faster as the TBC increases.

EBC Scalability. If the transaction volume increases, you can solve the problem of EBC performance shortage by increasing the EBC. Because all EBCs can run in parallel, so the processing speed of the system becomes faster as the number of EBCs increases.

Throughput and Delay. The trading of EBCS digital asset trading platforms is carried out in the internal TBC of the exchange. The TBC has good scalability, high throughput, and fast speed, so the delay is small. EBCS digital asset trading platform trading digital asset transferred is conducted on the EBC. At this time, the EBC has good scalability, so it has a large throughput, but the speed of asset transferred depends on the speed of other digital asset arrival confirmation. Delay in asset transfer may be higher.

Security. All data on the EBCS trading platform uses cryptographic algorithms that need to verify the customer's digital signature when initiating transactions. The use of decentralized ledger technology can both prevent external attacks and effectively prevent internal attacks and internal tampering with data. EBCS uses temporary accounts for asset custody, which transfers assets needed for trading from wallet to EBCS temporary accounts only when transactions are required, and the exchange returns the balance of the temporary account directly to the user's wallet after the transaction is completed in the withdrawal of funds. Therefore, it is difficult to be attacked and thus safer. During the asset transfer phase of the transaction, smart contracts are used. Smart contracts are executed on the EBC, and they are verified through formal methods and are therefore safer.

Privacy. EBCS system is composed of many exchanges, different exchanges have their own ABC and TBC, and each exchange is also a node of the EBC. ABC is used to store the account data and entrusted order records of their customers, TBC is used to store matching orders record, and customer account data is not easy to leak, with good privacy. EBC does not directly manipulate the customer's account data for the transfer of transaction assets, so the privacy is better.

In terms of asset custody, EBCS uses temporary accounts for custody. This mode transfers the assets needed for the transaction from the purse to the temporary account of EBCS only when the transaction is required. The temporary account of EBCS generated each time is the same and unrelated.

In the aspect of transaction matching, EBCS uses internal TBC to match orders, at this time does not involve customer account data, information is not easy to leak, and privacy is good.

In the perspective of transaction settlement, the use of EBC chain for asset transferred, smart contracts in the EBC chain for digital asset transfer, not directly manipulate customer account data, no storage of both sides of the transaction account information, privacy is very good.

EBCS is a distributed exchange system which is consists of many exchanges. Different exchanges have their own ABC and TBC. ABC is used to store their own account information and record entrustment orders. TBC is responsible for order matching within the exchange. User information is not easy to disclose and has good privacy.

Supervision. All transactions of the EBCS trading platform are recorded on the EBC. The supervision agency can comprehensively analyze the behavior of each user, thus promptly discovers the wrong information and preventing the occurrence of illegal activities. Using KYC and AML, the exchange can verify the identity of both parties in the transaction and analyze it to determine whether the transaction is legal. Supervisors can also perform big data analysis. Asset transferred transactions are recorded on the EBC. Supervisors can format all data in the system so that large data and data mining techniques can be used to effectively analyze the data.

5   Conclusion and Future Work

This paper compares DDAE platform and proposes principles that are applicable to most DDAEs. Based on these principles, this paper proposes a DDAE trading platform EBCS based on the permissioned BCs. Analysis of transaction speeds, transaction fees, scalability, throughput, delay, security, privacy and supervision shows that the EBCS platform has better performance and can meet the needs of users in terms of transaction speed, asset liquidity, and asset security. In the future, we will conduct large-scale testing for EBCS.

Acknowledgment. This work is supported by National Key Laboratory of Software Environment at Beihang University, National 973 Program (Grant No. 2013CB329601) and National Natural Science Foundation of China (Grant No. 61472032), (Grant No. 61672075) and (Grant No. 61690202).

References

1. Nakamoto, S.: Bitcoin: a peer-to-peer electronic cash system (2008)
2. Decker, C., Wattenhofer, R.: Bitcoin transaction malleability and MtGox. In: Kutyłowski, M., Vaidya, J. (eds.) ESORICS 2014. LNCS, vol. 8713, pp. 313–326. Springer, Cham (2014). https://doi.org/10.1007/978-3-319-11212-1_18
3. Baldwin, C., Poon, H.: Bitcoin worth $72 million stolen from Bitfinex exchange in Hong Kong. http://www.reuters.com/article/us-bitfinex-hacked-hongkong-idUSKCN10E0KP. Accessed 28 Oct 2018
4. A Timeline: ShapeShift Hacking Incident (2016)
5. Kim, C.Y., Lee, K.: Risk management to cryptocurrency exchange and investors guidelines to prevent potential threats. In: 2018 International Conference on Platform Technology and Service (PlatCon). IEEE (2018)
6. WISeKey. Annual Report (2017). https://docs.wisekey.com/site/justdownload.html?id=63. Accessed 28 Oct 2018
7. Bhaskar, N.D., Chuen, D.L.K.: Bitcoin exchanges. In: Handbook of Digital Currency, pp. 559–573 (2015)
8. 0x: An open protocol for decentralized exchange on the Ethereum blockchain. https://0xproject.com/pdfs/0x_white_paper.pdf. Accessed 28 Oct 2018
9. KyberNetwork: A trustless decentralized exchange and payment service. https://home.kyber.network/assets/KyberNetworkWhitepaper.pdf. Accessed 28 Oct 2018
10. AirSwap (AST)-Whitepaper. https://whitepaperdatabase.com/airswap-ast-whitepaper/. Accessed 28 Oct 2018
11. Tsai, W.-T., Bai, X., Yu, L.: Design issues in permissioned blockchains for trusted computing. In: 2017 IEEE Symposium on Service-Oriented System Engineering (SOSE). IEEE (2017)
12. Tsai, W.-T., et al.: Intellectual-property blockchain-based protection model for microfilms. In: 2017 IEEE Symposium on Service-Oriented System Engineering (SOSE). IEEE (2017)
13. Tsai, W.-T., et al.: Application of Blockchain to Trade Clearing. In: 2018 IEEE International Conference on Software Quality, Reliability and Security Companion (QRS-C). IEEE (2018)
14. Stex Whitepaper. https://stex.exchange/media/pdf/whitepaper.pdf. Accessed 28 Oct 2018
15. Loopring Whitepaper. https://github.com/Loopring/whitepaper. Accessed 28 Oct 2018
16. Etherdelta. https://etherdelta.com/. Accessed 28 Oct 2018
17. Tsai, W.-T., et al.: A system view of financial blockchains. In: 2016 IEEE Symposium on Service-Oriented System Engineering (SOSE). IEEE (2016)
18. Tsai, W.-T., Yu, L.: Lessons learned from developing permissioned blockchains. In: 2018 IEEE International Conference on Software Quality, Reliability and Security Companion (QRS-C). IEEE (2018)
19. Yu, L., et al.: Smart-contract execution with concurrent block building. In: 2017 IEEE Symposium on Service-Oriented System Engineering (SOSE). IEEE (2017)

Crux—A New Fast, Flexible and Decentralized Consensus Algorithm with High Fault Tolerance Rate

Pengfei Li[1,2(✉)], Jingtian Peng[1], Long Yang[2], Qian Zheng[3], and Gang Pan[2]

[1] LD Research, Shanghai, China
pfli0220@gmail.com, jingtian.peng@ldres.org
[2] Zhejiang University, Hangzhou, China
{yanglong,gpan}@zju.edu.cn
[3] Nanyang Technological University, Singapore, Singapore
csqianzheng@gmail.com

Abstract. This paper presents Crux, a new permissionless blockchain consensus algorithm that achieves higher fault tolerance rate with more flexibility than existing blockchains such as Bitcoin, Ethereum and EOS. Crux utilize a DPoS-XPaxos pipelined algorithm to achieve effective and efficient consensus. Those who hold tokens in Crux elect $2f + 1$ block producers called validators through a continuous approval voting system. The elected validators are scheduled in an order and produce blocks in turns agreed by all of the validators. XPaxos, guarantees $\frac{f}{2f+1}$ fault tolerance rate, is added to traditional DPoS to confirm blocks. Once $f + 1$ validators have signed a block, it is deemed irreversible. Analysis shows Crux provides higher securities, better flexibility, higher TPS (transaction per second) with little cost of centralization compared with existing blockchain consensus algorithms.

Keywords: Blockchain · Consensus algorithm · DPoS · XPaxos
Fault tolerance

1 Introduction

Traditional financial system is inefficient and expensive in global transaction: every participator (or a centre organization) should take part in the maintenance of its own account. Besides, the account in database cannot be fully trusted by all the participators in the multi-stakeholder transactions. Blockchain, a decentralized, tamper-resistant, traceable and distributed ledger, is a potential way to overcome above difficulties and improve traditional financial ecosystem.

Blockchain is originated in the technology of Bitcoin [22], and due to the success of Bitcoin crypto-currency, a lot of blockchain systems have been proposed in recent years, such as Ethereum [4], Hyperledger Fabric [5], BigchainDB [21]

The intellectual property right of this paper belongs to LD Research.

© Springer Nature Switzerland AG 2018
M. Qiu (Ed.): SmartBlock 2018, LNCS 11373, pp. 66–76, 2018.
https://doi.org/10.1007/978-3-030-05764-0_7

and et al. Comparing to traditional financial ecosystem, one of the most significant advantages in blockchain system is that it is unnecessary to ensure all the participators are trusted by each other and it is designed to achieve the Byzantine fault tolerance. Thus, consensus algorithm, the process of agreeing on a deterministic order of transactions and filtering invalid transactions is one of the core issues in blockchain. For example, Proof-of-Work (PoW) [22], Proof-of-Stake (PoS) [12], Delegated Proof-of-Stake (DPoS) [18] and Practical Byzantine Fault Tolerance (PBFT) [8] are typical approaches proposed to achieve agreement on the transactions.

Existing consensus protocols suffer from different shortcomings. For example, even though PoW guarantees a fault tolerance rate of 50%, it is computationally expensive with low utilization, and the forks produced by it makes the block chaim system less stable and reliable. Forks are also the main problem in PoS. People staking their coin can vote for both forks of the blockchain, and can even mine effortlessly in secret. Thus, PoS is not able to achieve consensus, unfortunately. In DPoS, only 21 nodes are elected as block producers and a block generation needs confirmations from at least 15 producers, $i.e.$, the fault tolerance rate is less than $\frac{1}{3}$. Similarly, PBFT can only achieve a fault tolerance rate of less than $\frac{1}{3}$—it is not high enough.

To address above problems, in this paper we propose Crux, a new consensus protocol that contains two parts: (1) a small subset of nodes (active delegates called "validators" in this paper) is elected firstly to produce blocks, (2) then confirm blocks by an XFT [20] model. Crux provides a fault tolerance rate of $\frac{f}{2f+1}$—larger than that of PBFT and DPoS. Moreover, it is unnecessary to generate forks and is more flexible and efficient.

For the delegates election step in Crux, we adopt the method introduced in Delegated Proof of Stake (DPoS) [1], the users (or nodes) who hold tokens in Crux elect $2f+1$ validators, $i.e.$, the block producers. Only the top $2f+1$ witnesses (who have collected the most votes) gain the right to turn to the following validate transactions part. In Crux, the voting power that the token holder has, otherwise known as voting weight, is determined by how many of the base token the account is holding. The roles of validators in Crux revolve around as follows: ensuring they are always up and running, collecting the transactions across the network into blocks, and signing and broadcasting those blocks, validating the transactions.

For the confirmation part in Crux, we use XPaxos protocol which is proposed in XFT model. This part makes the proposed Crux be an efficient resilient blockchain system that tolerates both Byzantine faults and crash faults (as well as network faults). Traditional consensus protocols such as Fault-tolerance based algorithms such as Practical byzantine fault tolerance [8] (PBFT), Zyzzyva [15] and Raft [23] give extraordinary power to the adversary, which results in there is no practical solution to effectively tolerate Byzantine faults. The XPaxos in Crux put a few restrictions on the power to the adversary and achieves higher fault tolerance rate. Besides, the XPaxos does not consume extra resources and preserve all reliability guarantees of asynchronous crash fault-tolerance

(CFT) [20], *e.g.*, Paxos [17]. It is an efficient and effective way to provide correct service as long as a majority of validators are correct and communicate synchronously.

Our contributions in this study are mainly the superior advantages of Crux, which can be summarized as follows:

- Crux provides a $\frac{f}{2f+1}$ fault tolerance rate. As long as more than f validators are correct and synchronous, it is guaranteed that blocks could be generated and confirmed correctly and efficiently.
- Crux will not generate forks. Upon a block is appended to the chain, it is stabilized and irreversible.
- Crux is flexible. The number of validators and the expiration time of validators' generating blocks could be dynamically adjusted.

This paper is organized as follows. Section 2 details our Crux. Section 3 reports the analysis of Crux. Section 4 reviews the related works. Finally, Sect. 5 concludes the paper and points to future work directions.

2   Crux Details

Existing blockchain consensus algorithms face many problems: Low fault tolerance rate (PBFT, DPoS); Huge computation resource consumption (PoW); Forks (PoW, PoS, DPos). These problems will bring insecurity or resource waste. To address these problems, we propose a scheme that a small subset of nodes is elected firstly to produce blocks. Then XPaxos, a novel state-machine replication (SMR) protocol designed in the XFT model [20], is used to confirm blocks.

2.1   Notations

We use N to denote the total number of all nodes in the Crux. Since any node is able to join or leave the Crux at any time arbitrarily, N is a dynamically changing number. These N nodes elect a group of validators, *i.e.*, block producers at intervals. We use *epoch* and Δep to denote the succession of node configurations from the beginning of one election to the next one and the expiration time of an epoch, respectively. In each epoch, $n = 2f + 1$ nodes are elected as validators.

Validators may suffer from the following kinds of faults: (1) Byzantine faults, where a validator act arbitrarily, *i.e.*, it fails to deliver blocks, delay them or duplicate them, but cannot subvert the cryptographic techniques we use (public-key signatures [26], message authentication codes [27], message digests produced by cryptographic hashes [7,25]); (2) crash faults [20], where a validator may suffer from a system crash or network break so that it stops all computation and communication. A node that is neither Byzantine faulty nor crash faulty is called *correct*.

We assume these validators are connected by point-to-point network asynchronously. Thus, validators may suffer network faults, *i.e.*, two replicas cannot deliver and process message within a delay Γ. We give the following definition to help quantify the number of network faults [20].

Definition 1 (Partitioned validator). *A validtor v is partitioned if it is not in the largest network-connected component, in which every pair of validitors can deliver and process messages among each other within Γ.*

Figure 1 shows an example about partitioned validators. We say a validator v is synchronous if v is not partitioned.

Having above descriptions, the number of three kinds of validator faults at a given moment s is modeled by

- $t_c(s)$: the number of crash-faulty nodes.
- $t_b(s)$: the number of Byzantine-faulty nodes.
- $t_p(s)$: the number of correct, but partitioned nodes.

Definition 2 (Anarchy). *The group of validators is in anarchy at a given moment s iff $t_c(s) + t_b(s) + t_p(s) > f$.*

Definition 3 (XFT protocol). *Protocol P is an XFT protocol if P satisfies safety in all executions in which the system is never in anarchy.*

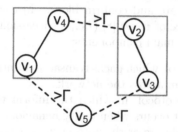

Fig. 1. An illustration of partitioned nodes: $\{v_1, v_4, v_5\}$ or $\{v_2, v_3, v_5\}$ are partitioned based on Definition 1 [20].

2.2 DPoS in Crux

Crux utilizes Delegated Proof of Stake (DPoS) [1], an existing decentralized consensus algorithm that is used in some popular blockchains such as EOS [2] and has been proven to be capable of meeting the requirements of applications on the blockchain, to elect validators on the beginning of each epoch. Under DPoS, those who hold tokens on Crux elect block producers through a continuous approval voting system. Anyone may choose to participate in block production and will be given an opportunity to produce blocks, provided they can persuade token holders to vote for them.

Under DPoS, the stakeholders can elect any number of nodes to be validators and generate blocks. Each account is allowed one vote per share per validator, a process known as approval voting. The top $n = 2f + 1$ nodes by total approval are selected. The number (n) of validators is defined such that at least 50% of voting stakeholders believe there is sufficient decentralization. Thus, it may be changed: when stakeholders think the speed of blocks generation is too low, the number will decrease; when stakeholders want more decentralizations, they will demand increase n. This process is also executed by voting: when stakeholders expresses their desired number of validators, they must also vote for that many validators. Crux will choose the median number of the voting numbers of n.

Each time validators produce a block, they will be paid for their services. If a validator fails to produce a block, then they will not be paid, and may be voted out in the future. In addition, those nodes participating the election and voting for the validators that generate blocks successfully will be also paid. This ensures that stakeholders are ultimately in control because stakeholders will get paid if they act correctly (*i.e.*, to vote for the ones that are most probable to become validators) but lose the most when they does not operate smoothly. For now, the pay rates of the validators that generated blocks and their voters are set by the stakeholders via their elected delegates, same with BitShares [18].

2.3   XPaxos in Crux

Crux utilizes XPaxos, a state-machine replication protocol in the XFT model [20] to make validators generate and confirm blocks. In each epoch *ep*, XPaxos is orchestrated in a sequence of *views* [8] (*i.e.*, a succession of validator configurations.). It consists of two main components:

- A common-case protocol, which packs transactions into blocks, then replicates and totally orders them across the networks.
- A new view-change protocol, in which the information is transferred from one view to another. It occurs when faulty behaviors of invalid validators are observed by valid validators or the current view expires. It is performed in a decentralized, leaderless fashion.

Each view is assigned to a unique number which is incremented once view-change occurs. For a given view i, we use a mapping known to all validators to determine a synchronous group sg_i which consists one *primary* and f *followers*— they are jointly called active validators. The remaining f validators in a given view are called *passive* validators. We denote the digest of a message m (maybe a block or some other kinds of information) by $D(m)$, where $\langle m \rangle_{\sigma_v}$ denotes a message that contains both $D(m)$ signed by the private key of validator v and m. We assume all nodes have public keys of all other nodes.

Common Case. In the common case, new digitally signed transactions are broadcast to all validators and each validator keeps a transactions pool. The primary collects transactions from his transactions pool into a block and sign it. Then this block is sent to other t active validators to be confirmed.

To be more specific, upon a block b is generated from the primary (says s_0), s_0 (1) increments the block number bn and assign bn to b; (2) signs a message $prep = \langle \text{PREPARE}, D(b), bn, i \rangle_{\sigma_{s_0}}$ and *prepares* the block b, *i.e.*, logs $\langle b, prep \rangle$

into its prepare log $PrepareLog_{s_0}[bn]$, and (3) forwards $\langle b, prep \rangle$ to all other active validators (*i.e.*, the f followers).

Each follower s_j $(1 \leq j \leq f)$ verifies the validity of each transaction in the block b and the primary s_0's signature. It will also be checked that if the local block number to be equal to $bn - 1$. If all of these validity verifications are achieved, s_j (1) logs $\langle b, prep \rangle$ into its prepare log $PrepareLog_{s_j}[bn]$, (2) update its local block number to bn, (3) signs the digest of the block b, the block number bn and the view number i, and (4) sends $\langle COMMIT, D(b), bn, i \rangle_{\sigma_{s_j}}$ to all active validators (including the primary).

If an active validator s_k $(0 \leq k \leq f)$ receives f signed COMMIT messages— one from each follower, it (1) *commits* the block b, *i.e.*, logs *prep* and the f signed COMMIT message into its commit log $CommitLog_{s_k}[bn]$, and (2) *confirms* the block b, *i.e.*, broadcasts the authentication message $\langle AUTHENTICATION, b, bn, ep, \rangle_{\sigma_{s_k}}$ to all other nodes (including those non-validator nodes) and remove all transactions in b from its transaction pool. A node accepts the block b and appends it to the chain of Crux when it receives $f + 1$ matching valid AUTHEN-TICATION messages. An AUTHENTICATION message is treated valid if (1) s_k is an elected validator in epoch ep, (2) the block number bn is larger than the local block number of a node and (3) every transaction in the block b is valid. Note that if a node cannot find the previous block of b based on b's previous block pointer, it will wait until b's previous block arrives, similar to Bitcoin [22].

The common-case message pattern of XPaxos in Crux is shown in Fig. 2.

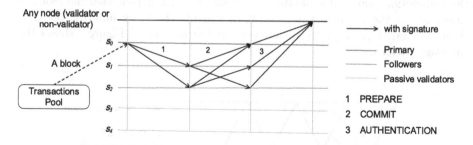

Fig. 2. Common-case message pattern of XPaxos in Crux when $f = 2$.

View-Change. Different from traditional view change techniques [9,10,14] where the view-change is led by a single node (usually the primary), in XPaxos view-change from view i to $i + 1$, every active validator in view $i + 1$ participate in the process.

We assign a expiration time Δv for each view. The objective is to make every validator have chances to be the primary. If view i expired, or sg_i, the synchronous group in view i does not make progress, *i.e.*, some faults are detected, a view-change occurs. Specifically, an active validator $s_k \in sg_i$ initiates a view change if (1) view i expires, or (2) s_k does not receive PREPARE message in Γ if it is not the primary, or (3) s_k does not receive enough COMMIT or AUTHENTI-CATION messages in Γ, or (4) s_k receives a message from other active validator that does not conform to the protocol (*e.g.*, an invalid signature or transactions in the block is invalid), or (5) s_k does not complete a view change to view i in a timely manner, or (6) s_j receives a valid SUSPECT message for view i from another active validator in sg_i, s_k will stop participate in the current view upon a view change is initiated. Then it will send $\langle \text{SUSPECT}, i, s_k \rangle_{\sigma_{s_k}}$ to all other validators (including the passive ones).

Upon receiving a SUSPECT message from an active validator in view i, validator s_k stops processing messages of view i and sends $\langle \text{VIEW-CHANGE}, i+1, s_k, PrepareLog_{s_k}, CommitLog_{s_k} \rangle_{\sigma_{s_k}}$ to the $f+1$ active validators of sg_{i+1}. Note that $PrepareLog_{s_k}$ and $CommitLog_{s_k}$ might be empty if s_k is passive. Besides, the synchronous groups of all views are deterministic to all validators, *i.e.*, each synchronous group uniquely determines the primary and every validator knows the members of the synchronous group in a given view. Active validator s_k in view $i+1$ waits for 2Γ time to collect as many VIEW-CHANGE messages. If at least $f+1$ VIEW-CHANGE message are received from all, s_k inserts all these messages into set $VCSet^{i+1}_{s_k}$. Afterwards s_k sends $\langle \text{VC-FINAL}, i+1, s_k, VCSet^{i+1}_{s_j} \rangle_{s_k}$ to every active validator in view $i+1$. Active validators are able to exchange the received VIEW-CHANGE messages through this process.

To start the new process of generating blocks and delivering messages, every active validator $s_k \in sg_{i+1}$ must receive VC-FINAL messages from all active validators in sg_{i+1}. Afterwards, the new primary ps_{i+1} collects transactions from its transaction pool and generate a new block b. Then it processes the block as described in the common case, *i.e.*, it increments the block number, prepares b and forwards $\langle b, prep \rangle$ to all followers in the new view. Figure 3 shows the message pattern.

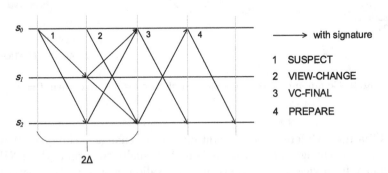

Fig. 3. XPaxos view change: the synchronous group is changed from $\{s_0, s_1\}$ to $\{s_0, s_2\}$.

3   Crux Analysis

3.1   Correctness of Crux

The correctness of Crux is guaranteed if the synchronous group contains only correct and synchronous validators. As long as the total number of Byzantine-faulty, crash-faulty and partitioned validators among $2f+1$ validators in an epoch is less than f, i.e., $t_b(ep) + t_c(ep) + t_p(ep) < f$, this can be achieved. Note that, there exists at least $f+1$ correct and synchronous validators, which are able to compromise a synchronous group sg—that is what we demand. Recall that, outside anarchy, in a given view i, at least one correct and synchronous active validator exists. These validators will report the invalid behaviors of faulty/partitioned validators and invoke a view change. A new synchronous group will replace the current one. The replacement process will continue until a synchronous group containing correct and synchronous validators only (sg is chosen). XPaxos guarantees that, eventually, view change will complete with $f+1$ correct and synchronous active validators. It is also indicated from above descriptions that the fault tolerance rate of our Crux is $\frac{f}{2f+1}$.

3.2   Confirmation of Blocks

As we described in Sect. 2.3, the process of a block generation needs $f+1$ confirmations, one from each active validator in a synchronous group. As we assume at most f validators are incorrect or partitioned, in this case a block in the chain is confirmed by at least one correct and synchronous active validator so that it is valid. In addition, Crux will not generate forks. Therefore, upon a block is appended to the chain, it becomes stabilized and irreversible.

In addition, due to our Crux confirm blocks based on messages deliveries and does not need to calculate nonces satisfied to some conditions like PoW, the blocks confirmation speed or transactions per second (TPS) of a blockchain system employing our Crux is much higher than that of blockchain systems using PoW as their consensus algorithm (e.g., Bitcoin [22] and Conflux [19]).

3.3   Flexibility of Crux

We provide two kinds of flexibility in Crux:

- The number of validators can be dynamically changed. In contrast, in DPoS, the number of delegated block producers is fixed to 21. By reducing the number, the COMMIT and AUTHENTICATION messages delivery time would be shortened so that the process of block confirmation can be finished in a shorter time period. This servers to be a kind of dynamics that controls the block generation speed. The function of adjusting the number of validators is similar to the difficulty adjustment in Bitcoin system [22].

- Δep and Δv—the epoch and view expiration time, respectively, can be changed. By decreasing Δep, more nodes have chances to become validators. On the contrary, if in a time period, elected validators are all correct and synchronous so that they can generate blocks efficiently and correctly. We can increase Γ to make trustable validators can generate blocks for longer time. Similarly, by changing Δv, we can adjust the speed of view change.

4 Related Work

In blockchain, how to reach consensus among the untrustworthy nodes is a transformation of the fault tolerant (FT) Problem, which was raised in [16]. In blockchain, there is no central node that ensures ledgers on distributed nodes are all the same. Some protocols are needed to ensure ledgers in different nodes are consistent.

The early BFT protocols are either too expensive, or intended for synchronous systems [11,24], which changes when PBFT is published. PBFT is a replication algorithm to tolerate Byzantine faults. PBFT or its variants are used in many existing permissioned blockchain systems, such as Hyperledger [5], Parity [3], Ripple [6] and ByzCoin [13]. However, the blockchain based on classic PBFT protocol keeps the fault tolerance rate of $\frac{f}{3f+1}$—which is low, the communication bound of $O(N^2)$ where N is the number of nodes. Thus, the performance of blockchain system based on PBFT algorithm is neither effective nor efficient at present, which implies the PBFT based protocols hurt scaling. Comparing to PBFT, XFT [20] can handle Byzantine, crash and network faults together whose fault tolerance rate is $\frac{f}{2f+1}$—higher than PBFT. In addition, it is more efficient than PBFT [20].

PoW (Proof of work) is a consensus strategy used in the Bitcoin network [22]. In PoW, each node of the network calculates a hash value of the block header. Generally the work means huge calculations. Thus it consumes much electricity and provides a very low TPS. To get a higher TPS, Conflux [19] represents relationships between blocks as a direct acyclic graph and achieves consensus on a total order of the blocks. But it sacrifice a lot of memories to save redundant transactions.

PoS (Proof of stake) is another energy-saving alternative to PoW [12]. Popular blockchain systems such as Ethereum [4] adopts PoS as their consensus algorithm. Miners in PoS have to prove the ownership of the amount of currency instead of the computation consumption. However, the selection based on account balance is quite unfair because the single richest person is bound to be dominant in the network. As a result, many solutions are proposed to improve PoS. For example, Blackcoin [28] uses randomization to predict the next generator and Peercoin [12] favors coin age based selection. However, both of them are not thorough solutions to the problem.

The major difference between PoS and DPoS [1] is that PoS is direct democratic while DPoS is representative democratic. In DPoS, stakeholders elect their delegates to generate and validate blocks. With significantly fewer nodes to validate blocks, the block could be confirmed quickly, leading to the quick confirmation of transactions. However, for DPoS, there are many difficulties in dealing with faulty nodes. The validator elections cannot effectively prevent the emergence of some destructive nodes and cause potential safety hazard to the network.

5 Conclusion and Future Work

In this paper, we propose Crux, a novel algorithm to achieve flexible, fast consensus with high fault tolerance rate in blockchain. Our algorithm first employs Delegated Proof of Stake to elect $2f + 1$ validators in every epoch to generate blocks and confirm them. Each epoch is composed of a series of views. In each view $f + 1$ validators are determined to be active which compromise the synchronous group. Among them, one is the primary that collect transactions and generate blocks and the others are followers which check the validity of the generated blocks through message deliveries. If invalid behaviors are detected, current active validators invoke the process of view change to alter the members of synchronous group in the new view until there is no incorrect or partitioned validator exists in the group.

There is a main disadvantage in our Crux now—when the number of incorrect or partitioned validators is large (*e.g.*, near f), the time consumption of view change will be huge. Therefore, a fault detection mechanism will be one of our future works. Fortunately, it may not be very difficult. An active validator in sg_{i+1} could detect which validator behaves invalidly based on the $CommitLog_*$ and $PrepareLog_*$ in the VIEW-CHANGE messages—this inspires us to make the VIEW-CHANGE messages contain both of commit and prepare logs. Moreover, we can also design an approach to directly select correct and synchronous validators in the process of view change.

References

1. Delegated proof-of-stake consensus. https://bitshares.org/technology/delegated-proof-of-stake-consensus/
2. EOSIO white paper. https://github.com/EOSIO/Documentation/blob/master/TechnicalWhitePapermd
3. Ethcore. parity: next generation ethereum browser. https://ethcore.io/parity.html
4. Ethereum blockchain app platform. https://www.ethereum.org
5. Hyperledger project. https://www.hyperledger.org/projects/fabric
6. Ripple. https://ripple.com
7. Bellare, M., Rogaway, P.: The exact security of digital signatures-how to sign with RSA and rabin. In: Maurer, U. (ed.) EUROCRYPT 1996. LNCS, vol. 1070, pp. 399–416. Springer, Heidelberg (1996). https://doi.org/10.1007/3-540-68339-9_34
8. Castro, M., Liskov, B.: Practical byzantine fault tolerance. In: OSDI, pp. 173–186 (1999)
9. Castro, M., Liskov, B.: Practical byzantine fault tolerance and proactive recovery. ACM Trans. Comput. Syst. **20**(4), 398–461 (2002)

10. Clement, A., Wong, E.L., Alvisi, L., Dahlin, M., Marchetti, M.: Making byzantine fault tolerant systems tolerate byzantine faults. In: NSDI, pp. 153–168 (2009)

11. Hopkins, A.L., Lala, J.H., Smith, T.B.: The evolution of fault tolerant computing at the Charles Stark Draper laboratory, 1955–85. In: Avižienis, A., Kopetz, H., Laprie, J.C. (eds.) The Evolution of Fault-Tolerant Computing. DEPENDABLECOMP, vol. 1, pp. 121–140. Springer, Vienna (1987). https://doi.org/10.1007/978-3-7091-8871-2_6

12. King, S., Nadal, S.: PPcoin: peer-to-peer crypto-currency with proof-of-stake. Self-published Paper, 19 August 2012

13. Kogias, E.K., Jovanovic, P., Gailly, N., Khoffi, I., Gasser, L., Ford, B.: Enhancing bitcoin security and performance with strong consistency via collective signing. In: USENIX Security, pp. 279–296 (2016)

14. Kotla, R., Alvisi, L., Dahlin, M., Clement, A., Wong, E.L.: Zyzzyva: speculative byzantine fault tolerance. ACM Trans. Comput. Syst. $27(4)$, 7:1–7:39 (2009)

15. Kotla, R., Alvisi, L., Dahlin, M., Clement, A., Wong, E.: Zyzzyva: speculative byzantine fault tolerance. ACM SIGOPS Oper. Syst. Rev. $41(6)$, 45–58 (2007)

16. Lamport, L., Shostak, R.E., Pease, M.C.: The byzantine generals problem. ACM Trans. Program. Lang. Syst. $4(3)$, 382–401 (1982)

17. Lamport, L., et al.: Paxos made simple. ACM SIGACT News $32(4)$, 18–25 (2001)

18. Larimer, D.: Delegated proof-of-stake (DPOS). Bitshare whitepaper (2014)

19. Li, C., Li, P., Xu, W., Long, F., Yao, A.C.: Scaling Nakamoto consensus to thousands of transactions per second. CoRR abs/1805.03870 (2018)

20. Liu, S., Viotti, P., Cachin, C., Quéma, V., Vukolic, M.: XFT: practical fault tolerance beyond crashes. In: OSDI, pp. 485–500 (2016)

21. McConaghy, T., et al.: BigchainDB: a scalable blockchain database. BigchainDB white paper (2016)

22. Nakamoto, S.: Bitcoin: a peer-to-peer electronic cash system (2008)

23. Ongaro, D., Ousterhout, J.K.: In search of an understandable consensus algorithm. In: USENIX ATC, pp. 305–319 (2014)

24. Paulitsch, M., Morris, J., Hall, B., Driscoll, K., Latronico, E., Koopman, P.: Coverage and the use of cyclic redundancy codes in ultra-dependable systems. In: DSN, pp. 346–355 (2005)

25. Rivest, R.L.: The MD5 message-digest algorithm. RFC 1321, pp. 1–21 (1992)

26. Rivest, R.L., Shamir, A., Adleman, L.M.: A method for obtaining digital signatures and public-key cryptosystems. Commun. ACM $21(2)$, 120–126 (1978)

27. Tsudik, G.: Message authentication with one-way hash functions. In: INFOCOM, pp. 2055–2059 (1992)

28. Vasin, P.: Blackcoin's proof-of-stake protocol v2 (2014). https://blackcoin.co/blackcoin-pos-protocolv2-whitepaper.pdf

Boost Blockchain Broadcast Propagation with Tree Routing

Jia Kan[✉]📖, Lingyi Zou📖, Bella Liu📖, and Xin Huang📖

XJTLU, Suzhou, China
Jia.Kan17@student.xjtlu.edu.cn
http://www.xjtlu.edu.cn/

Abstract. In recent years, with the rapid development and popularization of BitCoin, the research of blockchain technology has also shown
growth. It has gradually become a new generation of distributed, non-
centralized and trust-based technology solution. However, the blockchain
operation is expensive and transaction is delayed. Take BitCoin as an
example. On the one hand, a block is produced every ten minute. On
the other hand, once the new block is generated, it takes a certain time
to propagate world wide. The slow speed of propagation determines that
BitCoin can not use too small block interval time. Ethereum also faces
similar problems, so the concept of uncle block was introduced to reduce
blockchain forks. This paper introduces a new tree structure based broadcast propagation routing model, providing a novel method to organize
network nodes and message propagation mechanism. In oder to avoid
the single node failure problem, the tree cluster routing is proposed.
The research shows that the tree based routing can accelerate broadcast
convergence time and reduce redundant traffic.

Keywords: Blockchain · Broadcast network · Tree based routing
Tree cluster routing · Gossip protocol

1 Introduction

The concept of blockchain has risen rapidly, it has gradually become a hot spot of
technological innovation independent of BitCoin [2]. It creating a new distributed
data storage technology with an innovation change on system and programming
concepts [6]. Many financial institutions and related IT enterprises around the
world have set off a blockchain technology in the economic and Internet fields.
The development of blockchain has gone through three stages [14]. Blockchain
1.0 era is a cryptocurrency represented by BitCoin, which has the functions
of payment, circulation and other currencies. The Blockchain 2.0 era subverts
traditional currency and payment concepts through smart contracts, such as
Ethereum. In the era of blockchain 3.0, it goes beyond the financial field and provides decentralized solutions for various industries, including education, health,

Supported by Brahma OS.

culture, art and so on. Blockchain technology will change the deep structure of the enterprise, create new business model, and ultimately bring huge economic impact.

The blockchain network is a decentralized peer-to-peer (P2P) network that breaks the traditional Client/Server (C/S) model. In the original C/S model network [15], the server requirements are too high. It is increasingly difficult to provide satisfactory service performance. On the contrary, the decentralization of P2P technology is fully compatible with Internet protocol and structure. It has strong adaptability and network service capabilities. In recent years, with the broadband of users and the improvement of computer capacity, the advantages of P2P technology can be fully utilized.

Bitcoin's network uses a P2P network architecture which was based on the Internet, gossip protocol is used to propagate transaction and block information. In 1987, the gossip protocol was first proposed in Epidemic algorithms for replicated database maintenance [1]. The gossip protocol is also known as the epidemic algorithm. In a bounded network, each node communicates randomly with other nodes. After some messy communication, the state of all nodes will be agreed [10]. Figure 1 simulates the case where a message is propagated using the gossip protocol in the entire network nodes: The source node that starts the message will randomly select a peer node to send the message, then the infected node continues to select some peer node propagation. Repeat the process until all nodes are infected, until all nodes receive the message. The shortcomings of gossip are also obvious. In principle, mutual infection between nodes leads to repeated infections of some nodes. Although the reliability of information dissemination is ensured, duplicated contact affects the speed of network propagation convergence, especially for new block discovery. In term of speed, the slowness of propagation affects the efficiency to form a consensus [7].

In the blockchain protocol, after block data is generated, the node is broadcasting to all other nodes on the entire network for verification. However, due to the irregular connection between nodes, the message will propagated repeatedly, which ensures the reliability of information, but also causes redundancy and affects the broadcasting efficiency.In a large amount of nodes in the network, it is naturally desired to have a broadcast mechanism that more closely matching this mode to optimize the transmission of blockchain technology related services [4]. This paper designs a new tree structure model that supports blockchain broadcast services, proposing a complete information broadcast mechanism to reduce redundant traffic within the network and accelerate information propagation.

2   Blockchain and Broadcast Network

Microscopically, the essence of blockchain is a hash chain that cannot be tampered and traceable. Macroscopically, blockchain is a basic protocol with the characteristics of distributed storage, P2P network and consensus mechanism [2]. The reason why the P2P network is adopted is the blockchain nodes are characterized by openness, autonomy and anonymity.

In the traditional centralize mode, it's common to use a dedicated server from which multiple clients obtain data. The advantage of this mode is that the system is easy to manage and understand. However, the shortcomings of this model are also obvious: (1) due to the centralize mode, the system is prone to a single point of failure. (2) a single server faces a large number of clients, because CPU capacity, memory size and network bandwidth limitations, the number of clients that can be served concurrently is very limited. P2P technology is a network proposed to solve these problems [9]. In a P2P network, each node can either receive services from other nodes or provide services to other nodes. In this way, huge terminal resources are utilized, two drawbacks in the centralize mode are solved in one fell swoop.

Each node in a P2P network communicates and interacts with each other in a flat topology [9]. There are no special nodes and hierarchical structures. Each node will assume network routing, verify block data, broadcast block data, discover new nodes, etc. Because there are no special nodes in the whole network, he failure of any node will not pose a threat to the stability of the whole network. Different organizational structures are applied in different fields of computer network. In its network structure organization, such as gossip protocol, plays a huge role in BitCoin.

3 Gossip Protocol

In 1972, the emergence of the simple branch processing model of Galton-Watson made the research on gossip a solid theoretical tool [13]. The publication of "Epidemic algorithms for replicated database maintenance" [1] in 1978 pushed the research on gossip to a new height. The gossip protocol is simple and efficient, it also has good scalability and robustness. It is well adapted to a non-central, large-scale, highly dynamic distributed network environment, making it widely used in many fields [12].

The gossip protocol is also known as the epidemic algorithm. In a bounded size network, each node randomly communicates with other nodes. After some messy communication, the state of all nodes will be agreed. Each node may know only a few neighbor nodes. As long as these nodes are connected through the network, eventually their state is consistent.

In the gossip protocol [10], each node has the information about its neighbors. In every round of communication, each node selects one from the contacts to communicate, three communication methods as following: (1) Push, the A node sends the information to the Node B, Node B updates according to the received information; (2) Pull, Node B sends the information to Node A, Node A updates according to the received information; (3) Push/pull, in addition to the pull, A pushes the data that Node B does not have it, node B updates according to the received information.

There are three important factors in the gossip network [1]. (1) The number of nodes in the network, that means the size of the network. (2) The number of contacts saved by each node. In layman's terms, each node knows several nodes (number of friends). If the total number of nodes is 10000 and the number of friends is 100. The received message was transmitted multiple times though 100 friends, finally 10000 nodes received this message. (3) Rumor Mongering [11], the interest of rumors will be reduced with the same rumors received many times. When hearing this message many times, the node will instinctively believe that the rumor has spread widely, thus stopping its own spread. In 1/k, Increasing k will decrease the residue. This attenuation of interest helps to reduce rumor propagation, thereby reducing bandwidth usage, but also to some extent leads to the formation of isolated points.

Figure 1 simulates the case where a message is propagated using the gossip protocol in the entire network node: The source node that starts the message will randomly select a peer node to send the message, then the infected node continues to select some peer node propagation. Repeat the process until all nodes are infected, that is, all nodes receive the message. As shown in the Fig. 1,regardless repeating friends, in the first round, node 1–2; in the second round, node 1–3 and node 2–3; third round, node 1–4, node 2–4, node 3–4. It is known that its propagation amount is 2^{N-1}. However, in the actual simulation, nodes will have duplicate contacts. As soon as it reaches the boundary, most of the contacts who is spreading with may already know the message. In order to avoid the waste of bandwidth, the interest of mongering will decrease by the times of the contacts heard the news, in the case of the contacts amount of k. At the end of the spread, the feature of reduced interest does not guarantee 100% coverage.

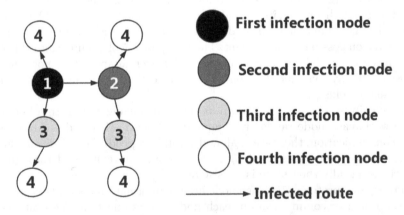

Fig. 1. The gossip protocol is used to disseminate messages in the network.

The advantages of gossip are also obvious. (1) Any node can spread the message to the whole network. When the central node has an error, the rectification system will not affects. (2) Any node can join or quit. (3) Fault tolerance, the downtime and restart of any node in the network will not affect the spread of messages. (4) Low CPU overhead and low network bandwidth are suit for large P2P networks. Figure 1 simulates the case where a message is propagated using the gossip protocol in the entire network node: The source node that starts the message will randomly select a peer node to send the message, and then the infected node continues to select some peer node propagation. Repeat the process until all nodes are infected, that is, all nodes receive the message. As we can see, we also clearly see the shortcomings of the gossip network. Since the node will only send messages to several nodes randomly, the message will eventually reach the whole network through multiple rounds of dissemination.

Some messages have to go very long. In order to reach the far node in the corner of the network, it will inevitably cause delay in the message. In addition, mutual infection between nodes leads to repeated infections of some nodes. It ensures the reliability of information dissemination, but also creates redundancy of information and increases the processing pressure on nodes.

4   Tree Based Broadcast Network

Inside blockchain, P2P network is a mandatory component. Among the three types of P2P communication models: pair-wise, group-wise and broadcast, broadcasting is the most common requirement for blockchain as every transaction or new block discovery requires to be announced in the whole network as efficiency as possible.

The broadcast network can be implemented with gossip protocol [1]. Gossip protocol [1] is extreme reliable, however it can not ensure the message can be arrived in every corner of network within fixed time. The propagation convergence time could last very long.

We proposed a tree based network in broadcasting use case. In tree based network topology, node join to tree as a leaf one by one, rules are set to ensure the tree is as balance as possible. In tree network, the longest distance between two nodes will be less than 2 times of tree height. That means even in a binary tree based topology, the message can be passed to the farthest node with less than 2 times tree height hops. It might be the most efficiency way for broadcasting in logic.

Compared with Figs. 1 and 2 simulates the case where a message is broadcasting through the tree structure throughout the network node: the source node that starts the message will broadcast the message along the branch to each node, assuming the depth of the source node is n, This infected node continues to propagate to the next deep (n+1) node until all nodes receive the message. As shown in the Fig. 2, without considering Rumor Mongering, in the first round, broadcasting depth n, broadcasting path node 1–2; in the second round, broadcasting depth n+1, node 2–3; in the third round, The propagation depth is n+2, 3–4. It can be seen that the rate of its propagation is 1+2+4+8.

In tree based broadcast network, message could be initialed from any tree branch node. A binary tree node will pass the message to its parent and two children from the original node. Any neighborhood receives the message, the message will be forward to other neighborhoods except the incoming one. For example, original node's parent receives the broadcast message, it will forward

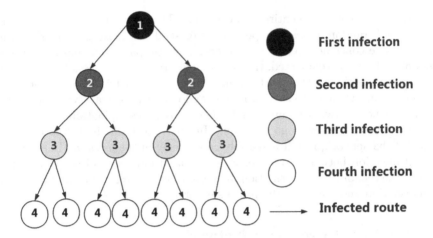

Fig. 2. Tree based broadcast network

the message to its parent node and another leaf node. If the original node's child receives the message, the message will be forward to both its children leaves.

However, tree based network also has its disadvantage compare to gossip protocol [1]: any single node failure will block the message propagation, because there is only one way for message to travel. To fix this issue, redundancy is required to add in this tree based broadcast network design.

5   Tree Based Network with Cluster Redundancy

The basic idea of adding redundancy to the tree based network, is to extend the single node to a cluster group. In Fig. 3 for the experiment purpose we assume a group contains 3 nodes. Inside the group, the nodes connect to each other. The nodes within one group can be located in different data center world wide. The broadcast message is passed to the group buddies if any node receives message from either parent or child.

Broadcast storm will happen as each message is hand to not only parent and children but also the group buddies. To prevent broadcast storm the node is required to remember the received message id. When the same message incomes, the node will refuse to forward it again.

The benefit of this design is it allows multi paths of routing from parent to child. If the direct connection between the parent and child is very slow or interrupted, the connection to buddy could be relatively fast. This relay could speed up the message propagation and ensure the reliable of whole tree network.

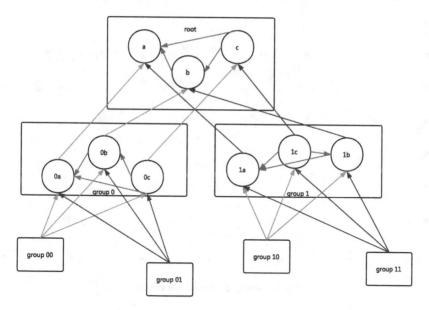

Fig. 3. Tree based broadcast network with cluster

6 Metric

For the gossip network, there are three key parameters: the network size, the number of contacts, and the message hotness decaying rate. Those parameters will impact the spreading speed. The tree network will reach the 100% convergence within fixed cycles, which is more efficiency.

In ideal situation, the gossip protocol and the tree based routing provides the similar propagation rate. The total nodes affected within N cycles in gossip protocol is 2^{N-1} and in binary tree based routing is $2^N - 1$, which is quite similar growth rate.

However, in reality, gossip network can not archive this rate because of nodes' duplicated contact. Let's say each node has enough contacts and the message hotness decaying rate is zero. As the message spreading showing in Fig. 4, node may talk to the contact which has already heard the message before. It slows down the whole network propagation, no matter the network size.

In tree based routing the nodes are organized in structure, it's a trade off between pure distributed system and centralized system. The node message always sends to unheard nodes in the next cycle. The convergence to all the nodes will be faster comparing to gossip protocol.

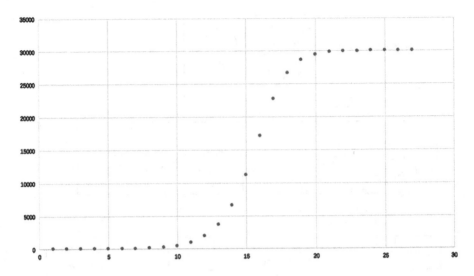

Fig. 4. Gossip protocol simulation

7   Evaluation

Tree based network routing plays quite similar way as gossip protocol did in blockchain broadcasting. Gossip protocol is simple, rousted, reliable, but sometimes it takes longer time to reach the 100% convergence. Tree based network is easy to understand, less traffic wasted, the disadvantage is obvious: the single node failure issue. Tree cluster network can fix this, although it makes the implementation a bit more complex, however it combines the advantages of both gossip protocol and tree network. This makes the following points a reality. Firstly, improving the integrating capability of P2P network. Secondly, this network Improves the efficiency of message transmission and avoids power consumption. Thirdly, Reducing the network bandwidth occupancy and improving the broadband speed.

8   Related Work

While we were working on the blockchain performance paper: Improve Blockchain Performance using Graph Data Structure and Parallel Mining [3], it's found that the blockchain performance has its bottle neck not only in the chain data structure, but also in the P2P network. Comparing to the blockchain, P2P technology is a big issue as the diversity of all kinds network situations. Lots of problem in reality would affect the P2P network performance, generally blockchain performance is limited. Oppositely, people believed improving consensus algorithm can increase blockchain performance, which is not true as expected. To improve blockchain's overall performance, P2P network is the critical part to work on.

In Seele's second yellow paper: An Accelerated Method for Message Propagation in Blockchain Networks [4], the performance requirement for a blockchain P2P network is affirmed. To build a high performance, a fast P2P network is necessary component.

Acknowledgment. The authors thank Brahma OS and the team advisors' help on information collection and idea pitching.

This work was supported in part by the National Natural Science Foundation of China under Grant No. 61701418, in part by Innovation Projects of The NextGeneration Internet Technology under Grant NGII20170301.

References

1. Demers, A., et al.: Epidemic algorithms for replicated database maintenance. In: Proceedings of the Sixth Annual ACM Symposium on Principles of Distributed Computing, pp. 1–12. ACM, December 1987
2. Nakamoto, S.: Bitcoin: a peer-to-peer electronic cash system (2008)
3. Kan, J., Chen, S., Huang, X.: Improve blockchain performance using graph data structure and parallel mining (2018)
4. Bi, W., Yang, H., Zheng, M.: An accelerated method for message propagation in blockchain networks (2018). arXiv preprint arXiv:1809.00455
5. Delgado-Segura, S., Pérez-Solà, C., Herrera-Joancomartí, J., Navarro-Arribas, G., Borrell, J.: Cryptocurrency networks: a new P2P paradigm. Mob. Inf. Syst. (2018)
6. Xie, H., Wang, J.: Study on block chain technology and its applications. Netinfo Secur. **9**, 192–195 (2016)
7. Watson, T.J., Golumbic, M.C.: The general gossip problem (1974)
8. Swan, M.: Blockchain: Blueprint for a New Economy. O'Reilly Media Inc., Newton (2015)
9. Decker, C., Wattenhofer, R.: Information propagation in the bitcoin network. In: 2013 IEEE Thirteenth International Conference on Peer-to-Peer Computing (P2P), pp. 1–10. IEEE, September 2013
10. Lind, P.G., et al.: Spreading gossip in social networks. Phys. Rev. E **76**, 036117 (2007)
11. Rosnow, R.L.: Rumor and gossip in interpersonal interaction and beyond: a social exchange perspective. In: Kowalski, R.M. (ed.) Behaving Badly: Aversive Behaviours in Interpersonal Relationships, pp. 203–232. American Psychological Association (2001)
12. Baumeister, R.F., et al.: Gossip as cultural learning. Rev. Gen. Psychol. **8**, 111–121 (2004)
13. Athreya, K.B., Ney, P.E., Ney, P.E.: Branching processes. Courier Corporation (2004)
14. Gu, X.L.: Research progress and development prospect of block chaining technology. Inf. Comput. 106–107+112 (2018)
15. Pourebrahimi, B., Vassiliadis, S., Bertels, K.: A survey of peer-to-peer networks. In: Proceedings of Annual Workshop on Circuits Systems & Signal Processing, vol. 94, no. 8–10, pp. 263–270 (2005)

A Simple Auditable Fingerprint Authentication Scheme Using Smart-Contracts

Xiaohu Zhou, Yousif Hafedh, Yonghao Wang, and Vitor Jesus[(✉)]

School of Computing and Digital Technology, Birmingham City University,
Birmingham, UK
vitor.jesus@bcu.ac.uk

Abstract. Biometric authentication, and notably using fingerprints, are now common. Despite its usability, biometrics have however a caveat which is the impossibility of revocation: once the raw fingerprint is breached, and depending on the technology of the reader, it is impossible to stop an illegitimate authentication. This places a focus on auditing both to detect fraud and to have clear indications that the fingerprint has been breached. In this paper we show how to take advantage of the immutability property of Blockchains to design an auditable protocol based on Diffie-Hellman key exchange with applications to fingerprint authentication.

Keywords: Biometrics · Authentication · Security · Blockchains
Smart-contracts · Auditing

1 Introduction

Fingerprint biometrics are nowadays a mature and widespread technology for authentication. It has several advantages being the two most important its usability (by being inherent to virtually any human) and accuracy since two people having the same fingerprint pattern is extremely rare. Fingerprint authentication has also seen commercial use in access control and application security and an example of such is seeing many modern mobile phones supporting it. There is however an important caveat which is the relative easiness of capturing fingerprints and later re-creating (say with wax fingers) and, post-incident, the impossibility of revoking a lost fingerprint in its original form.

In a world where one can only expect to have the identity stolen at some point in the future, biometric authentication is likely to become a reliable, yet non-authoritative (e.g., for legally binding actions), means of authentication. More than with any other security control, once an illegitimate attempt was successful, one can only expect more incidents to follow. Obtaining reliable evidence of the vulnerable step in the authentication flow where the invalid authentication happened is of paramount importance to harden systems, provide security checkpoints (such as multi-factor) and, in general, assess the risk against the sensitivity of the resources accessed. A simple example is with a bank account. If it is known that the fingerprint of a human has been illegitimately used, allowing bank transfers purely based on it is perhaps not advisable but viewing a bank statement is likely to meet the risk profile.

© Springer Nature Switzerland AG 2018
M. Qiu (Ed.): SmartBlock 2018, LNCS 11373, pp. 86–92, 2018.
https://doi.org/10.1007/978-3-030-05764-0_9

Audit trails, in the form of reliable and authoritative data on the process, along with real-time notifications, thus play a key role. Following the bank account example, after an incident has been recorded, it is likely that the bank will want to know where the vulnerable step happened; for example, if the authentication was successful because the fingerprint did match or whether it was deeper in the process and a mismatching fingerprint (or any other form of authentication) was accepted.

This paper proposes and discusses how blockchains can be used to provide an authoritative mechanism to prove, beyond any arbitrary level of doubt, that an illegitimate but successful identification took place at the fingerprint scan stage. Blockchains have the inherent property that, if enough time has elapsed (that depends on its size), whatever data is stored in it becomes immutable thus providing an excellent medium to store audit trails and reliable access notifications upon which one can act on.

The challenge we tackle is how to involve a blockchain in the authentication process. We do so by creating a protocol similar to Diffie-Hellman key exchange that, instead of running peer-to-peer, is ran intermediated by a blockchain. Considering that blockchains, whatever its form, typically require private keys to interface it, this scheme inherently provides multi-factor authentication. We envision our work to be, in fact, generic to any type of biometric authentication that relies on pre-acquired templates (such as images of fingers or iris) but we will keep the scope to fingerprints in order make the problem easy to discuss.

In Sect. 2 we present the technical background on fingerprint biometrics and blockchains. In Sect. 3 we present our approach and in Sect. 4 we illustrate with an implementation strategy using Ethereum and the Solidity language, a public blockchain supporting smart-contracts. We conclude our paper in Sect. 5.

2 Background

This section gives a technical background on fingerprint biometrics and blockchains; it further discusses related work in the area.

2.1 Fingerprint Biometrics

Fingerprint recognition is based on identifying a user by comparing stored fingerprint data (at enrolment stage) with input fingerprint data obtained in real-time. An automated fingerprint recognition system is concerned with fingerprint acquisition, minutiae extraction, minutiae match and storage [1]. There are two main phases: enrolment and authentication. Before a user can authenticate, s/he needs to record the images on an enrolment module. The minutiae (wiggling patterns virtually unique to everybody) are extracted and stored in a template with an associated user ID. The template is, typically, further transformed as explained below. On authentication, the authentication module extracts a minutiae pattern from the image (the probe) to compare with the corresponding user ID template in the system. A matching algorithm will then determine a matching score which, given a threshold, will then make a decision to accept or not.

Storing the templates of users is a central problem because, if breached in the raw form, it is impossible to revoke in the sense of revoking a certificate or changing a password. Cancellable biometrics is a key technique to help with this problem. Instead of storing the raw image or template, a distorted version is used either using a non-invertible transformation or biohashes [2] with the latter offering convenient fixed sizes templates.

2.2   Blockchains and Smart Contracts

Blockchains are a recent, and still maturing, technology having its first appearance to solve the "double-spending problem" in a digital currency and later recognised to solve the more generic "two generals' problem". It has evolved from its first application, Bitcoin, to now support generic scripting (smart contracts) as is the case of Ethereum. Whether it is information, in the sense of a ledger as in Bitcoin, or algorithmic methods and execution state, such as in Ethereum, Blockchains have the disruptive property of immutability: once stored, data is subject to cryptographic operations that are virtually impossible to reverse without abundant computing resources which is made further harder as time passes and as blocks (holding information) are added since they are interlinked. Therefore, if enough time is elapsed (i.e., enough computing effort is spent) it becomes virtually impossible to modify or destroy a record which brings auditing potential [3].

2.3   Related Work

Whereas literature is rich and abundant in biometrics authentication [4, 5], and Blockchains are already being analysed in research and academic literature, beyond commercial applications, very few works have approached the combination of the two techniques. Hammudoglu et al. [6] propose a mobile biometric-based authentication system for a self-sovereign identity solutions. It integrates a permissionless blockchain with identity and key attestation to be used in mobile phones. This work, however, is focused on how to implement self-sovereignty but storing secret and biometric material in full user control rather than the generic scenario of ours which is enhancing current biometric systems with auditing capabilities of blockchains. A similar remark can be made for Nandakumar et al. [7] which design a fairly complete system relying on private blockchains and mixing the blockchain's consensus layer with biometric material so that the decision of matching is distributed. This is further made secure by using secret sharing techniques such as Shamir's.

To the best of our knowledge, this is the first work to combine biometrics with blockchains and especially to use blockchains to enhance the auditability of an authentication process.

2.4   Problem Statement

The trace of the authentication is the central point of this paper. Our attacker model is simple: finger can be stolen or a copy of the fingerprint can be re-created. Our approach does not directly mitigate this problem; rather, it gives trusted means for a user to be notified and later audit the security breach since an adversary cannot delete records. Another possible attack vector is an inside malicious actor: no authentication was done but it is claimed to have happened. Since the insider is able to manipulate the logs, there is no way to credibly dispute or disprove there was, or was not, authentication via fingerprint. If an authentication point has been compromised, there will be no trace left in the blockchain.

3 Approach

Our approach is based on Diffie-Hellman Key Exchange (DHE) which allows the generation of a shared secret between two parties over an insecure channel. In order to make the authentication process auditable, while protecting the biometric material, we use the blockchain as a secure and immutable medium on which messages exchanged cannot be modified once written and enough time has elapsed. Figure 1 shows our scheme.

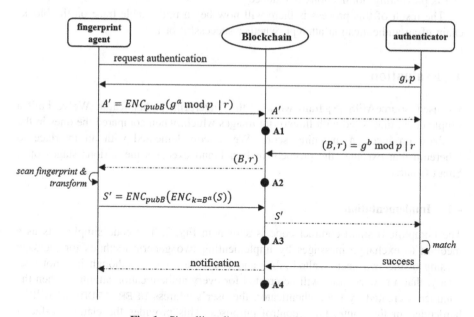

Fig. 1. Signalling diagram and audit points.

The user, previously enrolled, request authentication by using an agent application. This could be a mobile application. The authenticator responds with the following. It initiates the protocol by sending (random) parameters for the protocol (g, p) and (not shown in the diagram), the location of the smart-contract such as its address. It is assumed the user has secret keys to access the smart-contracts which, effectively, acts as a second-factor for the authentication process. The public key of the authenticator, perhaps obtained in real-time from a certificate sent by the authenticator (e.g., using

TLS), is used to encrypt both the remaining material of DHE and also to send a random nounce, r. Shown in dashed lines is the implicit broadcast process of a blockchain: once the block is mined, it is broadcast to all participating nodes. At this point, an audit point **A1** is created proving the user possesses the keys to interact with the blockchain.

The authenticator receives and decrypts the first message of DHE along with the nounce. Still using the blockchain, the authenticator publishes both its component of DHE and the nounce decrypted thus proving it possesses the public key and it is the right endpoint to send authentication material. This creates audit point **A2**. The user and the authenticator have now a shared secret, $k = A^b = B^a$. The user scans the finger (optionally transforming in the sense of cancellable biometrics) and encrypts with shared secret k its fingerprint. It further can encrypt with the receiver's public key for better privacy and forward-secrecy. This creates audit point **A3**. The client then publishes in the blockchain the result S' which holds the fingerprint scan. Upon a match, the authenticator records the result and the user is granted access. At any of the audit points, a notification to the user should be sent. Noting that these points are blockchain-wide, and any client for that blockchain can read it, the impact of a compromised agent that is preventing notifications is reduced.

The result of this process is there will now be an undeletable trace on the block-chain of an authentication attempt, whether successful or not.

4 Evaluation

We used SourceAFIS [8] framework as the fingerprint authenticator. We've built a simple client that is fed with fingerprint images which, when compared the ones in the database produces, a matching score. We've complemented with an interface to Ethereum that executes the protocol in Fig. 1 and executes the various stages on a Smart-Contract.

4.1 Implementation

The (simplified) smart-contract code is shown in Fig. 2. The code simply acts as a medium to exchange messages by implementing two generic methods for message passing of the two peers, called Alice and Bob. We assume, although it is not necessary, that a new contract will be created for every authentication attempt. When the contract is created by the authenticator, the user's address USER_ADDRESS will be hardcoded in the contract for control purposes. This provides the claimed 2-factor authentication as only the keys to that address will be able to interface the contract.

4.2 Evaluation

As expected, running a protocol over a smart-contract is significantly slow when compared with point-to-point protocols. We deployed and ran the contracts in a local Ethereum test network where no other contracts were being executed. This assured that every block was predictable given the low load in mining and confirmations occurring about every 15 s. Running the protocol took minutes as expected and one should note

```
contract Authentication {
  String message;

  constructor() public {
    supplicant = USER_ADDRESS;
    user_authenticated = false;
  }

  function bob( string msg ) public {
    if (msg.sender == authenticator) {
      message = msg;
    }
  }

  function alice( string msg ) public {
    if (msg.sender == supplicant) {
      message = msg;
    }
  }

  function auth_result() {
    if ( msg.sender == authenticator )
      user_authenticated = true;
  };
}
```

Fig. 2. Simplified smart-contract code.

that this is the simplest case where, e.g., no retries exist and the network has no load. A further practical issue is storage which, for the time being, makes this somewhat unfeasible. Since, at certain point, the user sends the fingerprint, regardless of how compressed it may be, it will take up space which, in a public blockchain may be unfeasibly expensive.

5 Conclusions and Outlook

This paper discussed the usage of a blockchain, and smart-contracts, to enable trusted audits of fingerprint biometrics. As seen, any biometric process that requires exchange of media can take advantage of this protocol to guarantee that actions leave an unmodifiable audit trail that can later be analysed.

Our scheme needs improvement, nevertheless, given its impracticalities, notably using the blockchain to store the candidate fingerprint. Furthermore, the time it takes to authenticate a user is also of consideration which may defeat the typical usability of biometrics as an authentication vector. These and other issues are the subject of our current and future work.

References

1. Jain, A.K., Nandakumar, K.: Biometric authentication: system security and user privacy. IEEE Comput. **45**, 87–92 (2012)
2. Ratha, N.K., Chikkerur, S., Connell, J.H., Bolle, R.M.: Generating cancelable fingerprint templates. IEEE Trans. Pattern Anal. Mach. Intell. **29**(4), 561–572 (2007)
3. Abreu, P., Aparicio, M., Costa, C.: Blockchain technology in the auditing environment. Caceres, CISTI (2018)
4. Pakutharivu, P., Srinath, M.V.: A Comprehensive survey on fingerprint recognition systems. Indian J. Sci. Technol. **8**(35), 1–7 (2015)
5. Meng, W., Wong, D.S., Furnell, S., Zhou, J.: Surveying the development of biometric user authentication on mobile phones. IEEE Commun. Surv. Tutor. **17**(3), 1268–1293 (2015)
6. Hammudoglu, J.S., et al.: Portable trust: biometric-based authentication and blockchain storage for self-sovereign identity systems, June 2017. http://cn.arxiv.org/pdf/1706.03744
7. Nandakumar, K., Ratha, N., Pankanti, S., Darnell, S.: Secure one-time biometric tokens for non-repudiable multi-party transactions. In: IEEE Workshop on Information Forensics and Security (WIFS), December 2017, Rennes, France (2017)
8. Vazan, R.: SourceAFIS. https://sourceafis.machinezoo.com. Accessed 26 Sept 2018

A Vision for Trust, Security and Privacy of Blockchain

Wenshi Wang[1,2]($\boxtimes$)

[1] Beijing Chain Space Information Technology Co., Ltd, Beijing, China
[2] AVIC Capital Building, Wangjing, Chaoyang District, Beijing, China
wangwenshi@aclub.io

Abstract. To introduce the latest technology of blockchain. In this paper, we discuss the problems from the aspect of reliability and security, which is encountered in the current blockchain technology and some research in the frontier field were introduced to develop the blockchain better. The scope of the discussion includes data availability issues, light client, fraud proof issues and zero knowledge proof issues.

Keywords: Blockchain · Trust · Security · Privacy

1 Introduction

In recent years, distributed computing is playing an increasingly important role. In 2008, satoshi published "Bitcoin: A peer-to-peer electronic cash system" [4] that brought us an e-cash system that can achieve peer-to-peer payment without the need for third-party authentication in the computer world. This experiment shows the potential of blockchain technology and distributed computing. Then the limited-function bitcoin script was replaced with the Turing-complete EVM virtual machine replaced. At the same time, the new and urgent problems need to be solved in the new field. Such as the security and privacy of blockchain.

This paper is organized as the follows. In Sect. 2 we described the trust mechanism in blockchain. In the Sect. 3 we discussed the security solution in blockchain. In Sect. 4 we gave the discussion on the privacy of blockchain. And in Sect. 5 we summarize the progress in our work.

2 Trust

In the world of blockchains, when we talk about trust, we usually use another term, called consensus. Consensus mechanism often defined as the following:

> Since most of the cryptocurrencies use decentralized blockchain design, nodes are scattered and parallel everywhere, so a system must be designed to maintain the order and fairness of the system, unify the version of the blockchain, and reward Resources maintain users of the blockchain and punish malicious people.

© Springer Nature Switzerland AG 2018
M. Qiu (Ed.): SmartBlock 2018, LNCS 11373, pp. 93–98, 2018.
https://doi.org/10.1007/978-3-030-05764-0_10

2.1   The Necessary of Consensus Mechanism

Back in the blockchain scenario, we hope to solve the problem of transaction credibility in a peer-to-peer environment where no one can control it. Essentially the consensus algorithm is expected in the following two environments:

1. There is no single entity that can own or control a resource.
2. Every subject get the resources they need in a certain amount of time.

It does means that this is necessary to find a feasible solution to a problem within a limited time and under limited resources.

2.2   Byzantine General Problem

The byzantine general problem is proposed by Leslie Lamport in The byzantine generals problem paper, which is the most complex and rigorous fault-tolerant model in the distributed domain. Analogy CAP theory is essentially solves it, and weighs the following three aspects:

1. The number of block producers.
2. The number of transactions per unit of time that the system can handle.
3. The cost of a malicious node initiating a Byzantine attack.

If no consensus is reached, the blockchain network will not work. In the typical Byzantine environment, $O(n)^2$ network communication efficiency makes it difficult to solve application problems. In 2009, Nakamoto led a solution for Bitcoin, and the workload proved that PoW's consensus network communication efficiency has achieved $O(n)$.

3   Security

The current blockchain technology is still constrained by the conditions that decentralization, security, and scalability cannot be met at the same time. We name it the impossible triangle problem.

3.1   Scalability

The root cause lies in ensuring the consistency of data on the blockchain in the future. Each node needs to verify all the data on the blockchain, thus bringing the block size limit; the physical limit of the block size is fundamentally limited TPS. One of the key points of solution to improve TPS:

1. The trade-off of the consensus mechanism yields higher TPS performance at the expense of neutralization and equivalent security.
2. Improve the book structure, Blockchain $\rightarrow$ DAG.
3. Introduce a network layered fragmentation architecture to achieve performance optimization with different security levels.
4. Offchain solution, the first layer Layer 1 guarantees network security, and the second layer Layer 2 pursues high scalability under the mechanism design that constrains data availability problems.

3.2 Data Availability

The data availability problem can be considered as one of the biggest and most difficult problems encountered in the current blockchain domain.

- Classical Blockchain: data on the blockchain → calculation, change → data on the blockchain
- Improved Blockchain: data on the blockchain ⊕ external data → calculation, change → data on the blockchain

This means that while ensuring that the data on the blockchain is correct, it is also necessary to ensure that the data in the entire blockchain p2p network is available. The current thinking in this industry is probabilistic optimization (Fig. 1).

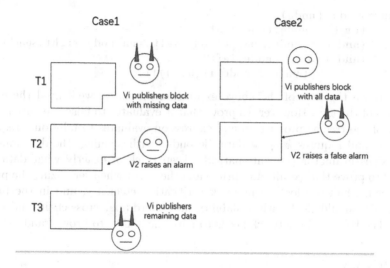

Fig. 1. Data unavailability problem

We consider introducing fraud proof, zero-knowledge proof, mechanism design and other schemes to optimize the problem of data unavailability [3].

3.3 Light Client and Fraud Proof Issues

Merkle trees allow us to map a large volume of data and easily identify where changes in the data occur. When we want to verifying membership in the bunck requires only a few computations (Fig. 2).

But if we want to relies on negative proof to proof fraud. In Petertodd's blog [6], he say we can see the lisp expression. A simple example is proving fraud in merkle-sum tree, where the validity expression would be something like:

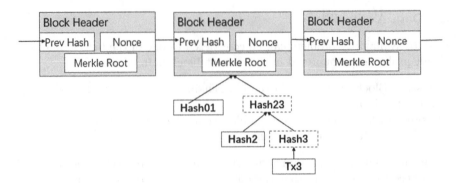

Fig. 2. Merkle tree

```
(defun valid? (node)
       (or (== node.type leaf)
       (and (== node.sum (+ node.left.sum node.right.sum))
       (and (valid? node.left)
            (valid? node.right)))))
```

To prove the true of the above expression evaluates, we'll need the entire contents of the tree. However, to prove that it evaluates to false, we only need a subset of the tree as proving an and expression evaluates to false only requires one side, and requires $k \log_2 n$ data. Secondly, with pruning, the deterministic expressions evaluator can automatically keep track of exactly what data was needed to prove that result, and prune all other data when serializing the proof.

It can achieve $O(\log(n))$ network verification efficiency, and in the future blockchain should deal with scalability and shardding, cross-chain and other fields. The blockchain network needs to have the ability to prove fraud.

4   Privacy

Blockchain technology has the characteristics of decentralization, encryption, and non-defective modification. The blockchain technology innovates our way of storing data and allow users to fully control their personal data share in public. The potential and fragmentation of blockchain technology may be the key to protecting our privacy.

4.1   Zero Knowledge Proof

The general concept of zero-knowledge proof is that I have to prove to others that I know fact A, but I can't reveal any information about A in my proof. The core problem of zero-knowledge proof is that it is being processed (Fig. 3).

1. Is it general?
2. Is it non-interactive?

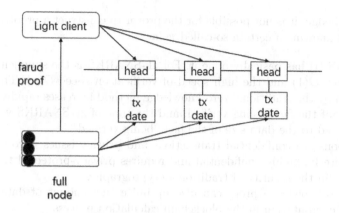

Fig. 3. Fraud proof framework

3. Operating efficiency?
4. Prove that the size varies with the size of the problem?

A general, non-interactive, efficient, constant-size zero-knowledge proof protocol is the goal of cryptography researchers for many years. zk-SNARKS [1] has basically done it, and the most popular place for zk-SNARKS is the simplicity of generating proof $O(1)$ and the high speed of verification speed $O(n)$. The time of verification by the traditional zero-knowledge method increases rapidly with the complexity of the facts being verified, and the time of zk-SNARKS verification is only related to the data size of the facts being verified. Technologies such as zk-STARKS and bulletproofs [2] are also advancing research in this field.

4.2 Advantage of Zero Knowledge Proof

In this general setting of so-called interactive protocols, there is a *prover* and a *verifier* and the prover wants to convince the verifier about a statement by exchanging messages. The generally desired properties are that no prover can convince the verifier about a wrong statement (*soundness*) and there is a certain strategy for the prover to convince the verifier about any true statement (*completeness*) [5].

- Succinct: the sizes of the messages are tiny in comparison to the length of the actual computation.
- Non-interactive: there is no or only little interaction. For zkSNARKs (succinct non-interactive arguments of knowledge), that a single message from the prover to the verifier. Furthermore, SNARKs often have the so-called "public verifier" property.
- ARguments: the verifier is only protected against computationally limited provers. Provers with enough computational power can create proofs/arguments about wrong statements.

– of Knowledge: it is not possible for the prover to construct a proof/argument
  without knowing a certain so-called *witness*.

zk-SNARKS [1] has basically done it. For zk-SNARKS is the simplicity of generating proof $O(1)$ and the high speed of verification speed $O(n)$. The time of
verification by the traditional zero-knowledge method increases rapidly with the
complexity of the facts being verified, and the time of zk-SNARKS verification
is only related to the data size of the facts being verified.

In response to confidential transactions and privacy issues, zero-knowledge
proof require be highly confidential and requires privacy-protected transaction
data hiding in the security of traditional cryptography.

The zero-knowledge proof can also optimize the amount of data and the
amount of computation in the blockchain calculation process.

5   Summary

On the road to the pursuit of more advanced blockchains, the problem becomes
more and more complicated. In this paper, we discuss the problems encountered
in the current blockchain technology in terms of scalability, security, and introduced some research in the frontier field to open up the future of blockchain.

References

1. Ben-Sasson, E., Chiesa, A., Tromer, E., Virza, M.: Succinct non-interactive zero
   knowledge for a von Neumann architecture. In: USENIX Security Symposium, pp.
   781–796 (2014)
2. Bünz, B., Bootle, J., Boneh, D., Poelstra, A., Wuille, P., Maxwell, G.: Bulletproofs:
   short proofs for confidential transactions and more. IEEE (2018)
3. Buterin, V.: A note on data availability and erasure coding (2017). https://github.
   com/ethereum/research/wiki/a-note-on-data-availability-and-erasure-coding
4. Nakamoto, S.: Bitcoin: a peer-to-peer electronic cash system (2008)
5. Reitwiessner, C.: zkSNARKs in a nutshell, May 2016. https://blog.ethereum.org/
   2016/12/05/zksnarks-in-a-nutshell/
6. Todd, P.: Building blocks of the state machine approach to consensus (2016).
   https://petertodd.org/2016/state-machine-consensus-building-blocks

A Blockchain-Based Data Hiding Method for Data Protection in Digital Video

Hongguo Zhao[1], Yunxia Liu[1(✉)], Yonghao Wang[2],
Xiaoming Wang[3], and Jiaxuan Li[3]

[1] College of Information Science and Technology,
Zhengzhou Normal University, Zhengzhou, China
liuyunxia0110@hust.edu.cn
[2] Computing and Digital Technology, Birmingham City University,
Birmingham, UK
[3] High Performance Blockchain Foundation LTD, Beijing, China

Abstract. The protection of secret data based on data hiding technique provides the basic security services for digital video through network transmission. However, the video with secret data is stored with centralized storage, which is vulnerable from external centralized attacks, such as the loss and tampering of the digital video. The protection of copyright and privacy data for digital video is still open issues. In this paper, we propose a blockchain-based data hiding method for data protection in digital video. To improve the integrity certification of secret data and the video, we combined the blockchain and data hiding techniques by adding the hash value to the block with a traceable hash value record; to improve the protection level of privacy data such as copyright related to digital video, we designed a DCT-based data hiding scheme which interact with the blockchain record, where the external chain is utilized as the controller for the privacy data into carrier video. Similar to Bitcoin, This system removes the need for a trusted third party, enabling autonomous control of privacy data.

Keywords: Data protection · Data hiding · Blockchain

1 Introduction

Blockchain is a brand-new decentralized infrastructure and distributed computing paradigm that has gradually emerged with the increasing popularity of digital cryptocurrencies [1]. Its application scope has gradually expanded to government departments, technology companies and capital markets. Blockchain has the characteristics of decentralization, traceability, and high credibility. Blockchain-based applications such as Bitcoin [2] and Ethereum [3], which can achieve the goals of transparency, irreversibility, and anonymity. That is, without the need of supervision by a third party organization, a consensus and trust can be reached between the two parties on themselves. Moreover, there exists technical inspiration significance for data protection such as the certification and protection of mass digital video existing on network.

The certification and protection issues of digital video have become an increasingly demand with the rapid development of internet video applications such as live

M. Qiu (Ed.): SmartBlock 2018, LNCS 11373, pp. 99–110, 2018.
https://doi.org/10.1007/978-3-030-05764-0_11

broadcasting, multimedia cloud [4], and 8K ultra-high definition (UHD) video applications [5]. So how to protect the legitimate interests of users and owners in the digital video that occupies the majority of the main internet traffic has become an active research area.

Based on the protection of the secret data (e.g., copyright information, and covert communication) inside the content of digital media, the technology of data hiding based on pictures as well as video has gradually caused more and more attention. Since the main focus of data hiding is to make best efforts to preserve the high visual quality of digital picture or video, it has a good data protection effect on copyright protection, and covert communication, especially for network video scenarios [6]. However, the traditional digital media on the network is always stored or utilized within centralized servers, distinguished from peer-to-peer transmission [7] (P2P service mode). In particular, with the rapid development of decentralization applications based on blockchain, the combination between data hiding and blockchain technologies has not received too much attention from scholars.

The main contributions and novelty of this paper are highlighted as follows: (1) Improved and expanded the applications of existing digital data hiding technology. The proposed data protection method is not only limited to digital media copyright protection, covert communications on the Internet transmission, but also can be effectively applied to blockchain application scenarios with respect of for digital media secret data protection. (2) Improved and enhanced the protection level for privacy data of video on chain. The integrity certification of digital video can be guaranteed with hash and encryption on blockchain technology. At the same time, the security of secret data can also be achieved with data hiding technology. That is, the security protection mechanism is derived not only from hash and encryption, but also data hiding technology.

The remainder of this paper is organized as follows: Sect. 2 introduces the related background, including the security mechanism and smart contract of blockchain, data protection on the chain, data protection on data hiding. Section 3 proposes the blockchain-based data hiding architecture for data protection in digital video and the preliminary evaluation is also presented in this section. Finally, the conclusion and the future challenges are shown in Sect. 4.

2   Related Background of Blockchain and Data Hiding

2.1   Data Protection on Blockchain

Data protection on blockchain mainly focuses on two aspects: the integrity certification and secret protection of data [8]. The integrity certification means that the data should be real, effective and not be unauthorizedly tampered. The secret of data means that the data on the blockchain is not accessible to the unauthorized users. For data protection on blockchain, there are already some scholars attempting to make efforts to develop the protection mechanism [8–14]. However, since the capacity of block on chain is limited, which makes it difficult to store and protect large-scale data. The existing data protection methods based on chain can be classified as follows:

(1) Data protection on the chain: The main goal of data protection on chain is that the implementation of comprehensive surveillance on chain, and averts illegal tampering about the transaction data into block. The authors in [11] proposed an encryption scheme for the transaction address with a random number to guarantee the protection for the transaction address. The authors in [8] utilized hash value, time stamp and Merkle root value which are recorded in the body of each block to guarantee integrity certification of data chain. As shown in Fig. 1, current block is connected to previous block with previous recoded hash value, and connected to the next block with storing the current block hash value. These techniques can guarantee the body of the block cannot be faked and tampered from the malicious attackers. For example, once the data of transaction 2 is illegal tampered, and then the hash value of current block could also be changed as depicted with shadow regions in Fig. 1, correspondingly. The result of these changes would not be consistent with the following block which has recorded the current block hash value, and the chain structure of block will be broken.

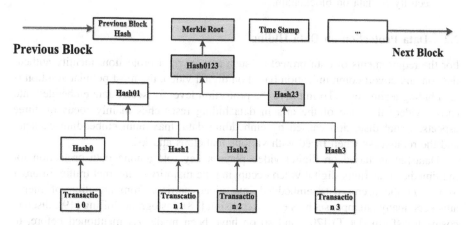

Fig. 1. Overview of security mechanism for blockchain

The authors in [15] proposed a control method based on blockchain data, which utilized publicly auditable contracts to automatically manage the tracking of the data source and logging data usage history. The method embedded the control requirements into smart contract to improve the transparency and security for the usage and protection of data on chain. However, the effort for data protection about multimedia on blockchain is noticed by few scholars. Bhowmik et al. [28] proposed a distributed and tamper-proof media transaction framework to protect data security, and the multimedia object is mainly focused on pictures. However, the challenge for data protection about digital video is that the bitstreams for the video content are too large to be incorporated into block on chain. Thus, there still exists a strong need for the researches about the protection of digital video data on chain.

(2) Data protection on and off the chain: data protection on and off chain has been provided for the limited storage capacity, which means that the blockchain technique has been utilized for the protection of the integrity and traceability, and the encryption are also used to ensure the secret of the large-scale data stored in a trusted database. The authors in [16] proposed a data protection model with the combination of user, service, blind escrow and blockchain. In this secret model, the blockchain is used to store the final hash value derived from the detailed data which has been stored in the specific database named Blind Escrow, the service and user are interacting with the encryption scheme. The authors in [17] further provided a secret distributed computing framework named Enigma, which distinguished the process of original data and data management. In the architecture of Enigma, the data are classified into three types: Public ledger stored the data which can be public to all nodes or users; distributed hash-table (DHT) and multi-party computation (MPC) are used to store the pointer index which is linked to the real database. The blockchain inherent character meets the demands of the integrity of data, and the utilization of DHT and MPC meet the demands of the security of data on blockchain.

2.2   Data Protection on Data Hiding

For the requirements of data protection such as copyright protection, identity authentication and covert communication based on digital video, the most popular solution is data hiding technology. To improve the protection level for secret data embedded into carrier video, the state of the arts in data hiding researches mainly focus on three aspects: visual distortion caused by embedding data, maximum embedding capacity and the robustness when faced with various malicious attacks.

Data hiding based on digital video plays a key role among data protection for multimedia concerning digital video occupying the majority of internet traffic. In order to protect the secret data embedded into video carriers from attention of illegal attackers, many attempts such as error expansion [18], histogram shifting [19], discrete cosine transform (DCT) [20], and so on have been made. As mentioned before, to reduce the visual distortion caused by embedding data, the authors in [21, 22] proposed the pair-coefficients to reduce the visual distortion of carrier video, and in [22] the authors proposed an improved method which combined the pair-coefficients and prediction modes to avert the distortion drift. To improve the embedding capacity, DCT coefficients have been proven an effective scheme for data hiding [23]. To strength the robustness of data hiding, the literatures in [24–27] used lots of pre-processing methods prior to embedding the secret data, for example, BCH codes and secret sharing techniques to resist various noise attacks and key data loss scenarios. However, the existing data hiding methods are mainly focused on the encoding and decoding procedures; the distribution multimedia application scenario on blockchain is not directly applied to data hiding.

3   Proposed Method and Evaluation for Blockchain Based Data Hiding

3.1   The Architecture for Blockchain Based Data Hiding

The architecture for blockchain based data hiding is composed with three sections: Data hiding servers & database with storing the real digital video, the blockchain with the signatures of specific video, and the data protection management with the format of smart contract. As shown in Fig. 2, if one certified blockchain user needs to inquire the secret data such as copyright of digital video C, the request for C is submitted to data protection management. Then the model of data protection management first checks the integrity of video C with the signature and second obtains the real digital video C index. After accessing the real index of the digital video C, the data protection management will post a request for copyright to data hiding servers. With extracting copyright data embedded into video C, the copyright data of video C will be transmitted to the certified user with encryption format.

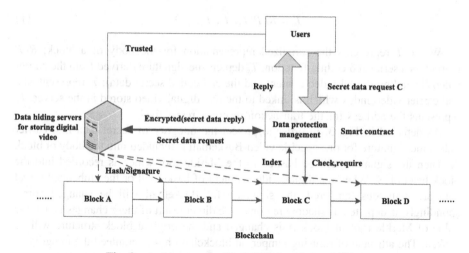

Fig. 2. Architecture for blockchain based data hiding

It can be seen from the architecture of blockchain based data hiding that the signatures of the digital video inside blockchain achieve the integrity goal of digital video data, and the trusted data hiding servers simultaneously guarantee the security of digital video data such as copyright, privacy data which are not suitable for presenting into the body of blockchain.

3.2   Protection Mechanisms Based on Blockchain

(1) *System Initialization*

Initially, each digital video should generate the signature (hash value) based on the specific video content and will be updated to the body of block data on blockchain. With the hashtable attribute of no tampering, the integrity of one specific digital video can be achieved with checking the signature stored on the chain. Also the data hiding servers should choose one outperformed data hiding algorithm which can achieve a good balance between visual distortion, embedding capacity and robustness.

2) *Protection Scheme for Data on Chain*

The protection scheme for digital video on chain mainly focuses on the integrity check and the security of sensitive data. In order to achieve the function of checking the integrity of digital video, the signature about one specific video content is uploaded to blockchian. Without the consideration of smart contract on blockchain, the transaction data on one block can be presented as follows:

$$T = RLP(T_s, T_i, T_a, \ldots) \tag{1}$$

Where T represents the serialized representation for the body of a block; RLP represents a serialized coding function; T_s depicts the signature derived from the carrier video (including digital video content and the embedded secret data); T_i represents the real carrier video index which is linked to the real digital video stored in the server, T_a represents the address for the transaction receiver, respectively.

As depicted in Fig. 3, in order to protect the integrity of secret data into carrier video, the signature for one specific video-Basketball is included into the body of block A. Then the signature will be hashed to the Merkle root which is recorded into the block head of A. When the digital video content of basketball or the embedded secret data are malicious tampered, the signature for Basketball will be changed correspondingly as depicted as shadow regions. The direct result of these changes is that the value of Merkle root of block A is changed and the original block structure will be broken. The attribute of refusing tamper on blockchain has guaranteed the integrity of secret data about digital video Basketball. Moreover, since the body of block A is open access for other nodes on blockchain, the carrier video index should be encrypted with respect of the security of the database storing the carrier video of Basketball.

(3) *Protection Scheme for Data off Chain*

The protection scheme for data off chain mainly focuses on the security level of the traditional data hiding technology and our previous study [25] has been adopted for the protection scheme of data off-chain. As mentioned before in Sect. 2.2, the security level of data hiding is determined by visual distortion, embedding capacity and robustness. In order to eliminate the visual distortion and improve the visual quality of carrier video, the paired-coefficients and prediction modes are adopted to avert the distortion drift introduced by embedding data. In order to enlarge the embedding capacity, DCT coefficients are considered for the actual syntax elements to embed data

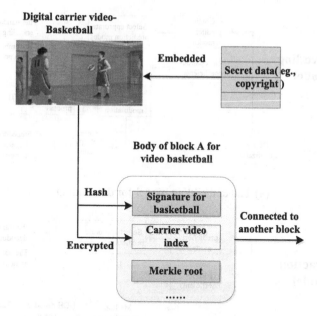

Fig. 3. Data protection on blockchain

since the DCT coefficients occupy the majority of video content. To improve the robustness of data hiding, BCH code scheme is also provided in case of unpredictable error bits scenes. The detailed protection scheme is shown in Fig. 4. In Fig. 4, the embedding model is depicted in (a) and the extraction model is also depicted in (b). Moreover, in order to ensure the security of secret data during the network transmission, the secret data which are embedded into carrier video should also be encrypted correspondingly.

To protect the real address for data hiding servers, the index transmitted from the blockchain network is also encrypted with the public key in case of unknown malicious attackers or unauthorized users. First, the data hiding servers should decrypt the index. If the request for secret data into digital video such as copyright is received, the extraction model is called to extract these secret data. If the request for adding the copyright data into digital video is received, the embedding model would be called to embed data. After that, the signature of the carrier video and the encrypted index would be transmitted to blockchain to preserve the integrity and security of the copyright information corresponding to the specific digital video.

The evaluation for data protection of chain can be classified into two aspects: visual quality of the carrier video and the robustness of embedded data. The Peak Signal-to-Noise Ratio (PSNR) is used to measure the visual quality of data hiding method, and the evaluation of PSNR can be defined as follows:

$$PSNR = 10 \times Log_{10}(\frac{MAX_A^2}{MSE})(dB) \tag{2}$$

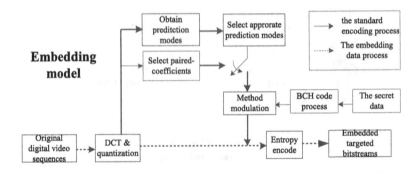

(a) The embedding model for data hiding

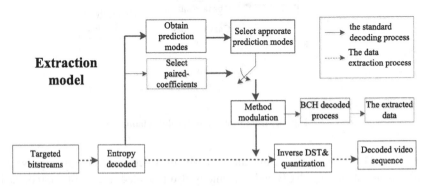

(b) The extraction model for data hiding

Fig. 4. The entire procedure for data hiding

$$MSE = \frac{\sum_{i=1}^{a}\sum_{j=1}^{b}\sum_{k=1}^{c}[A(i,j,k) - B(i,j,k)]^2}{a \times b \times c}$$

Where A and B represent the original and carrier video, a and b represent the resolution of the carrier video, c refers to the RGB color components. MAX represents the highest pixel value in frame A. Figure 5(a) provides the performance of PSNR between the proposed data hiding scheme and data hiding methods without consideration of distortion eliminated. Simultaneously, the survival rate is also used to measure the robustness of data hiding method, and The survival rate is calculated in the following formula:

$$Survival\ rate = \frac{Size\ of\ the\ extract\ secret\ data}{Size\ of\ original\ secret\ data} \times 100\% \qquad (3)$$

Figure 5(b) provides the performance of robustness between the proposed data hiding scheme and data hiding without robustness. The proposed data hiding scheme

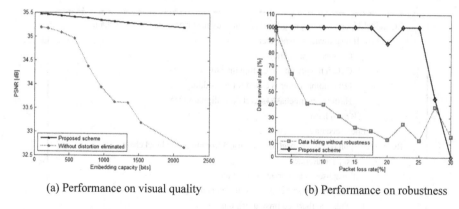

(a) Performance on visual quality   (b) Performance on robustness

Fig. 5. Evaluation on the proposed data hiding scheme

get better performance on visual quality and robustness. That is, the security of secret data off-chain is effectively outperformed than the methods without distortion eliminated and robustness. Moreover, we can get the embedding capacity by using more video sequences because the infinite video sequences just meet the requirements for the strict visual quality demand scenario.

(4) *Data Protection Management Agreement*

The data protection management agreement is based on the smart contract, and consists of Registration Contract (RC), an Inquiry Contract (IC) and a Transfer Contract (TC) models, respectively. Figure 6 also depicts our proposed data protection management agreement for registration, inquiry and transfer, respectively.

- RC: The RC model is designed for the registration of private data such as copyright to the owner of digital video. When the author of digital video is signing up an account on blockchain, the owner of contract about this video is also determined by confirming RC. Once the confirmed RC is re-called, the information of the transaction initiator will be checked. If the caller of contract is illegal, the request of re-updating privacy data would be rejected. However, after the legitimate account is registered, the RC will generate the hash value form the specific digital video.
- IC: The IC model is designed for the management of authorized users and query service for one worthy video content. The owner of digital video can manage the lists of authorized users by calling RC model. And only the authorized users are permitted to inquiry the secret data (e.g., Copyright). In order to preserve the secure transmission of secret data, the inquired secret data could be encrypted with the authorized users' public key, and the authorized user can decrypt the transmitted secret data with private key, corresponding.
- TC: The TC model is designed for the scenario that the ownership of the digital video can be transferred between the owners and the authorized users, which makes the data protection method more flexible. For example, if the secret data of digital video is copyright data, the transfer request for the copyright of digital video can be

```
RC model:Upon receiving msg("registration", owner) from users on blockchain
        If msg.owner =owner then
            Creat new transaction
            Obtain the privacy data from msg.owner
            Data hiding server is called for embedding
            Hash = generatehash (secret data, digital video)
        Return hash
    End procedure
RC model:Upon receiving msg("query", user) from users on blockchain
        List [ ] authorized
        If msg.user in authorized = True then
            Data hiding server is called for embedding
            Puk = authorized [msg.user]. puk
            Data = encrypt(secret data, Puk)
            Return Data
    End procedure
TC model:Upon receiving msg("transfer", buyer, owner) from users on blockchain
        If msg.owner =owner then
            If owner.operation = True then
                Transfer(buyer.to, owner.from)
                Data hiding server is called:
                    linkTo(buyer.data, digital video)
                Return the result of transfer.
    End procedure
```

Fig. 6. The procedure for data protection management agreement

made between the two parties of transaction. Then the TC will be called. If the copyright owner agrees to this transaction, the TC contract will be executed automatically. If the owner disagrees to this transfer transaction, the transaction will be discarded.

4   Conclusions and Future Challenges

In this paper, the solution of blockchain-based data hiding method has been proposed with respect of data protection for privacy data on digital video. The proposed blockchain based data hiding methods include data protection on chain, data protection off chain with data hiding technology, and data protection management agreement based on smart contract.

As shown in this work, the combination of blockchain and data hiding technologies can be a desirable tool to improve the protection level of secret data on digital video. The blockchain is a powerful technique explored for the integrity protection of data inside digital video, and the data hiding is also an effective technique for the secret protection, especially for privacy data inside digital video, and covert communication.

There remain some essential improvements of data protection with blockchain based data hiding method for future work. One is the continuous research for the combination between blcokchain and data hiding technologies. Even though the combination of the blockchain and data hiding can solve the problem of data protection inside digital media (integrity and security), the protection for data hiding servers, especially for the decentralized distribution of servers, still needs to be considered in the future. Another potential area of improvement is the continuously expanded researches on off-chain data protection, which means enhancing the security level of data protection in more digital applications, not only with digital video, but also with images and audios.

References

1. Christidis, K., Devetsikiotis, M.: Blockchains and smart contracts for the internet of things. IEEE Access **4**, 2292–2303 (2016)
2. Nakamoto, S.: Bitcoin: a peer-to-peer electronic cash system (2008). Consulted
3. Atzei, N., Bartoletti, M., Cimoli, T.: A survey of attacks on ethereum smart contracts (SoK). In: Maffei, M., Ryan, M. (eds.) POST 2017. LNCS, vol. 10204, pp. 164–186. Springer, Heidelberg (2017). https://doi.org/10.1007/978-3-662-54455-6_8
4. Zhu, W., Luo, C., Wang, J., Li, S.: Multimedia cloud computing. IEEE Signal Proc. Mag. **23** (3), 59–69 (2011)
5. Sze, V., Budagavi, M.: High throughput CABAC entropy coding in HEVC. IEEE Trans. Circuits Syst. Video Technol. **22**(12), 1778–1791 (2012)
6. Tew, Y., Wong, K.S.: An overview of information hiding in H. 264/AVC compressed video. IEEE Trans. Circuits Syst. Video Technol. **24**(2), 305–319 (2014)
7. Ha, P.H., Tsigas, P., Anshus, O.J., Sname, F.: SocioNet: a social-based multimedia access system for unstructured P2P networks. IEEE T. Parall. Distr. **21**(7), 1027–1041 (2010)
8. Liu, A.D., Du, X.H., Wang, N., Li, S.Z.: Research progress of blockchain technology and its application in information security. Journal of Software (2018)
9. Bogner, A., Chanson, M., Meeuw, A.: A decentralised sharing app running a smart contract on the ethereum blockchain. In: International Conference, pp. 177–178 (2016)
10. Kosba, A., Miller, A., Shi, E., et al.: Hawk: the blockchain model of cryptography and privacy-preserving smart contracts. In: Proceedings of the 2016 IEEE Symposium on Security and Privacy. Piscataway, NJ, pp. 839–858. IEEE (2016)
11. Monero: A note on chain reactions in traceability in Cryptonote 2.0 (2017). https://lab.getmonero.org/pubs/MRL-0001.pdf
12. Miers, I., Garman, C., Green, M., et al.: Zerocoin: anonymous distributed E-cash from bitcoin. In: IEEE Symposium on Security and Privacy Conference, Piscataway, NJ, pp. 397–411. IEEE (2014)
13. Ben-Sasson, E., Chiesa, A., Genkin, D., Tromer, E., Virza, M.: SNARKs for C: verifying program executions succinctly and in zero knowledge. In: Canetti, R., Garay, Juan A. (eds.) CRYPTO 2013. LNCS, vol. 8043, pp. 90–108. Springer, Heidelberg (2013). https://doi.org/10.1007/978-3-642-40084-1_6
14. Azaria, A., Ekblaw, A., Vieira, T., Lippman, A.: MedRec: using blockchain for medical data access and permission management. In: International Conference on Open and Big Data, pp. 25–30 (2016). https://doi.org/10.1109/OBD.2016.11

15. Neisse, R., Steri, G., Naifovino, I.: A blockchain-based approach for data accountability and provenance tracking. In: International Conference on Availability, Reliability and Security, p. 14. ACM (2017)

16. Lazarovich, A.: Invisible ink, blockchain for data privacy, Massachusetts Institute of Technology, Boston, Massachusetts (2015)

17. Zyskind, G., Nathan. O., Pentland, A.: Enigma: decentralized computation platform with guaranteed privacy. Computer Science (2015)

18. Kumar, M., Agrawal, S.: Reversible data hiding based on prediction error expansion using adjacent pixels. Secur. Commun. Netw. 9(16), 3703–3712 (2016)

19. Rad, R.M., Wong, K., Guo, J.-M.: Reversible data hiding by adaptive group modification on histogram of prediction errors. Signal Process. 125 C, 315–328 (2016)

20. Mstafa, R.J., Elleithy, K.M., Abdelfattah, E.: A robust and secure video steganography method in DWT-DCT domains based on multiple object tracking and ECC. IEEE Access PP (99), 1 (2017)

21. Ma, X.J., Li, Z.T., Lv, J.L., Wang, W.D.: Data hiding in H.264/AVC streams with limited intra-frame distortion drift. In: International Symposium on Computer Network and Multimedia Technology, pp. 1–5 (2009)

22. Ma, X.J., Li, Z.T., Tu, H., Zhang, B.: Data hiding agorithm for H.264/AVC video streams without intra frame distortion drift. IEEE Trans. Circuits Syst. Video Technol. 20(10), 1320–1330 (2010)

23. Swati, S., Hayat, K., Shahid, Z.: A watermarking scheme for high efficiency video coding (HEVC). PLoS One 9(8), e105613 (2014). https://doi.org/10.1371/journal.Pone.0105613

24. Liu, Y.X., Li, Z.T., Ma, X.J., Liu, J.: A robust without intra-frame distortion drift data hiding algorithm based on H.264/AVC. Multimed. Tools Appl. 72(1), 613–636 (2014)

25. Liu, Y.X., Jia, S.M., Hu, M.S., Jia, Z.J., Chen, L., Zhao, H.G.: A reversible data hiding method for H.264 with Shamir's (t, n)-threshold secret sharing. Neurocomputing 188, 63–70 (2016)

26. Yoo, H., Jung, J., Jo, J., Park, I.C.: Area-efficient multimode encoding architecture for long BCH codes. IEEE Trans. Circuits Syst. II Express Briefs 60(12), 872–876 (2013)

27. Liu, Y.X., Ju, L.M., Hu, M.S.: A new data hiding method for H.264 based on secret sharing. Neurocomputing (2015)

28. Bhowmik, D., Feng, T.: The multimedia blockchain: a distributed and tamper-proof media transaction framework. In: International Conference on Digital Signal Processing (2017)

A Novel Sustainable Interchain Network Framework for Blockchain

Qi Yang[1,2(✉)], Hong Guo[1,2], Vic Zhu[3], Xiang Fan[3], Xin Cui[3], Xiangrui Kong[3], and Bobinson Kalarikkal Bobby[3]

[1] College of Computer Science, Wuhan University of Science and Technology, Wuhan, Hubei, China
kidandkite@163.com, guohong@wust.edu.cn
[2] Hubei Province Key Laboratory of Intelligent Information Processing and Real-Time Industrial System, Wuhan, China
[3] UINP Lab, Hangzhou, Zhejiang, China
{vic,steve,scofield,eric,bobinson}@uinp.io

Abstract. The traditional online data exchanges are processed through the third-parties' support. However, such mode is facing the problem on personal privacy disclosure and relate issues. Blockchain has been proposed as a promising diagram as the new approach for data organization and management, especially for the online data exchanges. It can provide reliable and credible service for business and related requirements as the decentralization technology. The blockchain network itself is always the focus of the whole system for it's the foundation of all the services. When more than one blockchains is proposed to provide different services for different using environments, it is becoming a challenge on how to exchange the data between the different blockchains. In this paper, we provide the design of unitary, which a novel sustainable interchain network framework for blockchain. Unitary Interchain Network is a network consists of infinite parallel global blockchain networks. It is a distributed P2P network of decentralized networks. It can provide sustainable service as the basic blockchain network.

Keywords: Cross chain · Blockchain · Observer chain

1 Introduction

When computer technology and network technology are introduced into our technology system, the virtual world has been constructed as the infrastructure of the real world. Today, the virtual world is almost as powerful as the real economy, which has served as the basis for the business system [1]. With the continuous

---

This work was sponsored by Key Project of Hubei Provincial Department of Education under Granted No. D20181103.

M. Qiu (Ed.): SmartBlock 2018, LNCS 11373, pp. 111–119, 2018.
https://doi.org/10.1007/978-3-030-05764-0_12

development of the virtual world, online and offline business are closer when they are crossing closer and closer [2]. However, when the data are exchanged online, especially the business data, a trusted third-party is needed and necessary to guarantee the authenticity of the information and the true value that can be mapped to the real world [3]. Such mode is the basic business mode of the Internet now. However, these so-called trustworthy companies may also be likely and able to do some deceptive and harmful things intentionally or unintentionally, such as monitoring or selling user data for commercial use [4]. This is not good for the whole system.

Blockchain is proposed as a potential solution for the above problem. The emergence of blockchains provides the trustworthy data management and exchange methods, which can make online transactions more real, and it allows them to be free from third-party or intermediary companies [5]. More and more blockchain based applications have been used to provide services in business and other areas, which has great influence on the online business system. Blockchain provides non-modifiable data records for the online transactions, which makes the transaction be more reliable. The booming of blockchain is very important to the Internet, especially to the online business [6,7]. Blockchain based applications can help to build the reality to the Internet and achieve fairness, equality and sharing between virtual reality online and real reality in the real world. The things, which are constructed through blockchain technology in the virtual world, become valuable and real for the confirmed information [8]. When privacy and reliability become more and more important online, blockchain will also play more important role in the future. Blockchain based systems will be the basic infrastructure, which can provide plenty of services to the people.

With the rapid development of blockchain technology, there are more and more blockchains, which are designed and implemented to provide different types of services [9]. And each blockchain has its own virtual reality construction, which makes the data exchange between blockchains be difficult. Each blockchain has its own network protocol after this blockchain is born [10]. In this paper, we provide the design of unitary, a novel blockchain sustainable interchain network framework that connects all possible blockchain networks in the future through the decentralization.

This paper is organized as the follows. In Sect. 2 we describe the latest researches in this direction. In the Sect. 3 we introduced the framework of unitary. In Sect. 4 we will analyze our study. In Sect. 5 we summarize this study and make some explanations for future research directions.

2   Related Work

Bitcoin is the first real application based on blockchain technology. This virtual money was designed and developed in 2009. After the widely use of Bitcoin, a variety of blockchain systems or blockchain-based applications have been designed, developed and applied to a large number of scenarios for different targets, and the blockchain technology itself is constantly in progress and improved in recent years [11]. The blockchain is also known and used as a distributed ledger, which can be the public basis for the business, which corresponds to a traditional centralized ledger, such as the service provided by a bank. Distributed ledgers based on blockchain technology rely on redundantly storing ledger data in all participating nodes to ensure the security of the ledger, which is very different from the centralized accounts [12]. The blockchain technology is based on three underlying technologies including peer-to-peer networking, cryptography and distributed consistency algorithms. When a blockchain based system is constructing, it will have a feature called a smart contract. The smart contracts are not an necessary part of the blockchain-based systems, blockchains provide the natural support for them [13].

When a blockchain system is to be established for different scenarios, the blockchain system will often need some modifications on the basic structure and mechanism of the blockchain itself to meet specific business requirements. What need to be modified are including the identity authentication, consensus mechanism, key management, throughput, response time, and privacy, protection, regulatory requirements, etc. Thus, when the blockchain based system is constructed, it should be customized for the special business requirements [14].

There are many such customized blockchain based systems to provide services for the companies. Bitcoin has been used widely for the businesses online, which is based on blockchain. Though bitcoin is called as a type of electronic money, it features for its number limitation and generation algorithm. Ethereum is another type of such design and implementation. Ethereum is designed to provide a blockchain, in which the contracts can be created and recorded according the transactions. It provides the simple logic design and implementation routine, which makes it clear to create a blockchain-based application and then use this application in special using scenarios without currency [15]. Fabric is a blockchain framework designed by IBM and DAH. It is a project of the Superbook, which has the similar functions Ethereum, and it also provides the service as a distributed intelligent contract platform. However, it is just an open framework not a public chain or having no built-in tokens at the beginning, which are different from Ethereum and Bitcoin.

When the blockchains are used for online transactions, how to exchange data between them is a problem. Each blockchain system has its own ecologic environment, which means when the users need to exchange information between different blockchains, they have to exchange the information between two different ecology [16]. It is very hard to complete such tasks. Though some mechanisms are provided as the solutions, the efficiency and complexity are always the bottlenecks when the information is exchange. In this paper, we proposed a novel sustainable interchain network framework for blockchain, which is called utinary. Utinary has provided a network structure in which every blockchains in the virtual world can be connected, exchange data, and even disconnect again. Those virtual realities constructed by the corresponding blockchains can be mapped as a single unitary reality. Thus, they can communication with each other. The unitary has been used in real application, which can provide better efficiency with logic simplicity.

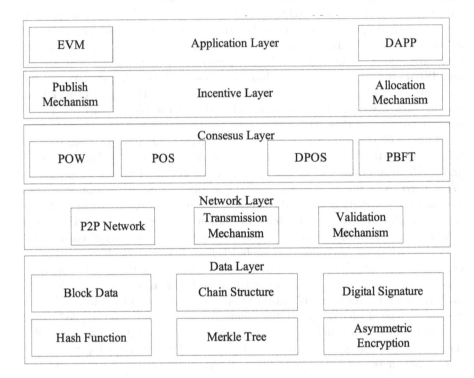

Fig. 1. OTechnique stacks of blockchain network.

3 Overview of Unitary

3.1 Technique Stacks of Blockchain

When blockchain is emerging as the potential technology for data management, a serial related techniques are provided to support it. It can be organized as a technique stack for blockchain technology as shown in Fig. 1. There are five layers including application layer, incentive layer, consensus layer, network layer, and data layer. There are many different techniques in this stack in each layer. When a blockchain based system is constructed, it means this system will need support from all of these layers. Such system can be customized through the existing projects.

3.2 Unitary Framework

Unitary is designed as an interchain network, which consists of nodes plugged in the nodes of other blockchain network. This makes unitary can construct an infinite parallel global blockchain network and connect the other blockchain networks. It is a distributed network with decentralized network topology, which is powered by the decentralized ultra blockchain engine framework which is called unitary parliament in charge of network parameters, and the unitary interchain network protocol set (UINP) which is suitable for building the interoperability of all the global blockchain networks. In the concept of unitary, each blockchain network is an independent system which is defined as a membrane. Unitary needs to provide the whole architecture to connect the different nodes in the membranes. The interoperations can be carried on through the unitary interchain network.

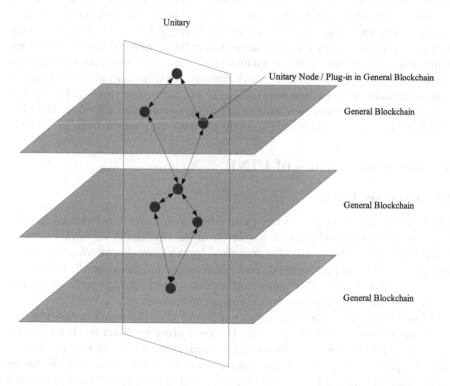

Fig. 2. Unitary universe.

Unitary interchain network is distributed network, which uses POU (Proof of United) consensus algorithm to construct the basic component called plug-ins. The plug-ins can be forked and installed pluggable installed by the nodes of any public, consortium, private chains, or other cross-chains. And then unitary will connect the different nodes through the plug-ins by using UINP. UINP with plug-ins provide a novel interchain network to cross different blockchains. Each independent blockchainis considered as a universe (called membrane). Because the blockchains have no relationship according to their own definition, these universes are parallel and UNIP will connect these universes through the plug-ins, which will build the Unitary chain. This chain has provided a powerful blockchain interconnection as shown in Fig. 2.

Unitary constructs the interchain network parallel universes, which is a network of the blockchain networks. This is a multi-dimensional cross-chain network, which has the auto increasing and decreasing scale. Each universe can have its own features to provide customized service. These universes are considered as the atomic blockchain networks. Thus, unitary interchain network can provide the interoperability, autonomy, elasticity, scalability, tradability and exchangeability for the blockchain virtual reality world. And it will make it suitable for the applications to connect these independent blockchain networks when necessary.

The independent blockchains can map to their single real reality, or they can map with each other by interconnection through UINP. UNIP provides the necessary protocols with the plug-ins as the gateway network of these realities, which can connect the different membranes. That is to say that the different blockchains can join the UNIP network through UNIP protocols and plug-ins. It is an interchain network that can link every virtual reality through this special tunnels. The independent blockchains are still parallel with each other. But they can share the same timeline and can exchange data through the tunnels in UINP.

4   Key Components of UINP

4.1   Observer Chain

UINP uses observer chains as the basic fabric to connect the blockchains. The observer chain is formed through two layers of the traditional network structure. If the target blockchains are also organized by traditional network structure, it will go to work as being designed. Such implementation based on the traditional infrastructure helps UINP to connect the blockchains with higher efficiency. The traditional communication protocols can be used as usual.

Observer chain is used to connect different and independent blockchains, which are parallel in the whole space. It means observer chain needs to provide the connection between the blockchains. Each observer chain can be divided into two parts. One part is a normalized chain, which is similar to the target blockchain. This normalize chain is implemented in the application layer, which is used to connect observer chain and the target blockchain. The other part is called the router chain, which is used to connect the two nodes of observer chain. Router chain is implemented in the transport layer. The two sub-chains can work together to help connecting the nodes in different blockchain membrane. POU consensus structure is used as the consensus algorithm for observer chain including both the normalized chain and router chain.

As we can see from Fig. 3, observer chain has its own nodes, which makes itself work as a blockchain. Each node of observer chain can be connected to a node of another blockchain. The data, which need to be exchanged, will be transferred from one node of observer chain to another node of observer chain. The information will go through the observer chain to its target. In fact, observer

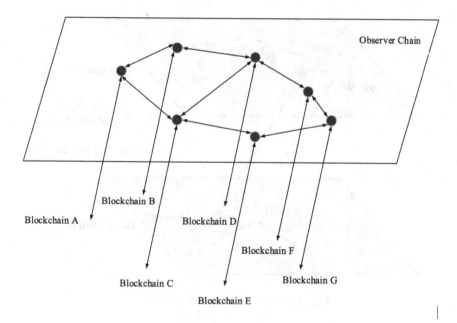

Fig. 3. Observer chain.

chain can be considered as a special flat. And then all the nodes need to be connected to the nodes to other blockchains can be projected to observer chain flat. Thus, observer chain can be obtained clearly with natural logic.

4.2 Dapps' Interaction with Parliament Chain

When observer chain is trying to connect the blockchains, it cannot connect the nodes directly. It just connects to a target blockchain through its nodes. Plug-ins are used as the basic nodes of UINP as shown in Fig. 4. Plug-ins does not exist independent in parallel with the nodes of the other blockchains. These plug-ins are plugged into the nodes of the target blockchains. When a node of one blockchain has a plug-in of UINP, it can now have the potential to connect some node of another blockchain. In fact, the node of one blockchain is connected to plug-in, which is considered as a node of UINP interchain network. And then this plug-in is connected to another plug-in of UINP. This another plug-in is connected to another node of some other blockchain. Thus, the two nodes or the two blockchains are connected through UINP.

When a public blockchain A and blockchain B enter the UINP universe, the corresponding nodes of this public blockchain have plug-ins first. These plug-ins will directly begin to exchange information first to observer chain. And then the target nodes of some other blockchain will be found. As shown in Fig. 4, node NA is a node of blockchain A and node NB is a node of blockchain B. Blockchain A and blockchain B both enter UINP network. When node NA needs

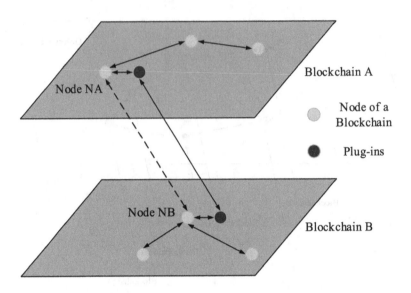

Fig. 4. Connection through plug-ins.

to connect to node NB, node NA will communication with its UINP plug-in, and node NA's plug-in will connect to node NB's plug-in. node NB's plug-in then connects to node NB. Though the connection is not really directly, it's logic direct connection to blockchain A and blockchain B. The data exchange has been complete according to the communication requirements of these two blockchains.

5   Discussions and Conclusions

When there are more and more transactions online, privacy and some other requirements are becoming more important to the users. The traditional mode based third-party is now becoming the bottleneck to meet these requirements. Blockchain is proposed to solve the above problem as the online data management and exchange approach. The data and transactions on blockchain are reliable, untamed and private. Such advantages make blockchain become one of the mainstreams to provide the new network infrastructure. Different blockchain based applications are designed, developed and used for different using environments. When more such blockchains are used in the transactions, the data exchange between different blockchains is becoming the new challenge. In this paper, we propose a novel sustainable interchain network framework for blockchain. The design is described and the key components are depicted in details. This framework is implemented as the Unitary network which has a blockchain protocol set named UINP. Unitary has been used in real world for cross-chain data exchange with high efficiency.

References

1. Lin, I.-C., Liao, T.-C.: A survey of blockchain security issues and challenges. IJ Netw. Secur. **19**(5), 653–659 (2017)
2. Tapscott, D., Tapscott, A.: The impact of the blockchain goes beyond financial services. Harv. Bus. Rev. **10** (2016)
3. Zyskind, G., Nathan, O., et al.: Decentralizing privacy: using blockchain to protect personal data. In: 2015 IEEE Security and Privacy Workshops (SPW), pp. 180–184. IEEE (2015)
4. Eyal, I., Gencer, A.E., Sirer, E.G., Van Renesse, R.: Bitcoin-NG: a scalable blockchain protocol. In: NSDI, pp. 45–59 (2016)
5. Vukolić, M.: The quest for scalable blockchain fabric: proof-of-work vs. BFT replication. In: Camenisch, J., Kesdoğan, D. (eds.) iNetSec 2015. LNCS, vol. 9591, pp. 112–125. Springer, Cham (2016). https://doi.org/10.1007/978-3-319-39028-4_9
6. Back, A., et al.: Enabling blockchain innovations with pegged sidechains (2014). http://www.opensciencereview.com/papers/123/enablingblockchain-innovations-with-pegged-sidechains
7. Kshetri, N.: Can blockchain strengthen the internet of things? IT Prof. **19**(4), 68–72 (2017)
8. Xu, X., et al.: A taxonomy of blockchain-based systems for architecture design. In: 2017 IEEE International Conference on Software Architecture (ICSA), pp. 243–252. IEEE (2017)
9. Gai, K., Choo, K.K.R., Qiu, M., Zhu, L.: Privacy-preserving content-oriented wireless communication in internet-of-things. IEEE IoT J. **5**(4), 3059–3067 (2018)
10. Gai, K., Qiu, M.: Blend arithmetic operations on tensor-based fully homomorphic encryption over real numbers. IEEE Trans. Ind. Inform. **14**(8), 3590–3598 (2018)
11. Kraft, D.: Difficulty control for blockchain-based consensus systems. Peer-to-Peer Network. Appl. **9**(2), 397–413 (2016)
12. Sikorski, J.J., Haughton, J., Kraft, M.: Machine-to-machine electricity market: blockchain technology in the chemical industry. Appl. Energy **195**, 234–246 (2017)
13. Iansiti, M., Lakhani, K.R.: The truth about blockchain. Harv. Bus. Rev. **95**(1), 118–127 (2017)
14. Crosby, M., Pattanayak, P., Verma, S., Kalyanaraman, V.: Blockchain technology: beyond bitcoin. Appl. Innov. **2**, 6–10 (2016)
15. Zhu, L., Wu, Y., Gai, K., Choo, K.K.R.: Controllable and trustworthy blockchain-based cloud data management. Futur. Gener. Comput. Syst. **91**, 527–535 (2018)
16. Gai, K., Qiu, M., Zhao, H., Tao, L., Zong, Z.: Dynamic energy-aware cloudlet-based mobile cloud computing model for green computing. J. Netw. Comput. Appl. **59**(C), 46–54 (2016)

Economic Incentive Structure
for Blockchain Network

Huanhuan Sheng[1,2(✉)], Xiang Fan[3], Wei Hu[1,2], Xing Liu[1,2], and Kai Zhang[1,2]

[1] College of Computer Science, Wuhan University of Science and Technology,
Wuhan, Hubei, China
2690717019@qq.com, {huwei,liuxing1975,zhangkai}@wust.edu.cn
[2] Hubei Province Key Laboratory of Intelligent Information Processing
and Real-Time Industrial System, Wuhan, China
[3] UINP Lab, Hangzhou, Zhejiang, China
steve@uinp.io

Abstract. Traditionally the transactions need middleman or the third-party to keep them trustworthy. However, the middleman itself may be the bottleneck of the trust model. When all the transactions are dealt with by the third parties, these third parties may not be trustworthy any more. Blockchain is proposed to eliminate the third parties of the transactions, which will make the trading parties of the transactions "face to face". Though blockchain can provide the potential solution, it is still in rapid progress. At present, blockchain technology has been widely used to provide reliable transaction support. But the application mechanism is too complex and the demand for high concurrency is strong in some specific industries. This paper introduces a delegated parliament, which is selected from the unified node, whose role is to unite different blockchains and adjust the economic system of the network within a single chain, automatically form a decentralized marked financial market and an economy consensus law that complies with community laws and regulations. This structure is used in Unitary blockchain network, which provides the proof of its efficiency.

Keywords: Blockchain · Delegated parliament · Economic incentives

1 Introduction

The blockchain has developed rapidly in information technology. It can identify the identity of the signer in the digital accounting process and ensure that the signature content cannot be tampered with based on the development of cryptography, digital abstracts and digital signatures. The traditional distributed databases cannot meet the requirements of the new transactions and there is

This work is supported by the Basic and Frontier Technology Research of Henan Province Science and Technology Department (No. 162300410198), and is partially supported by the National Science Foundation of China under Grant 61472293.

M. Qiu (Ed.): SmartBlock 2018, LNCS 11373, pp. 120–128, 2018.
https://doi.org/10.1007/978-3-030-05764-0_13

a huge change in the scale, speed and complexity of data recording according to the improvement of computer processing power. With the emergence and widespread utilization of decentralized peer-to-peer networks [1,2], the resolution of consensus issues in distributed systems has made it possible for multiple parties to jointly maintain the same trusted digital record. From this perspective, the blockchain is the first efficient and reliable implementation of distributed digital recording technology.

The blockchain was first used in Bitcoin. Its core technologies are distributed technology, cryptography, consensus mechanisms and timestamps, and these four technologies are organically combined. Blockchain technology is a decentralized, trust-free open data maintenance technology. The distributed structure can save a lot of intermediary costs in the transaction process. The non tamperable timestamp feature can solve the problem of data tracking and information security [3,4]. The problem of trust mechanism that is difficult to solve in the Internet of Things technology, to achieve stability and transparency of the market order. In 2015, it was called the first year of blockchain development by the industry. Since then, blockchain technology has developed rapidly. The most important application of the blockchain is digital currency. The digital currency derived from bitcoin can solve the algorithm problem and can realize free exchange between large exchanges and French currency, making blockchain digital currency possible.

The main applications of blockchain technology in the financial industry include international payments and settlement, data instruments, customer identification and antifraud and antimoney laundering, securities asset transactions, and small and micro enterprise credit rationing. In addition to its use in the financial sector, blockchain technology has also been studied in different fields such as accounting and ecommerce [5]. The distributed bookkeeping advantages of the blockchain make it possible for future accounting to realize the encrypted storage of the books on different nodes by means of blockchain technology, and the accounting documents are more credible based on the irreversible modification of the blockchain technology. The blockchain can also be used to solve the credit problems in international trade, so as to achieve commercial synergy between buyers and sellers, solve the problem of document circulation through smart contracts, and use the combination of blockchain and Internet of Things to break through the different aspects of financing difficulties and promote international trade. The use of blockchains in innovative areas such as finance also presents challenges, including system building, technology bottlenecks, and safety oversight. However, scholars have high hopes for the development of future blockchains. They believe that blockchain technology will rely on new technologies and technologies such as big data and cloud computing to process information data more accurately, thus boosting industry upgrades and efficiency.

This paper is organized as the follows. In Sect. 2 we describe the latest researches in this direction. Section 3 gives the description of the delegated parliament infrastructure. In Sect. 4 we will analyze our study. In Sect. 5, we give the conclusions of our work.

2   Related Work

In the past 20 years, the virtual economy Internet has dominated other economic forms [6], but the rapid rise of blockchain has caused widespread concern in various markets [1,7], which will inevitably lead to the establishment of business models and society far beyond virtual The economic Internet (including the mobile Internet) [8], a new generation of comprehensive economic digital transformation is taking shape [9]. From the connection between people in the Internet age to the complete P2P link between people and people in the blockchain era [9], people and machines, and machines and machines, the era of value based digital economy is coming [10]. Replacing connections through links has become an inevitable requirement for the sustainable development of traditional shared economies driven by the information Internet and machine intelligence economy [11].

The nodes of the blockchain system generally have the characteristics of distributed, autonomous, open and free access [12], so the peer-to-peer network (P2P network) is generally used to organize the global participation data verification and accounting nodes [13]. Each node in a P2P network is peer-to-peer and communicates and interacts with each other in a flat topology. There are no centralized special nodes and hierarchical structures. Each node will assume network routing and verify block data, spreading block data, discovering new nodes, etc [14]. According to the amount of data stored by the node, it can be divided into full node and lightweight nodes. The former holds the complete blockchain from the creation block to the current latest block data, and dynamically update the main chain by checking and accounting the block data in real time. The advantage of the whole node is that it can independently verify, query and update any block data without relying on any other nodes. The cost of maintaining the entire node is higher [15].

The rapid development and popularity of blockchain technology has led to increasingly complex production needs [1]. A variety of industry and technical issues have caused developers to encounter bottlenecks when creating Dapps, and Dapps links the real world to virtual worlds that are implemented through blockchains [16]. Especially in certain industries, the application mechanism is too complicated and the demand for high concurrency is strong. These require targeted and customized blockchain operating systems to meet the needs of their commercial loans [17].

In the network, the economic structure of the network within the unified chain is extremely important. Because the unified intrachain network is one of many blockchain networks, equivalent to the "United Nations" in cyberspace. The delegating parliament introduced in this article is a "network UN" with a decentralized version of a single intranetwork. It can combine different blockchains, adjust the economic system of a single intranetwork, automatically form a decentralized financial market and comply with community laws. The economic consensus law of regulations. By delegating parliament to meet the economic incentive needs of the blockchain network. The delegating council will build a blockchain engine framework. This blockchain engine framework can meet the requirements of Dapp for processing large amounts of data. This article will add and improve functionality at the blockchain middleware service layer to support evolving Dapps requirements.

3   Delegated Parliament Infrastructure

3.1   Communication Protocol

The delegated parliament is very important in the DAO and shading mechanism of unitary interchain network protocol. It uses a random delegation algorithm to select committees from POS observer nodes. In the network, the parliament adopts a P2P network structure, communicates based on the unitary interchain network protocol stack, and strives to create an effective communication protocol.

Each node in the P2P network always listens to the data broadcasted in the single intranetwork and the new block. After receiving the data sent by the neighboring node, the node will first verify the validity of the data. If the data is valid, a storage pool is created for the new data in the order of receipt to temporarily store valid data that has not been credited to the block while continuing to forward to the neighboring node. If the data is invalid, the data is immediately discarded, ensuring that invalid data does not continue to propagate over the blockchain network.

There are two types of nodes in the delegated parliament, block producers and block witnesses. Nodes can broadcast, receive and forward blocks and transactions. During the node scheduling process, the witness arrives and becomes the block generator. The block is packed every 1.5 s. Other nodes authenticate after they are received. When most nodes receive a successful witness, the block is successfully linked in the longest chain.

Since the P2P network does not have a trusted central server and cannot achieve accurate time synchronization, there may be a delay in each node time. There may be cases where different nodes receive inconsistent information during the transaction. In order to avoid this problem, the interactive data is packaged by artificially setting a period of time to form a block. The generation of the block is generated by the client that first completes the specific number operation. When multiple nodes get the correct answer, the block with the longest transaction chain is used as the main chain, and the other is discarded. The blockchain solves the ordering problem of blocks by means of timestamps. When the client generates the block, the hash value obtained by the hash algorithm of the previous block is recorded, and the block generation order is decoupled from the system time. In addition, once the order of the blocks is solidified, when an attacker attempts to change a transaction within a certain block, it is necessary to recalculate and modify the block and subsequent blocks, which is almost impossible to achieve in a P2P network, and is better achieved security requirements.

3.2   Ultra Blockchain Engine Framework Structure

The delegated parliament of the unitary interchain network is built based on the Ultra Blockchain Engine Framework. This is the first Dapp or genesis Dapp in the engine. The Ultra Blockchain Engine Framework is an application-layer blockchain engine framework.

While the blockchain focuses on system block production, consensus and transactions, the Blockchain Middleware Service (BMS) provides data management and identity management support for Dapps in the hyperblockchain engine framework. The Ultra Blockchain Engine Framework uses proven graphene technology and extends it. The consensus mechanism used is SDPoS (Statistic Delegated Proof of Stake).

The RPC (Remote Procedure Call) and JSON (JavaScript Object Notation) RPC APIs (Application Programming Interfaces) provided by the blockchain are considered to be part of BMS and must be separated from the blockchain and moved to the BMS layer to reduce the performance impact on the blockchain.

The BMS function is:

- Identity Management and SSO.
- Data ingestion.
- consolidation of accounting data.
- real-time streaming and transformation of data from the blockchain.
- Blockchain provides data interfaces as well as a user interface to present the consensus, account status and other features. It will be possible to implement the entire BMS functionality by a third party other than Ultra and the Blockchain is completely independent of the BMS.

Blockchain functionalities are:

- Coin generation
- block production
- consensus
- account creation
- Transaction management

There is no clear distinction between the Ultra Blockchain Engine Framework and the blockchain middle layer functionality, as some components of middleware like the APIs are exposed from the blockchain itself. The Super Platform includes features that provide end users with the ability to develop and interact with blockchains in a variety of applications.

Future expansion of the system can facilitate component design and prevent intrusive integration into existing functions, that is the underlying blockchain will remain more or less the same with minimal changes.

4   Dapp (Decentralized Application) Based on Blockchain

4.1   Components of a Dapp

Dapp will have two basic components. One layer is to present the data to the end user, and the other layer will interact with the blockchain itself or various other layers in the middleware, or read ACTIONS or in some cases invoking changes to the data stored in the blockchain.

- Presentation (view).
- Operation.
- Information storage-an RDBMS, ODBMS or NoSQL.
- Data Storage-IPFS, Amazon S3 compatible object storage, Alibaba storage.
- Identification and SSO client.

Most Dapp frameworks include mobile apps-iOS, Android, Samsung-follow and object-oriented methods. Ultra's BMS will provide an object-oriented interpretation of the blockchain and its data where applicable. This will ensure a one-to-one mapping between entity-driven development in the Microsoft ecosystem and class-driven design and development in the rest of the system.

We expect the Dapp framework and platform to be connected-Python Django, Python Flask, GoLang framework, such as leaf framework for game development, RoR, NodeJS, PHP framework, .NET ecosystem and mobile technology such as Phone Gap, Xmarin and transition iOS And the Android development environment.

In addition, in the above programming environment, we hope that Alibaba's cloud platform, Google's Firebase, Amazon's Echo and machine learning tools can take advantage of Ultra's BMS.

4.2   Dapps' Interaction with Parliament Chain

This section follows a top-down approach that discusses the architecture of the Ultra platform and the Dapp that interacts with the chain, and then lists the components. Figure 1 summarizes the logical aspects of Dapp and blockchain interaction.

4.3   Dapps Will Be Provided with the Following Features and Services

Dapps will provide the following features and services:

- JSON RPC APIs.
- Identity management.
- Data storage-IPFS and object storage.
- Log management.

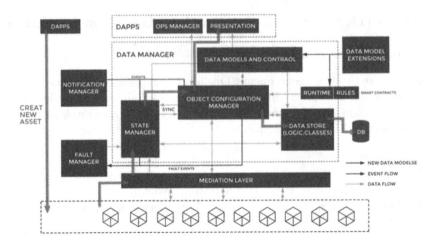

Fig. 1. Logical aspects of the Dapp and blockchain interaction.

Together with JSON RPC, we will make RPC calls to a large number of data transfers.

Identity Management. The identity management mechanism provides a universal account system and extensive identity management and SSO capabilities. This layer constitutes an important aspect of platform and Dapp security. By providing a federated login, we can use other identity management solutions such as WeChat, Facebook, etc. to connect with the blockchain. OAuth 2.0 will achieve the same functionality.

Blockchain APIs Exposed to the Dapps. A subset of the blockchain APIs will be exposed to the Dapps to perform various operations. The following Table 1 gives the APIs and corresponding operations.

Table 1. Table gives the APIs and corresponding operations

API	Action/Transactions	Scope
Transfer funds	Transfer funds between two blockchain accounts	Blockchain
Escrow	Initiate an escrow between two parties	Blockchains
Login	Identify	BMS
Fetch history	Fetch historical information of blockchain transactions	BMS
Reports	If we are deciding to add report generation a group of APIs will be added	BMS
Federated login APIs	SSO and enterprise identity management features	BMS

Dapp Provisioning. The first step of the Dapp creation is to create a corresponding blockchain account for the Dapp. A simple UI will be provided for the same.

Aspects provisioned:

- account name.
- access credentials-usernames, passwords, permissions.
- secure tokens.
- federated logins with Okta, WeChat, Facebook etc.
- support for Multifactor authentication.

Dapp Store. Ultra Blockchain Engine Framework can be enlarged to a Dapp Store (including the Random DPOS main chain, side-chains for Dapp as well as cross-chains universe described in the previous chapter). For the Dapp developers, if they want to use to develop, this section is useful for them.

5   Discussions and Conclusions

At present, the blockchain is still in its infancy, and the technology itself is not mature. From a technical point of view, blockchain involves many technical fields, including: cryptography, distributed systems, network and computing architecture, databases, game theory, and so on. These technologies are the basis for the generation and development of blockchains, but these technologies still need to be further refined. At the application level, the token introduced in the blockchain can be considered as an incentive for system expansion and a tool for changing the rules of interest distribution. Therefore, many people believe that blockchain is a technology that changes the relationship of production and interests. The blockchain establishes a reliable trust between the two parties, which do not understand each other and disperse the realization of credible value transfer. Therefore, the blockchain is called the Internet value or the second generation Internet. By entrusting the parliament, uniting different blockchains and adjusting the economic system of the network within a single chain to meet the economic incentive needs of the blockchain network.

References

1. Eyal, I., Gencer, A.E., Sirer, E.G., Renesse, R.: Bitcoin-NG: a scalable blockchain protocol. In: 13th USENIX Symposium on Networked Systems Design and Implementation, NSDI 2016, Santa Clara, CA, USA, 16–18 March 2016, pp. 45–59 (2016)
2. Zhu, L., Wu, Y., Gai, K., Choo, K.K.R.: Controllable and trustworthy blockchain-based cloud data management. Futur. Gener. Comput. Syst. **91**, 527–535 (2018)
3. Gai, K., Choo, K.K.R., Qiu, M., Zhu, L.: Privacy-preserving content-oriented wireless communication in internet-of-things. IEEE IoT J. **5**(4), 3059–3067 (2018)
4. Gai, K., Qiu, M.: Blend arithmetic operations on tensor-based fully homomorphic encryption over real numbers. IEEE Trans. Ind. Inform. **14**(8), 3590–3598 (2018)
5. Gai, K., Qiu, M., Zhao, H., Tao, L., Zong, Z.: Dynamic energy-aware cloudlet-based mobile cloud computing model for green computing. J. Netw. Comput. Appl. **59**(C), 46–54 (2016)
6. Swan, M.: Blockchain: Blueprint for a New Economy, 1st edn. O'Reilly Media Inc., Sebastopol (2015)

7. Zyskind, G., Nathan, O., Pentland, A.: Decentralizing privacy: using blockchain to protect personal data. In: 2015 IEEE Symposium on Security and Privacy Workshops, SPW 2015, San Jose, CA, USA, 21–22 May 2015, pp. 180–184 (2015)
8. Griggs, K.N., Ossipova, O., Kohlios, C.P., Baccarini, A.N., Howson, E.A., Hayajneh, T.: Healthcare blockchain system using smart contracts for secure automated remote patient monitoring. J. Med. Syst. **42**(7), 130 (2018)
9. Kosba, A.E., Miller, A., Shi, E., Wen, Z., Papamanthou, C.: Hawk: the blockchain model of cryptography and privacy-preserving smart contracts. In: IEEE Symposium on Security and Privacy, SP 2016, San Jose, CA, USA, 22–26 May 2016, pp. 839–858 (2016)
10. Pappalardo, G., Di Matteo, T., Caldarelli, G., Aste, T.: Blockchain inefficiency in the bitcoin peers network. EPJ Data Sci. **7**(1), 30 (2018)
11. Mettler, M.: Blockchain technology in healthcare: the revolution starts here. In: 18th IEEE International Conference on e-Health Networking, Applications and Services, Healthcom 2016, Munich, Germany, 14–16 September 2016, pp. 1–3 (2016)
12. Münsing, E., Mather, J., Moura, S.: Blockchains for decentralized optimization of energy resources in microgrid networks. In: CCTA, pp. 2164–2171 (2017)
13. Yuan, R., Xia, Y., Chen, H.: Private smart contract on public blockchain. J. Comput. Sci. Technol. **33**(3), 542–556 (2018)
14. Huckle, S., Bhattacharya, R., White, M., Beloff, N.: Internet of things, blockchain and shared economy applications. In: The 7th International Conference on Emerging Ubiquitous Systems and Pervasive Networks (EUSPN 2016), The 6th International Conference on Current and Future Trends of Information and Communication Technologies in Healthcare (ICTH-2016), Affiliated Workshops, 19–22 September 2016, London, United Kingdom, pp. 461–466 (2016)
15. Ma, Z.: Digital rights management: model, technology and application. China Commun. **14**(6), 156–167 (2017)
16. Käll, J.: Blockchain control. Law Crit. **29**(2), 133–140 (2018)
17. Kim, H.-W., Jeong, Y.-S.: Secure authentication-management human-centric scheme for trusting personal resource information on mobile cloud computing with blockchain. Hum.-Centric Comput. Inf. Sci. **8**(1), 11 (2018)

An Improved Consensus Mechanism for Blockchain

Hong Guo[1,2], Hongqiang Zheng[1,2](✉), Kai Xu[3], Xiangrui Kong[4], Jing Liu[1],
Fang Liu[5], and Keke Gai[3]

[1] College of Computer Science, Wuhan University of Science and Technology,
Wuhan, Hubei, China
{guohong,luijing_cs}@wust.edu.cn
[2] Hubei Province Key Laboratory of Intelligent Information Processing and
Real-time Industrial System, Wuhan, China
378845238@qq.com
[3] School of Computer Science and Technology, Beijing Institute of Technology,
Beijing, China
{3220180758,gaikeke}@bit.edu.cn
[4] UINP Lab, Hangzhou, Zhejiang, China
eric@uinp.io
[5] City College of Wuhan University of Science and Technology, Wuhan, Hubei, China
Liufangling007@gmail.com

Abstract. When consistency and stability is becoming more and more important in network, blockchain is emerging as a potential solution for this challenge. The network is always the focus of the blockchain for it is the foundation of all the services. It is still a challenge on how to improve the performance of the network especially in the implementation of a real blockchain. In this paper, an improved network for blockchain is proposed to combine different blockchain networks together. It uses POU consensus mechanism to make the blockchain network environment better, which consists of Proof of Stake Entrance, Hash Net Verification and Delegated Parliament. This improved consensus mechanism is used in Unitary blockchain network. It can provide stable and credible network services for business and related requirements.

Keywords: Consensus mechanism · POU · Blockchain

1 Introduction

The Bitcoin network based on the blockchain structure came out quietly in January 2009, which combined important achievements such as modern cryptography and distributed network technology [1]. In recently years, the Bitcoin

This work is partially supported by the Basic and Frontier Technology Research of Henan Province Science and Technology Department (No. 162300410198), and was partially supported by the National Science Foundation of China under Grant 61602350, and the support from Beijing Institute of Technology Research Fund Program for Young Scholars (Dr. Keke Gai).

M. Qiu (Ed.): SmartBlock 2018, LNCS 11373, pp. 129–138, 2018.
https://doi.org/10.1007/978-3-030-05764-0_14

network stably supported massive transfer transactions in a purely distributed scenario. Gradually it is realized that the blockchain which is a data structure seems to be simple, but it can solve the basic requirements of distributed accounting [2], when the distributed accounting technology which is based on blockchain structure began to be popular. These technologies are collectively referred to as blockchain technology [3] because most of them use the blockchain structure as their core ledger structure.

Blockchain, which has attracted intense attention only after the introduction of Bitcoin, is considered as one of the most potential technologies for the future network transactions [4–9]. Normally, when people make payments through the Internet, they have to trust a third party, who would verify the validity of their transactions before putting them into action. For instance, people who use shopping apps such as Taobao and JD believe things or services can be mapped to real staffs because of the trusted background companies. However, big companies can cheat and do harmful things such as conducting surveillance or selling users' data for commercial use. Consistency and stability are becoming more and more important in network for the trustworthiness.

This paper proposes an improved network for blockchain [10], which can combine the existing different blockchain networks together. It uses POU consensus mechanism to make the blockchain network environment better. The remainder of this paper is organized as the follows. First, in Sect. 2, we describe the latest researches in this direction. Next, in the Sect. 3, we introduce the basic theories of our study. Furthermore, in Sect. 4, we present the key algorithms that are implemented for the proposed system. Finally, in Sect. 5, we summarize our works and make some explanations for future research directions.

2   Consensus Mechanism

2.1   Background

The emergence of blockchain makes the transactions [11] better without being assured by a third party or a middleman company on which staff is real and which is fake in the virtual world. The revolution of the virtual world lead by blockchain is booming now, which influences backward to the reality and the whole world. Moreover, it is totally different from the first revolution of the Internet when the reality was going to be virtualized initially. The blockchain technology is the revolution of the virtual world and the second revolution of the Internet [10], which builds the reality in the virtual world and makes it fair, equal, and sharing in both the virtual reality and the real reality indirectly.

In order to understand how the blockchain works, it is necessary to introduce concepts such as transaction, block and chain, etc. The transaction is an operation which result the state of the ledger change [12]. Block is a consensus on the current state of the ledger which is a record of all transactions, state and results in a period of time. Chain is the whole ledger status change log and composed of blocks according to the order of generation.

Generally speaking, when any transaction is proposed, its validity is verified by some nodes [13]. If a transaction is valid, which means the sender has enough money to spend (proved by the past transactions in the old blocks), and also the sender has confirmed this transaction by signing his or her digital signature inside, it will be included in a block [12]. From here, in order to make the transaction really valid, the block containing this transaction should be added to the chain, which must be recognized by all the other nodes. A node will try to append a block containing many transactions by broadcasting it to the rest [12], which proposes them to add this block to their current chain. However, if the transactions are verified in this way, there could be confusion when every node tries to broadcast their found block. For purpose of preventing this situation, an agreement, which is called consensus algorithm [14], should be made between all nodes about which blocks should be appended, and which nodes are permitted to append their proposed blocks. To date, many consensus mechanisms have been proposed. The introduction of several common consensus mechanisms will be given in the next section.

Consensus is a classic technical problem in the field of distributed systems. Academia and industry have a large number of research results in consensus mechanism, such as POW, POS [15], etc. The core of consensus mechanism is to ensure that an operate in a distributed network produce the consistent execution result, which is irrefutable and recognized by most of parties in the network [16]. Next part will introduce several popular consensus mechanisms from three aspects: principle, applicable scenarios and defect.

2.2   Proof of Work

Proof of Work (POW) is mainly to use the calculation cost which is required to solve the computational difficulty problem as the credential of the new-add block and obtain income as rewards. Satoshi Nakamoto proposed the POW consensus mechanism in the paper on Bitcoin, which is used to ensure the consistency of data and the security of consensus by computational power competition of distributed nodes. In the Bitcoin system, all nodes compete to solve a SHA256 math problem by their respective computing powers [2]. Which the problem is complex to compute but easy to verify. The node which is the first one that solves this problem will get the account rights of block and the Bitcoin is automatically generated as reward.

The mathematical problem can be expressed as: according to the value of current difficulty, a suitable random number (Nonce) is found by searching, which satisfied that the double SHA256 hash value of the block header metadata is less than or equal to the hash value of the target, and the Bitcoin system adjust the difficulty of finding the random number flexibly to guarantee that generating a block every 10 min. Normally, the process of random number searching consists three steps. Firstly, all the transactions which are unconfirmed at the current time are collected in whole network, and a Coinbase transaction which is used to issue a new Bitcoin reward is added to form a transaction set of the current block. Second, the Merkle root value of the block transaction set is calculated and added to the block header with the other metadata, and then the random number (Nonce) is set to zero. Third, the random number (Nonce) is incremented by one, and if the Nonce meets the condition that the double SHA256 hash value of the current block header is less than or equal to the hash value of the target, the appropriate random number is found and the node obtain the counting right of the block. Otherwise continue to the third step until the random number meet the condition. Finally, if the timeout is unsuccessful, the timestamp and unconfirmed transaction set are updated, and the Merkle root is recalculated and the search continues.

The hash value of block header that meets the requirements usually consists of multiple leading zeros. The smaller the target hash value, the more leading zeros of the block header hash value, and it is more difficult to find the appropriate random number and dig out the new block, so the security and non-destructive modification of the Bitcoin blockchain system is guaranteed by the powerful computing power of the POW consensus mechanism. Any attack or tampering on block data must recalculate the SHA256 problem of all the blocks, and the speed of calculation must make the length of the forged chain exceed the main chain. The cost of this attack will far exceed the cost. It is precisely that this mechanism guarantees the data consistency and irreparable modification of the blockchain, but it also wastes lots of resources, and even loses the advantage of the decentralization due to the emergence of the super large mining pool.

2.3 Proof of Stake

Proof of Stake (POS) mainly replaces the workload proof with the equity certificate, and the node with the highest interest have the right to add new blocks and obtain income as rewards. The POS Consensus is an alternative for the POW consensus mechanism to reduce the waste of resources and improve the security of system. Its essence is to use the equity proof to replace the hash-based workload proof in the POW, which is obtained by the node with the highest interest rather than the highest power in the system. The equity is reflected in the Coindays, which is the ownership of the node to a specific amount of currency. The Coindays is the product of the specified number of coins and the length of time of their last transaction. Each transaction will consume a certain amount of Coindays. For example, if someone receives 10 coins in a transaction and keep it for 10 days, they will get 100 Coindays. Then they will spend 50 Coindays after spending five coins. Obviously, the system using POS consensus mechanism is specific. The total number of currency ages at the time point is limited, and longterm holders prefer to have more Coindays, so the Coindays can be seen as an interest in the POS consensus system.

In addition, the difficulty of mining in the POW consensus process is equal in each node, but it is inversely proportional to the number of Coindays in the transaction in the POS consensus process. The more Coindays consume, the lower difficulty of mining is, and the more likely to become the accounting node. The block which is the most cumulative consume of Coinday will be added to the main chain. If a new POS block was found, the Coindays will be cleared to zero. When the Coindays are emptied by 365 times, you will receive an interest of 0.05 coins from the block. The criterion for the node to judge the main chain is changed from the highest cumulative difficulty of the POW consensus to the highest consumption of the Coindays. Each block transaction will submit the Coindays which was consumed to the block, and the block with the highest consumption of the Coindays will be linked to the main chain. The POS algorithm allows all nodes of the network to participate in defense, which defend against attacks and ensure the security of the network. Any adversary attempting to conceal a blockchain containing more than the main chain to destroy the currency requires more cost.

It can be seen that the POS consensus process mainly relies on the Coindays and rights, without the need of much external computing power and resources, reduce the waste of computing power and accelerate the consensus to a certain extent.

2.4 Delegated Proof of Stake

Delegated Proof of Stake (DPOS) is an evolutionary version of POS which selects representatives by POS and then selects the representative from generate-block and gains incomes.

DPOS consensus mechanism is similar to the "board decision", each shareholder node in the system can award they shares as a ballot to the representative. The top 101 nodes that have the most votes which are willing to become representatives will enter the "board of directors", according to the established schedule, the node of representative pack the transactions and produce a new block. Before each block is signed, it must be verified that the previous block has been signed by the trusted representative node. The authorized representative of the "Board" can earn income from the transaction fee of each transaction, and to be the authorized representative node need pay a certain amount of margin which is equivalent to 100 times the income of a block. The authorized representative node must be responsible for other shareholder nodes. If it misses signing the corresponding block, the shareholder will reclaim the ballot and "drop" the node. Therefore, authorized representative nodes usually guarantee more than 99% of online time to achieve profitability goals.

Each node autonomously determines the node which is trusted to the authorized nodes in the DPOS consensus mechanism and these nodes take turns to record new blocks. This consensus mechanism greatly reduces the number of nodes participating in verification and accounting and can achieve fast consensus verification.

2.5 Shortages of Existing Consensus Mechanisms

The above three consensus mechanisms have their shortcomings. The POW consensus wastes lots of computing power and the confirmation time is difficult to shorten. What's more, the new cryptocurrency needs to find a updated hash algorithm, if not, it will be attacked by the Bitcoin. The confirmation in POS consensus is just a probabilistic expression and an uncertainty one. There may be attacked by other effects in theory. DPOS consensus mechanism relies on token, and many commercial applications require not to use tokens. In order to make the blockchain technology developed better and the application scenario is wider, according to the current blockchain network, we use a hybrid consensus algorithm to improve the consensus mechanism. In the next section, we will introduce the improved consensus algorithm POU for Unitary Interchain Network.

3   Interconnect Blockchain Network Membranes

3.1   The Unitary Interchain Network

Unitary Interchain Network is the world first multi-dimensional blockchains' network, which consists of a Unitary Parliament and an auto increasing and decreasing scale of parallel universes or infinite parallel global blockchain networks. It is a distributed P2P network of decentralized networks powered by the decentralized Ultra lock chain Engine Framework (Unitary Parliament which in charge of network parameters) and the Unitary Interchain Network Protocol Set (form Unitary Interchain Network Parallel Universes) which are suitable for building the interoperability of all the global blockchain networks.

This Unitary Interchain Network Universe (parallel blockchain networks along without the Unitary Parliament) is a blockchain network of blockchain networks formed by the Unitary Interchain Network Protocol Set. Each blockchain network is named as an independent parallel reality (the blockchain network membrane) within the Unitary Interchain Network Blockchain Identity Space.

Unitary Interchain Network Protocol Set is a set of protocols built on the transport-layer as well as application-layer of the TCP suite which is the structure of the Internet using currently. Each new joint blockchain can be connected to the Unitary Interchain Network Universe by the community using the Unitary Interchain Network Protocol Set (install the Unitary Plug-in or implement UINP). In the Unitary Interchain Network which is distributed, the Ultra Blockchain Engine Framework Unitary Interchain Network Protocol Set uses POU (Proof of United) consensus algorithm to build the opensource Unitary Plug-in which can be forked or pluggable installed by any public, consortium, private chains, or other cross-chains nodes to connect to each other.

POU is a three-layer consensus algorithm that can unite all the sharing nodes that connect different blockchain network to the Unitary Interchain Network, and it assumes that the blockchain network environment is very bad, information may be lost, in-complete, delayed, sent multiple times, and the order of sending and receiving is very different. At the same time, any single node is untrustworthy and may be discarded, forged messages and node failures.

4   The Organization of POU

4.1   Proof of Stake Entrance

In the Unitary Interchain Network, everyone can use UINP nodes to connect a blockchain network membrane into the Unitary Interchain Network Universe through POS entrance.

Unlike the normal proof of stake system, which requires the user to show ownership of a certain number of cryptocurrency units to validate transactions and creates new blocks. UINP's POS sub-consensus is used by nodes to show the evidence of entrance into Unitary paradigm translation network, i.e. be qualified observer nodes. While if a node is a qualified observer node, then it can receive transactions from the source network and translate it to unitary transaction paradigm or vice versa (from unitary transaction paradigm to the target network transaction format and broadcast).

In most proof of stake cases, digital currency units are created at the launch of the currency and their number is fixed. Therefore, rather than using cryptocurrency units as the rewards, the forgers receive transaction fees as rewards. However, in Unitary Interchain Network Universe, new currency units can be created by inflating the coin supply, and forgers can be rewarded with new currency units created as rewards, rather than transaction fees. While in the next section, the verification of paradigm transactions rewards as well, which is the main progress of producing "block" or atomic units in DAG.

Coins at 'stake' firstly. Think of this as their holdings being held in an escrow account: if they validate a fraudulent transaction, they lose their holdings, as well as their rights to participate as a forger in the future. Once the forger puts their stake up, they can partake in the DAG forging process, and because they have staked their own money, they are in theory now incentivized to validate the right transactions.

4.2   Hash Net Verification

Hash Net consensus uses "redundancy reduced gossip" and "virtual voting" protocols based on a distributed computation and algorithms from theoretical computer science which provides a fair and fast, Byzantine fault tolerant consensus algorithm. It is a new consensus substitute platform inspired by the innovative development of Hash graph methodology and is designed to run on a non-permissioned (public) network thereby reaching a larger community.

For nodes community who is going to be paid by the server, the Unitary Interchain Network, after entrance in the network with POS consensus, the nodes now have the right and responsibility to verify the atomic paradigm transactions within the network and get their major payment by the Unitary Interchain Network Reward Pool. When a cross-chain transaction (either P2P, A2A, A2P or P2A) is initiated, the staked observer node receives it and broadcasts to the Unitary Interchain Network Universe to verify the paradigm transactions use HashNet consensus.

4.3   Delegated Parliament

SDPoS (Statistic Delegated Proof of Stake) is an Agent Election Rights Certification Consensus. The Parliament Network consists of the group of nodes, of which the size is the numbers of blockchain networks connect (Let's say N networks connected to the Unitary Interchain Network Universe). All the nodes are community-selected votes after the election by each networks' community. Additionally, there is one node selected by computer operation forensics, which means the total number of parliament nodes are N+1.

It is responsible for the proportionate and time-shared voting. The sequence of node connection in each link is generated by the Ultra Blockchain Engine Framework random algorithm. Nodes after the previous node cannot be predicted in advance, and the nodes in each link are guaranteed to be packaged at the same time. Meanwhile, the malicious nodes are fundamentally prevented from escaping. The situation arises.

After each round of link, packing is confirmed by 2/3+1 of total nodes, the block is completed. Each block generates a rate of 1.5 s. If the packet timing of a node exceeds the threshold, it is passed to the next random node for packet generation. If a node misses three packing orders in succession, there will be a 12-h time window for recovery. If the packing ability cannot be restored, there will be alternative nodes to replace.

The selected nodes are block producers and are elected by the entire network. At the same time, there are 200 candidate nodes and numerous verifiers in the entire network from the unitary community. All verifiers run full-node data.

Agent Random Production Mechanism. After 1–4 generations of graphene are elected in the witness node, round-robin around robin circulation is used in each link to perform round-by-block production. After each link is closed, the number of polling points for the next link node changes. This mechanism can ensure that there will be the longest chain in most cases, except when the Byzantine nodes in the network appear to be grouped together.

In the 1–4 generation graphene system, if most of the block producers in the chain become corrupt, they can produce countless forks, each of which will be confirmed by a 2/3 majority. In this case, the last irreversible block algorithm will revert to the longest chain algorithm. Then the chain recognized by the largest majority will be the longest chain, and the largest majority will be determined by the few remaining honest nodes. This behavior will not last long because stakeholders will eventually choose to vote for these block producers. However, if the chain blocks, the majority of block producers are corrupted, resulting in the sharing of the chain of forces "gangs", the direction of the longest chain cannot be determined, such as the eight agent nodes. If agent nodes generate interest groups in twos, the network will fail. At the same time, jointing corruption may also occur in the longest chain in the absence of warnings. For example, a five-person interest group will have a high probability of controlling the entire chain.

The agent's stochastic production mechanism guarantees that, even if the interest group node has a group, it cannot produce the problem that the internal interest group generated by the "board" agency or "shareholders' meeting" to perform the network operation right makes the network unfair.

Parliament consensus mechanism SDPOS, based on the 1–4 generation graphene consensus kernel, introduced a "Number in Once" random mechanism, called "Vector in Once". In each link, the scheduling order of the nodes is all random, and the first producer of the block is generated from the random vector of the last producer in the previous link. For example, if there are 17 nodes blockchain networks connect in the Unitary Interchain Network, the first producer randomly generates a random vector of 17 dimensions, each dimension represents a node and polls the notification (the notified node is likely to be in a failed state). The queue FIFO remove the invalid state node in first-arrive, first-out order, until a certain node handshake becomes the next producer. After the next producer produces a block, remove the first producer randomly and generate a random vector of 16 dimensions, and so on.

The net result is that all elected agents, even if they have interest groups, will have a stochastic mechanism to remove the corruption of the nodes in the chain. And the internal pecking order of each node in each round is unpredictable.

5   Summary

Unitary Interchain Network uses Proof of United (POU) consensus to organize all the unitary nodes community, which will be a community of communities. Unitary Interchain Network Protocol Set open a totally new technology stack for the worldwide blockchain industries to evolve to the next age-interconnection of blockchains, by introducing the most recent concept of physics achievements-parallel universe to describe and build Unitary Interchain Network Parallel Universes (network of blockchain networks) with an auto increasing and decreasing scale of multidimensional cross-chain networks, which are based on the many atomic global blockchain networks. Thence, the Unitary interchain network can provide the Interoperability, Autonomy, Elasticity, Scalability, Tradability, Exchangeability for the blockchain virtual reality world.

References

1. Juan, F., Galvez, J., Me, J.: Future challenges on the use of blockchain for food traceability analysis. J. Comput. Sci. Technol. **33**(3), 527–537 (2018)
2. Zheng, B., Zhu, L., Shen, M.: Scalable and privacy-preserving data sharing based on blockchain. J. Comput. Sci. Technol. **33**(3), 557–567 (2018)
3. Yuan, R., Xia, Y., Chen, H.: Private smart contract on public blockchain. J. Comput. Sci. Technol. **33**(3), 542–556 (2018)
4. Dorr, A., Steger, M., Kanhe, S., Jurdak, R.: A distributed solution to automotive security and privacy. IEEE Commun. Mag. **55**(12), 119–125 (2017)
5. Gai, K., Qiu, M., Xiong, Z., Liu, M.: Privacy-preserving multi-channel communication in edge-of-things. Futur. Gener. Comput. Syst. **85**, 190–200 (2018)

6. Gai, K., Choo, K.R., Qiu, M., Zhu, L.: Privacy-preserving content-oriented wireless communication in internet-of-things. IEEE Internet Things J. **5**(4), 3059–3067 (2018)

7. Gai, K., Qiu, M., Ming, Z., Zhao, H., Qiu, L.: Spoofing-jamming attack strategy using optimal power distributions in wireless smart grid networks. IEEE Trans. Smart Grid **8**(5), 2431–2439 (2017)

8. Gai, K., Qiu, M., Zhao, H.: Energy-aware task assignment for mobile cyber-enabled applications in heterogeneous cloud computing. J. Parallel Distrib. Comput. **111**, 126–135 (2018)

9. Gai, K., Qiu, M.: Blend arithmetic operations on tensor-based fully homomorphic encryption over real numbers. IEEE Trans. Ind. Inf. **14**(8), 3590–3598 (2017)

10. Mylrea, M., Gourisetti, S.: Blockchain for smart grid resilience: Exchanging distributed energy at speed, scale and security. In: 2017 Resilience Week (RWS), pp. 18–23, Wilmington, USA (2017)

11. Huckle, S., Bhattacharya, R., White, M., Beloff, N.: Internet of things, blockchain and shared economy applications. In: The 7th International Conference on Emerging Ubiquitous Systems and Pervasive Networks (EUSPN 2016)/The 6th International Conference on Current and Future Trends of Information and Communication Technologies in Healthcare (ICTH-2016)/Affiliated Workshops, 19-22 Sept 2016, London, UK, pp. 461–466 (2016)

12. Kosba, A.E., Miller, A., Shi, E., Wen, Z., Papamanthou, C.: Hawk: the blockchain model of cryptography and privacy-preserving smart contracts. In: IEEE Symposium on Security and Privacy, SP 2016, CA, USA, 22–26 May 2016, pp. 839–858 (2016)

13. Valenta, L., Rowan, B.: Blindcoin: blinded, accountable mixes for bitcoin. In: Brenner, M., Christin, N., Johnson, B., Rohloff, K. (eds.) FC 2015. LNCS, vol. 8976, pp. 112–126. Springer, Heidelberg (2015). https://doi.org/10.1007/978-3-662-48051-9_9

14. Münsing, E., Mather, J., Moura, S.: Blockchains for decentralized optimization of energy resources in microgrid networks. In: 2017 IEEE Conference on Control Technology and Applications (CCTA), pp. 2164–2171 (2017)

15. Eyal, I., Gencer, A.E., Sirer, E.G., Renesse, R.: Bitcoin-NG: a scalable blockchain protocol. In: 13th USENIX Symposium on Networked Systems Design and Implementation, NSDI 2016, Santa Clara, CA, USA, March 16–18, 2016, pp. 45–59 (2016)

16. Zhu, L., Yulu, W., Gai, K., Choo, K.-K.R.: Controllable and trustworthy blockchain-based cloud data management. Futur. Gener. Comput. Syst. **91**, 527–535 (2019)

A Novel Cross-Chain Mechanism for Blockchains

Yucen He[1], Xinyi Zhu[1], Fangfang Xu[2,3]($\boxtimes$), Yulu Wu[4], Xiang Fan[1], Xin Cui[1], Xiangrui Kong[1], and Bobinson Kalarikkal Bobby[1]

[1] UINP Lab, Hangzhou, Zhejiang, China
{heyucen,vic,steve,scofield,eric,bobinson}@uinp.io
[2] College of Computer Science, Wuhan University of Science and Technology, Wuhan, Hubei, China
xuff@wust.edu.cn
[3] Hubei Province Key Laboratory of Intelligent Information Processing and Real-Time Industrial System, Wuhan, China
[4] School of Computer Science and Technology, Beijing Institute of Technology, Beijing 100081, China
2120171080@bit.edu.cn

Abstract. With the popularity of online transactions, a large number of online transaction data has caused people to pay more attention to the privacy and security of data. The emergence of blockchain has brought the credibility of data to get rid of the limitations of trusted third parties and brought a secure distributed trading environment'. However, as the volume of transaction data increases, people will choose to trade on multiple blockchains. But establishing transactions between different blockchains is difficult. In this paper, a novel cross-chain mechanism for blockchains is proposed to provide basic support to the interconnection between blockchains. We stated our research and analyzed the feasibility of our research.

Keywords: Blockchain · Cross-chain · Plug-in · Privacy · Membranes

1 Introduction

In recent years, trading through Internet has become one of the most popular trade model. The large amount of trades produce huge number of data circulated in the network [1], which need to be protected to keep the data private and secure. The privacy protection of data is crucial recently. So, a dynamic privacy protection model is proposed to optimize privacy-preserving levels getting rid of the volume of data in [2,3].

This work is supported by the Basic and Frontier Technology Research of Henan Province Science and Technology Department (No. 162300410198). This paper was sponsored by Key Project of Hubei Provincial Department of Education under Granted No. D20181103.

© Springer Nature Switzerland AG 2018
M. Qiu (Ed.): SmartBlock 2018, LNCS 11373, pp. 139–148, 2018.
https://doi.org/10.1007/978-3-030-05764-0_15

The existing trading systems are based on the credit model with the support of the third parties as the basic infrastructure. The third parties are considered as the reliable ones to keep the transactions secure and give the trustworthy communications. However, these trusted third parties may cheat and do harmful things conducting surveillance or selling the user's data for commercial use. The privacy problem is one of the most prominent problems [4]. The security of the transactions has made it be an important issue to find a safe, transparent and more efficient way for the online trades.

Blockchain was proposed as the new technology for the above problem. It was designed for the online money system, which was called Bitcoin [5]. Blockchain could be used to keep the consistency, which was very important in distributed systems. When the practice provided the demonstration of the security and efficiency of block-chain technology [6], blockchain has attracted many concerns and becomes a popular technology for online trades. Blockchain has eliminated the third parties, which are set as the reliable middleman [7]. Blockchain provides the direct transactions between the sellers and buyers because that there are no centers to act as the intermediate trading platforms. Now the transactions can be operated in a decentralized way with blockchains, without the need of a central authority to achieve the same functionality with the same certainty.

When blockchains are widely used in different industries, it does not mean all the blockchains are the same. Different blockchains are designed with special concepts, which will bring us a new challenge that these blockchains were independent and could hardly to exchange data [8]. The interconnection operations between the different blockchains are getting more and more attention, which makes the traditional blockchain network structure need the improvements [9]. Though some existing mechanisms were proposed to solve this problem, the efficiency is still the bottleneck.

In this paper, a novel cross-chain mechanism for blockchains is proposed to provide basic support to the interconnection between blockchains [10]. "Plug-In" is used to add new nodes and "tunnel" is used to provide the connection to the cross-chain transactions. Such mechanism can provide the fast adding of new codes and efficient cross-chain service. Main contributions of our work are summarized in the followings:

- We proposed a novel cross-chain mechanism to provide interconnection between different blockchains by means of Plug-In added to applications.
- We introduced the concept of membrane to describe the cross-chain mechanism easily.

This paper is organized as the follows. In Sect. 2 we describe the latest researches in this direction. In the Sect. 3 we introduced the basic theories of our study. In Sect. 4 we will analyze our study. In Sect. 5 we summarize this study and make some explanations for future research directions.

2   Related Work

Blockchain is a promising technology for the online trading and other applications with high security and efficiency. It provides the new form of online service support through the encrypted chains [7]. The blockchains can be classified into three types: public blockchain, consortium blockchain, and private blockchain according to the organizational scope, the organizational structure, and the level of transparency. They can provide different services through their own definitions and rules. However, almost all the blockchains are independent and parallel, which means it is very hard to exchange their information. There are almost no related mechanisms within the blockchains to support the cross-chain [11] exchange.

In order to realize information exchange between the traditional blockchains, cross-chain technologies [12] are proposed to interconnect different blockchains. There are three relatively mature (in spite of there are some problems) solutions: the notary mechanism [11], the side chain/ repeater mode [11] and hash lock mode [13].

The first is the notary schemes. This model is well understood and similar to the real world. The notary schemes assume that A and B do not trust with each other, then a third party that both A and B trust is an intermediary as a notary. In this case, A and B indirectly trust with each other. The representative solution is Interledger, which is not a ledger and does not need any consensus. Instead it provides a top-level encryption hosting system called a "connector" with the help of this intermediary, allowing funds to flow between ledgers. The benefits of this model are simple and well understood, but the disadvantages are also existed. There is some conflict between this model and the decentralization of the blockchain, so many people don't think it is a blockchain. To the contrary, consider it as a centralized product.

The second is the side chain or repeater mode (sidechains/relays) that is used in cross-chain technology. In general, the main chain is not aware of the presence of the side chain, and the side chain must be aware of the existence of the main chain. RootStock [14] is a smart contract distributed platform base on the Bitcoin blockchain. The representative of the repeater mode is the polkadot relay chain. The relay chain is the tunnel between the chain and the chain and the tunnel is also blockchain. This project adopts a multi-signature mechanism which locks the main chain assets, anchors and executes them on the side chain, and whether the transaction on the side chains is valid determined by multiple signatures. The other one is Cosmos HUB [4]. This project is the hub and space communicate with each other by the blockchain communication protocol, and compliances with the link agreement.

The third model is hash-locking. Hash lock is based on the Bitcoin lightning network. The lightning network was a means of fast payment. The key technology of the lightning network is hash time lock contract which was applied to the cross-chain technology. Although the hash locking implements the exchange of cross-chain assets, it does not realize the transfer of cross-chain assets and cross-chain contracts, so the application scenario is relatively limited.

We propose a novel cross-chain mechanism in this paper. In this mechanism, the membranes containing the blockchains are organized as a 4-dimensional space. The plug-ins can be added to the nodes. The plug-ins can provide the interconnection tunnels through the interconnections between the plug-ins in the nodes of different membranes. These tunnels are just considered as the wormhole to connect the membranes, which are still independent in parallel. The details of the mechanism is discussed in the following.

3   Concept and Definitions

Though the blockchain is called a "chain", the blockchain is not just only a "chain". Each blockchain has its own data blocks in the network. Such data blocks can be considered as the nodes. All the nodes should be connected directly or indirectly via some type of interconnection methods. The blockchains have different types of networks as the basic structures to connect their nodes by the edges. There are three typical topologies using for blockchains including centralized topology, decentralized topology and distributed topology as shown in Fig. 1. The basic topologies can provide the support for the blockchains to organize the nodes. If the blockchains can be considered as a plane, the nodes and edges in the same blockchain can be projected to the same plane.

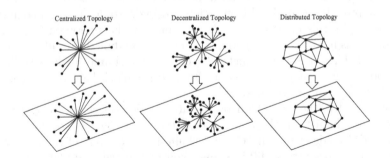

Fig. 1. Topologies of blockchains projected to the planes.

Each blockchain in real world is an independent system to provide corresponding services. Different blockchains will never mutual relationship if the applications do not need the information exchanged among them. It means that all the planes are parallel after all the blockchains are mapped to these corresponding planes.

Definition 1 blockchain membrane. Each plane is defined as a blockchain membrane, which contains an independent blockchain. When there are multiple blockchains, it means that there are multiple planes, which also means there are multiple membranes. The membrane containing a blockchain is named as an independent parallel reality (the blockchain network membrane).

The membranes are independent with each other. The blockchain in one membrane will fulfill its transactions according its own definitions and rules. It will not be intervened by the other blockchains. Now when a transaction needs to be dealt with between two blockchains, it means the cross-chain operation is required between these two blockchains. And two corresponding membranes will have some relationship through special mechanism.

All the membranes can be organized as a special 3-dimensional space. However, the blockchain itself is changing frequently for the changed data or new data. Because blockchain is changing all the time, the blockchains will be different from themselves from the past. The membrane contains the changing blockchain, which means the membranes are also changing. The static space cannot express such dynamic changes. The time dimension is added for the changing of whole space. Thus, a 4-dimensional space-time is organized as shown in Fig. 2.

These blockchain network membranes are just organized as a hierarchical architecture. Such an architecture can give a clear relationship among the different blockchains. All the blockchains are self-consistent. They do not need to join with the other blockchains to complete their transactions. Different blockchains can work at the same time. Each membrane can give us the chain's states of the corresponding blockchain. The membranes are parallel and have no relationship between each other. In this architecture, all the membranes are existing in the same universe and still independent.

The most important thing is to connect the different membranes. Each blockchain has its own definition of its features, which are used in this blockchain to deal with the data. Obviously, most blockchains are different according to their detailed using targets in special environments. When the data should be exchanged among the different blockchains, the data transferred should be accepted by the other blockchains. The membranes have to be connected at some special time when the corresponding blockchains have to finish some type of data exchange. It means that an interconnection mechanism should be provided to give the bridges to communicate with different membranes in the architecture shown in Fig. 2. This cross-chain mechanism is described in the next section.

4   Proposed Model

We would state our proposed model from three important parts as followings: plug-in based swap design, observer chain organization and wormholes based on plug-ins.

4.1   Plug-in Based Swap Design

Different blockchains may need to exchange information for the crossing applications. It means that there should be a special mechanism to provide the exchange path for the membranes. There are some limitations when it tries to connect different membranes. Each blockchain is running independently from the others. All of the blockchains have their own definitions and rules when they begin working.

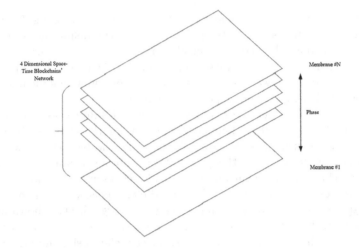

Fig. 2. Blockchain network membranes.

The existing blockchains will not be changed to connect to the other blockchains and other blockchains cannot be changed either. It means if the membranes need to exchange with others, we have to provide the exchange mechanism for membranes.

Traditionally, a public blockchain can provide the exchange between different blockchains which is a direct solution to this problem. The public blockchain will act as the bridge between the different blockchains and the data will be transmitted from one blockchain to the public blockchain and then to the other blockchain. When the number of exchange data increases, the public blockchain will be the bottleneck of the whole mechanism for the rapid increasing data quantity. Though there are some improved methods which can provide better performance, efficiency and convenience are still the problems.

A Plug-in based on cross-chain mechanism is proposed in this paper to connect the membranes. A pluggable connector named Unitary Plug-in (application-layer observer chain and transport-layer router chain) is built between the blockchain membranes, which forms the Unitary Interchain Network Universe, thereafter the Unitary Interchain Network.

As an instance, there is an example for plug-in based cross-chain mechanism. When NEO nodes connect to the Unitary Interchain Network Universe. The NEO blockchain network membrane integrates a Unitary plug-in connector produced by the Unitary Interchain Network Protocol Set, which is used to provide the basic communication support. When the observer connector is working, it can route to connect with every existing cross-chain inside the Unitary Interchain Network and map the corresponding elements indirectly through the transport-layer route tunnel. As visualized by Fig. 3, for instance, accounts, tokens, transactions, and information set can be mapped through the NEO-Unitary, ETH-Unitary observers' general transaction model.

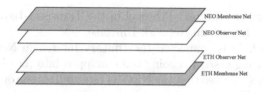

Fig. 3. Observer chain.

Therefore, NEO universe and ETH universe can do the four types of transactions: P2P (NEO to ETH), P2A (such as NEO to ETH smart contract), A2P (such as ETH smart contract), and A2A (NEO smart contract to ETH smart contract). If there already exist many XXX-Unitary observers, each pair of parallel reality can jump from one to others freely (e.g. NEO universe to BTC universe, NEO universe to ETH universe, NEO to Thorn universe, etc.). Therefore, after the linkage by the observer chain, NEO's citizens in NEO network cyberspace can jump from NEO virtual reality to another existing virtual reality (e.g. ETH) smoothly.

4.2 Observer Chain Organization

This plug-in based cross-chain mechanism connects every blockchain network through the Observer Chain, which is formed through two layers of the traditional Internet infrastructures, according to the principle that all the blockchain networks are based on the traditional Internet infrastructures, which means it is more efficient to cross chains by the cross layers (TCP suite Internet model) protocol set.

Each observer chain consists of two parts of "sub-chain" components: one is the normalized chain of the target blockchain in the application-layer (named observer), while the other is the router chain in the transport layer. The consensus algorithm of both observer and router (nodes of both subnetworks are named by unitary nodes) are within POU consensus structure. Within the POU structure, everyone can enter to the network by a substructure of POS which means the community can vest their U token to become either observer nodes or router nodes (or both, for those, install the Unitary Plug-in directly instead of fork and implement specific protocol in UINP), supply services to different blockchain network parallel virtual reality jumping one to the other, and get paid by the Unitary Interchain Network Reward Pool.

Observer nodes can use DAG consensus algorithm to verify the transactions, router in the transport-layer and get paid, while nodes elected to the parliaments from the observer nodes groups (each blockchain connecting to the Unitary Interchain Network will have a group of observer nodes) can monitor the health of the running network, forecast and execute adjustment on the parameters of the network. Unitary Interchain Network Protocol set (UINP) is the protocol that Unitary nodes plug-in can be used to connect the target blockchain using the observers (abided by the "Observer" Protocol in the Application-Layer), and the routers (abided by the "Router" Protocol in the Transport-Layer), which route within the Unitary Interchain Network Universe.

When a blockchain is connected the Unitary Interchain Network Universe, the identity producing system is going to be mapped into the observer's general identity producing system so that the NEO 34 bits address has one to one relation with ETH 40 bits address, as well as with others. The unitary interchain network general address is just the general account system that acts as a supplement and backup (only in account mapping process, one still need a Unitary account if he wants to have the reward from UNIP), but in implementing mapping, it is not necessary to have it as a must as one account system can automatically map to the other.

If the citizen of one virtual reality community, say NEO's wallet account, want to change the NEO to ETH, firstly, a mapping of NEO to ETH account system is built. Then it will create directly an account in ETH namespace if the user doesn't have one ETH wallet (If have, he can input the already existing ETH account to binding, so does to other digital currency). But only when he transfers assets to ETH wallet, the wallet is going to be confirmed by the ETH community, i.e. ETH mining nodes.

To build the Unitary Interchain Network, the complicity is high. For three chain crossing net like cosmos, polka dot etc. The dimension is 3, while to cross infinite chains besides public chains, consortium chains, and private chains will be multi-dimensional. Therefore, existence should be in a highlevel Hilbert virtual world i.e. the network of many networks. ETH users may not feel his existence of other blockchain networks, while if the chain is crossed, he can jump to the parallel.

However, we implement this in an engineering way by writing a transport-layer protocol to work with the application layer and will illustrate the detailed implement structure and simplified methods in the following sections. While for Information, Computers, Internet, Blockchain (network global computer, state machine etc.), Economy etc. which are mathematics, this paper doesn't aim to give too much mathematic conduct, one can go into the UINP Yellow Paper of UNIP to see the statistic model, game theory economic design, mathematics behind of perceptual hash, etc. used in UNIP, in another word, the mathematic proof of concept (POC) behind UINP.

4.3   Wormholes Based on Plug-ins

When plug-ins are inserted into the nodes, one membrane will have special tunnels to connect to the other membranes. When the node in one membrane has plug-in, the plug-in can connect the other plug-ins within the other nodes of the other membranes as shown in Fig. 4. There are five nodes with plug-ins including node A and node B of membrane N3, node C and node D of membrane N2, and node E of membrane N1. All the nodes in the same membrane can complete the operations according the rules of their own blockchains. The nodes without plug-ins cannot communication with the nodes in other membranes. The nodes with plug-ins can connect to the nodes with plug-ins in the other membranes.

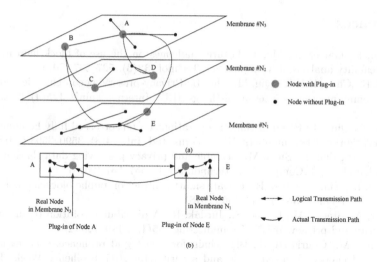

Fig. 4. Wormholes between different membranes.

For example, node A is in membrane N3 and node E is in membrane N1. The plug-ins can help node A and node E to connect with each other. As shown in Fig. 4(a), membrane N3 can connect to membrane N1 through the connection between node A and node E. There is a tunnel between node A and node E, which can help to complete the data exchange between node A and node E. This tunnel is just a wormhole between membrane N1 and membrane N3. When there are more membranes, the wormholes can connect the necessary membranes for the data exchange. In fact, the connected membranes are not connected directly, which are still independent. As shown in Fig. 4(b), the plug-ins in node A and node E make themselves be connected. And then they connect to node A and node E respectively. Thus, the connection between plug-ins provide the wormhole to node A and node E, which means membrane N1 and membrane N3 are connected.

5   Conclusions

In this paper, we propose a plug-in based cross-chain mechanism. The membranes containing blockchains are organized as a 4-dimensional space. The plug-ins are added into the nodes, which can give "gate" to the nodes in one membrane to connect to the nodes in other membranes. The worm-holes are kept to provide the tunnels between the membranes by these plug-ins. This mechanism is implemented in Unitary blockchain network with the support of a set of protocols (UINP). The use of blockchain may cause time delay due to its time consuming for minners' confirmation. The use of reinforcement learning in [15] has reduced the stress of resources decreasing the delay for the resource shortage. In the future, we can combine our proposed model with the cloud computing [16] to achieve higher efficiency.

References

1. Juan, F., Galvez, J., Me, J.: Future challenges on the use of blockchain for food traceability analysis. J. Comput. Sci. Technol. **33**(3), 527–537 (2018)
2. Gai, K., Choo, K.K.R., Qiu, M., Zhu, L.: Privacy-preserving content-oriented wireless communication in internet-of-things. IEEE Internet Things J. **5**(4), 3059–3067 (2018)
3. Gai, K., Qiu, M.: Blend arithmetic operations on tensor-based fully homomorphic encryption over real numbers. IEEE Trans. Ind. Inf. **14**(8), 3590–3598 (2018)
4. Zheng, B., Zhu, L., Shen, M.: Scalable and privacy-preserving data sharing based on blockchain. J. Comput. Sci. Technol. **33**(3), 557–567 (2018)
5. Yuan, R., Xia, Y., Chen, H.: Private smart contract on public blockchain. J. Comput. Sci. Technol. **33**(3), 542–556 (2018)
6. Dorr, A., Steger, M., Kanhe, S., Jurdak, R.: A distributed solution to automotive security and privacy. IEEE Commun. Mag. **55**(12), 119–125 (2017)
7. Mylrea, M., Gourisetti, S.: Blockchain for smart grid resilience: exchanging distributed energy at speed, scale and security. In: 2017 Resilience Week (RWS), Wilmington, USA, pp. 18–23 (2017)
8. Huckle, S., Bhattacharya, R., White, M., Beloff, N.: Internet of things, blockchain and shared economy applications. In: The 7th International Conference on Emerging Ubiquitous Systems and Pervasive Networks (EUSPN 2016)/The 6th International Conference on Current and Future Trends of Information and Communication Technologies in Healthcare (ICTH-2016)/Affiliated Workshops, 19–22 Sept 2016, London, UK, pp. 461–466 (2016)
9. Zhu, L., Yulu, W., Gai, K., Choo, K.-K.R.: Controllable and trustworthy blockchain-based cloud data management. Futur. Gener. Comput. Syst. **91**, 527–535 (2019)
10. Gai, K., Qiu, M., Zhao, H., Tao, L., Zong, Z.: Dynamic energy-aware cloudlet-based mobile cloud computing model for green computing. J. Netw. Comput. Appl. **59**(C), 46–54 (2016)
11. Kosba, A.E., Miller, A., Shi, E., Wen, Z., Papamanthou, C.: Hawk: the blockchain model of cryptography and privacy-preserving smart contracts. In: IEEE Symposium on Security and Privacy, SP 2016, San Jose, CA, USA, 22–26 May 2016, pp. 839–858 (2016)
12. Valenta, L., Rowan, B.: Blindcoin: blinded, accountable mixes for bitcoin. In: Brenner, M., Christin, N., Johnson, B., Rohloff, K. (eds.) FC 2015. LNCS, vol. 8976, pp. 112–126. Springer, Heidelberg (2015). https://doi.org/10.1007/978-3-662-48051-9_9
13. Münsing, E., Mather, J., Moura, S.: Blockchains for decentralized optimization of energy resources in microgrid networks. In: 2017 IEEE Conference on Control Technology and Applications (CCTA), pp. 2164–2171 (2017)
14. Eyal, I., Gencer, A.E., Sirer, E.G., Renesse, R.: Bitcoin-NG: a scalable blockchain protocol. In: 13th USENIX Symposium on Networked Systems Design and Implementation, NSDI 2016, Santa Clara, CA, USA, 16–18 March 2016, pp. 45–59 (2016)
15. Gai, K., Qiu, M.: Reinforcement learning-based content-centric services in mobile sensing. IEEE Netw. **32**(4), 34–39 (2018)
16. Gai, K., Qiu, M., Zhao, H.: Energy-aware task assignment for mobile cyber-enabled applications in heterogeneous cloud computing. J. Parallel Distrib. Comput. **111**, 126–135 (2018)

How to Detect and Contain Suspicious Transactions in Distributed Ledgers

Ralph Deters[(✉)]

Department of Computer Science, University of Saskatchewan,
Saskatoon, Canada
deters@cs.usask.ca

Abstract. Distributed Ledger Technology (DLT) like Blockchain Technology (BCT) enables the development of *trust-free* P2P networks, consisting of nodes that process and propagate transactions in form of messages. Trust into other nodes and/or messages is replaced by trust into the protocols that are governing the network; most notably the message signature and consensus protocols. Depending on the chosen consensus protocols, resilience towards malicious/faulty nodes and messages ranges between $1/3$ and $1/2 - 1$ of all nodes. However, an often overlooked aspect within the resilience/security aspects of DLT networks is that they tend to interact with other components that are often less resilient e.g. clients/wallets. This, in turn, allows attackers to issue forged transactions that are formally correct. This paper focuses on detecting and containing such transaction using metadata and event propagation.

Keywords: Distributed ledger · Blockchain · Malicious transactions
Fraud · Awareness · Metadata

1 Distributed Ledger Technology

The term Distributed Ledger Technology (DLT) refers to a class of P2P networks that are fully decentralized and physically distributed transaction-processing systems. Due to their trustless design, these P2P transaction-processing networks are designed to be highly resilient towards malicious/faulty nodes and messages. As indicated in the name, the ledger (record of all transactions) is distributed across the autonomous nodes that form the DLT network. While the specifics of the distributed ledger structure varies within DLT systems (e.g. use of sharding), the distributed ledger is expected to contain a record of the accounts and the approved transactions. Re-Executing the approved transactions allows a node to calculate the current state of each account. DLT networks use a single-writer, all-reader model to manage access towards individual accounts. The owner of an account is expected to digitally sign a transaction that alters the state of that account e.g. moves an asset contained in the account to another account. To be accepted by a node and ultimately the DLT system, each transaction must be signed by the involved account owners and fulfill certain ledger/application specific constraints e.g. no double spending. In the absence of trusted components, the nodes of a DLT network have to use a consensus algorithm to ensure the eventual consistency of the distributed ledger. Blockchain Technology (BCT) (aka Blockchain) is a subclass of

M. Qiu (Ed.): SmartBlock 2018, LNCS 11373, pp. 149–158, 2018.
https://doi.org/10.1007/978-3-030-05764-0_16

DLT networks, that deploy consensus algorithms that create blocks of verified transactions. These blocks are linked which leads to a chain (list) of blocks (aka blockchain). While BCT networks tend to face higher latency and lower throughput when
processing transactions, they remain popular due to the larger number of deployments
and simpler consensus algorithms (typically PoW). A key issue in the deployment of
DLT networks is the management of these systems especially in terms of performance
and the detection of malicious/fraudulent transactions. For DLT/BCT networks a
variety of hacking attacks are well documented e.g. Man in the middle attacks (MitM),
malware on clients, malware on miners, etc.. Especially the MitM class of attacks in
which an attacker installs malware on the victim's computer tends to be difficult to
handle in current DLT/BCT systems. Once an attacker manages to install malware on
the victim's computer, it becomes possible to change the destination address of assets
and/or obtain/steal the signing/private keys. The MitM & malware attacks become even
more challenging once software components act on behalf of users e.g. in an IoT
scenario. The problem of securing and preventing MitM & malware attacks increases
with the number of computers that host software components that act (sign transactions) on behalf of the user since each component presents a possible target for an
attacker. This paper focuses on the prevention and detection of a malicious/fraudulent
transaction due to compromised signing keys by adding a management layer that uses
metadata and event propagation. The remainder of the paper is structured as follows.
Section two introduces the most known security threats for DLT/BCT networks connected to other software components. This is followed by a section on suspicious
transactions and the use of anomaly detection in section three. Section four focuses on
the problems of needing data for the context-dependent analysis of transactions and the
privacy implications. To overcome this challenge the use of policies and metadata is
presented. Section five focuses on the information stored in the metadata accounts and
the use of event processors to determine actions in case suspicious transactions are
discovered. The process of the detecting is presented in section six. Section seven
presents a comparison of the proposed metadata account with the existing smart
contracts and chain code. Section eight focuses on the event processors and is followed
by a presentation of preliminary results of the evaluation in section nine. The paper
concludes with a summary and an outlook on future work.

2   Security and Distributed Ledger Technology

Security is one of the most common features associated with the various subclasses of
Distributed Ledger Technology (DLT) like Blockchain Technology (BCT). Since DLT
networks are trustless P2P networks, they can continue to operate even when significant parts of the network have been compromised. Depending on the consensus protocol, only more than half (PoW) or two-thirds (PBFT) of nodes are required to be
operating correctly. The different percentages of required uncompromised nodes reflect
different underlying assumptions and different performance characteristics of the
consensus protocol e.g. PBFT is generally faster since only a few dedicated nodes
perform critical operations. This, in turn, gave rise to the notion of *unhackable*
DLT/BCT networks. However, it is important to realize that DLT/BCT networks

interact with other software components that are far less resilient towards faulty/malicious nodes. Consequently, the security of a system/solution that is comprised of a DLT/BCT network and other software tends to be vulnerable towards attackers. As the deployments of DLT/BCT networks increased in recent years, it became apparent that there are real security challenges. Broadly speaking, the various challenges can be categorized into three broad groups:

1. Infrastructure attacks e.g. miner attacks [1], eclipse attacks [2].
2. Communication attacks designed to isolate or overwhelm the DLT nodes e.g. DoS [3].
3. *Attacks on components/clients that interface the DLT network e.g. Wallet theft, malware, Man-in-the-middle attacks* [4].

This, in turn, leads to the challenge of detection, containment, and prevention of attacks. This paper focuses on the security challenges that arise when signing keys have been obtained by an attacker (e.g. as a result of a malware or man-in-the-middle attack [4]). Using stolen keys, an attacker can inject transactions that appear to be legitimate and thus are processed by the DLT/BCT network. Since the abuse of signing keys is a known challenge, commercial tools for monitoring cryptocurrency accounts have emerged e.g. CHAINALYIS [5]. These tools focus on defining triggers and issuing alerts and allow monitoring of individual accounts. One underlying assumption of these tools is that the owner of an account is *aware of all activities* involving the account e.g. knows what transactions she/he has issued. Similar to a credit card statement, the transactions are reviewed and flagged in case they seem suspicious. However, once the owner of an account has transferred the signing authority to trusted parties e.g. other users or software agents, a significantly more complex situation emerges. In IoT where Capability-Based Access Control [6] is often used, it is fairly common that software components (e.g. agents) issue transactions on behalf of a user. In such a scenario it is extremely difficult to distinguish valid from suspicious transactions. BlockSci [7] tries to address this issue by providing a general purpose analysis platform. This platform is designed to offer a suite of APIs to enable developers to build analysis tools that offer a wide range of approaches. However, it is in its current state more a proposal and little is known on what kind of support is provided and what has to be developed by its users.

3 Suspicious Transactions Within DLT Networks

Suspicious transactions with DLT/BCT systems are transactions that meet all formal criteria of a valid transaction but don't seem to conform to expected behavior. In other words, a suspicious transaction is an anomaly. Detection of anomalies [5], especially in the field of financial transactions [8], is a well-established field. To detect anomalies and thus patterns that indicate suspicious transactions a context-dependent analysis of transactions is needed. Each transaction must be evaluated using the transaction history of accounts, patterns that indicate suspicious or unsuspicious transaction sequences and semantics of transactions. The key challenge in the detection of suspicious/abnormal transactions is in the development of a classifier with sufficient accuracy. This, in turn, leads to the question of how to obtain the "knowledge" that can be used for the classification. The continuum of possible approaches is marked by the two extremes:

- A posteriori: Based on analyzing past experiences e.g. using machine learning or other statistical approaches [9]. These approaches focus on "learning" from past experiences.
- A priori: Utilize an already existing theory/model [10] to determine how to classify transactions correctly. These models can be represented in various ways e.g. rules, cases or a state-transition graph. Model/theory-driven approaches tend to be more declarative and allow for the generation of explanations.

4   Context, Semantic and Privacy

To determine if a transaction has been signed by an attacker using stolen keys is a *context-depend* classification. If knowledge about "normal" behavior for accounts and the agents that control them is available, the task becomes easier. If it were known that an account is owned by user X and that X is currently unable to access it, transactions signed by X can be easily flagged as suspicious. Similarly, in an IoT scenario where a transaction signed by an agent of the user that transfers access tokens at an unusual rate, time or to an unusual destination may be flagged. Besides context, *semantic* is another important aspect of the classification. What is the meaning of the transaction? What does this transaction enable? Transferring a read-access token or transferring a write-access token are two very different operations. While being able to understand the operational semantics of a transaction and putting it in a context is very helpful in identifying suspicious transactions it does raise privacy concerns. By combining the semantic of transactions and their context, it becomes possible to infer private information e.g. in the context of IoT location profiles of users. Revealing such information to all nodes of a DLT/BCT network in order to minimize suspicious transactions seems rather unappealing even if it is encrypted/hashed e.g. zk-snarks [11] are used. However, instead of revealing data and establishing a context to evaluate transactions, it is also possible to define *policies* and associating them with accounts as *metadata*. The policies that govern the classification of transactions can be presented as workflows. While this appears to be similar to the concept of chain code or smart contracts [12–14] there is a major difference. Smart Contracts represent agreements between parties that don't change. Policies that define when to consider a transaction suspicious and when to accept it are subject to change. By changing policies frequently it becomes harder for an attacker to successfully inject fake transactions.

5   Account Metadata

Linking metadata to accounts can be achieved by viewing accounts as tuples consisting of a data field and a metadata field. However, it is more secure to store the metadata in a separate account. By using two accounts, an attacker would have to obtain not only the signing key of the account but also the signing key of the metadata account. In the context of DLT/BCT, metadata is often used to semantically enrich the transactions [15], but not to manage accounts and the transactions that interact with them. Adding metadata accounts into DLT/BCT introduces the challenge of managing two different types of accounts and managing the relationships between them. Instead of storing just the set of (data) accounts and the list of approved transactions we now also need to store in addition the set of metadata accounts and the relationships between the accounts. In the simplest case, each metadata account has a 1:1 relationship with a (data) account. However, it is also possible to have a metadata account linked to multiple data accounts. Finally, the metadata accounts themselves can have metadata accounts. This leads to the emergence of DAGs in which the (data) accounts form the leaf nodes and metadata accounts the parents. In many ways, metadata accounts represent a decentralized control layer in the DLT/BCT network. Having metadata accounts governing other metadata accounts leads to hierarchies of control which in turn increases the resilience of the DLT network. The concept of metadata accounts does not define what type of metadata is to be stored. In our implementation metadata accounts are 5-tuples consisting of:

{
- version number
- policy
  verification workflow
- verification functions
  list of functions to be used in verification workflow
  [{url_function_1, hash} .... {url_function_n, hash}]
- URLs of event brokers
  [url_eventprocessor_1 ..... url_eventprocessor_n]
- Whitelisted transactions
  [transaction_1, ... transaction_n]
  }

The version number is a counter that is increased with every change. It is used to synchronize the behaviors of nodes and to resolve conflicts due to using outdated metadata. A verification workflow is a finite-state machine that executes/uses the evaluation functions. These functions are defined in verification functions (list of functions). Verification functions are identified by the URL and the associated hashcode and are executed in each node. Finally, a list of event processors is provided that receive the results of the verification workflow for each received transaction.

6 Detecting Suspicious Transactions

Metadata accounts are used to guide the initial transaction verification step. Upon receiving a transaction, each node will perform a basic check if the transaction is well-formed and properly signed. The next step is to identify the accounts involved in the transaction. Upon identifying the accounts the related metadata is retrieved and if necessary the new verification functions and workflow is downloaded. The workflow is now executed using transaction, current account status of involved accounts and log of approved transactions. If the workflow creates an {approved, transaction} event, the transaction is considered non-suspicious and can be processed by the node. However, if the workflow creates an {suspicious, transaction, explanation} event, the transaction is not processed and the transaction flagged and will not be processed any further by the node. The messages produced by the workflow is always sent to the specified event processors. While approval events are used to track the processing of the transaction in the network, suspicious transaction events indicate a potential problem. Upon receiving a suspicious transaction event, the event processor can decide to still approve the transaction by adding it to the list of whitelisted transaction and/or changing the verification functions or workflow. The described event processors have some similarity with the coordinators in the Manifold coordination language [16]. However, unlike the coordinators in the Manifold model, the event processor doesn't manipulate the nodes (e.g. their input/output relations). Event processors just redirect the report of a suspicious transaction to the owner of the account or an agent of the owner. It is the owner or her/his agent that decides if the transaction is legitimate. If it is legitimate it requires a change in the metadata e.g. adding it to the whitelisted transactions and/or changing the code and/or workflow.

7 Metadata Versus Smart Contracts

Ethereum [17] is generally credited with introducing the concept of smart contracts in the area of BCT/DLT. While it was possible to define in Forth [18] code snippets that are linked to the transaction in Bitcoin [19], Ethereum generalized and extended the notion of using code in BCT networks. Generally speaking, enabling custom code to be executed in a DLT/BCT network dramatically increases the deployment possibility. It is, therefore, no surprise that smart contracts are at the center of most of the proposals for DLT/BCT networks targeting access control issues. In these proposals, access control is viewed as capability-based access control [28]. Transferring tokes in a DLT/BCT network from one account to another is used as a means for enabling/granting access. Software components that have such an access token can execute operations on resources. The access token is used to signal and specify the type of access the holder has e.g. how often which operations can be invoked. The main problem in using smart contracts as a means for checking if and what access token can be transferred from one account to another is their immutability and accessibility. Smart contracts and chain code are by design meant to be immutable since they represent a binding *contract between parties*. In addition, they need to be accessible since they are to be executed on many nodes. This allows an attacker to study them and design the attack in a manner that passes the rules of the smart contract/chain code. Smart contracts and chain code can be programmed to exhibit behaviors that depend on the values of other data accounts but this doesn't change the ability for an attacker to study them. In addition, it is hard to change smart contracts/chain code in light of an ongoing attack. Metadata accounts on the other side can be changed at any time and thus they are harder to handle for an attacker. For example, an owner of an account may use different workflows e.g. more/less restrictive based on the factors outside the

DLT/BCT. An owner of smart home devices may choose to use very restrictive settings when she/he is unlikely to add new components. The ability to change anytime the content of the metadata account adds a very effective control layer. Instead of directly influencing nodes, the metadata can be used to change the behavior of nodes when processing transactions on a per account base. This is particularly interesting if control loops are desired. In such a case the workflow and its verification functions are providing input on the state of the transaction processing on a per account base. The event processor receives the events and decides if it has to intervene by changing the whitelisted transaction list, the workflow, the verification functions or even the event processors that need to be informed. By changing the metadata accounts the behavior of the nodes in the DLT/BCT network are changed. Since metadata accounts can also be governed by metadata accounts hierarchical control loops are possible. This, in turn, allows for an autonomic computing [20–22] like control.

8 Event Processors

Each account has at least one event processor linked to it. The task of the event processor is to monitor all transactions that relate to the account and to determine which are legitimate and which are forgeries. While this enables very effective monitoring of single accounts it fails to ensure that patterns observed in one account are made know to other accounts. A very effective way of dealing with this challenge is to interconnect the event processors and create hierarchies. by letting event processor correlate events of one account and send these as events to other hierarchically higher event processors it becomes possible to effectively process a large number of events from all accounts in a distributed manner [23, 24]. By sharing the found patterns of illegitimate transactions (cases) the various event processors can learn and continuously adapt [25] towards novel attacks.

9 Evaluation

Given that a DLT/BCT network needs to exceed several hundred nodes for any realistic setting, simulation emerges as the only viable approach. However, evaluation of DLT networks is a still-evolving area of research [26]. The absence of workloads, benchmarks, and simulation approaches makes the evaluation of DLT/BCT networks challenging. To evaluate the use of metadata accounts, event processors as an effective means of detecting and containing transactions signed with stolen keys, an Erlang simulation of a network of 5,000–50.000 nodes is used. The simulation abstracts the nodes of the DLT/BCT network as Erlang processes that communicate via messages. The event workflows are also modeled as Erlang processes that receive messages from the simulated nodes. Using a load generator 1000 messages are sent into the network to test the ability to respond to suspicious transactions. The network connection between the DLT/BCT nodes were configured as Fully Meshed (each node sees every other node. Nodes send messages in one step to all other nodes) and Kademlia [27] (nodes see only a subset of nodes and messages are routed). As expected the costs for evaluating a transaction is very low and thus presents negligible costs in both network configurations. The main difference between the network configuration is the time it takes to inform all nodes. Kademlia is slower since messages are routed and require log (number of nodes) hops. Please note that

- the arrival rate of the transactions was between 0–300 ms
- the workflows were designed to detect the suspicious transactions,
- the nodes evaluate concurrently their workflows,
- the costs per workflow are low and that
- communication with the event processor is also minimal.

Consequently, the result is as expected. Changing the arrival rates or increasing the costs for the verification would require the use of more physical machines to ensure that the simulated nodes are not starved for computing resources. Please note that 4 google compute engine VMs (8 core, 30 GB) were used in this experiment and that one Erlang virtual machine was used per machine. All virtual machines run in the same subnetwork and are connected as a fully meshed network. 1 machine was used as the load generator and the remaining 3 other used to host the Erlang processes representing the nodes 5 K–50 K, their workflows 5 K–50 K and their event processors 5 K–50 K. As a result, the 3 machines hosting the virtual machines were exposed to very low loads given that Erlang VMs are designed to handle significantly higher numbers of processes. Please also note that each of the 3 machines hosts only 5 K–50 K Erlang processes.

10 Summary and Future Work

An often overlooked aspect within the resilience/security aspects of DLT/BCT networks is that they often need to interact with other components that are often less resilient e.g. clients/wallets. This, in turn, allows attackers to issue fake transactions that are formally correct. This paper focuses on detecting and containing such transaction using metadata and event propagation. Using simulation it was possible to test the effects the use of metadata and event processors on larger DLT/BCT networks. The simulation showed that there is a minimal overhead indicating that this is a viable option. Compared with the use of smart contracts and chain code, the use of metadata and event processors offers better protection since the metadata can be changed easily at runtime. One of the most interesting aspects of using workflows for verification and event processors for dealing with potentially harmful transactions is the possibility to enable different evaluation and processing workflows based on account on perceived threat status. this, in turn, leads to the possibility of heterogeneous DLT in which different accounts can enforce different workflows for evaluating and processing transactions. We also consider the use of hierarchical control loops very interesting and plan to investigate this further. Using the extensive research on autonomic computing and linking it to accounts within DLT networks promises interesting future research.

References

1. Eyal, I., Sirer, E.G.: Majority is not enough: Bitcoin mining is vulnerable. Commun. ACM **61**(7), 95–102 (2018)
2. Heilman, E., Kendler, A., Zohar, A., Goldberg, S.: Eclipse attacks on Bitcoin's peer-to-peer network. In: USENIX Security Symposium, pp. 129–144 (2015)
3. Dorri, A., Kanhere, S.S., Jurdak, R., Gauravaram, P.: Blockchain for IoT security and privacy: the case study of a smart home. In: 2017 IEEE International Conference on Pervasive Computing and Communications Workshops (PerCom Workshops), pp. 618–623. IEEE (2017)
4. Man-in-the-middle attacks on wallets. http://news.bitcoin.com/ledger-addresses-man-in-the-middle-attack-that-threatens-millions-of-hardware-wallets/
5. Chandola, V., Banerjee, A., Kumar, V.: Anomaly detection: a survey. ACM Comput. Surv. (CSUR) **41**(3), 15 (2009)
6. Hernández-Ramos, J.L., Jara, A.J., Marın, L., Skarmeta, A.F.: Distributed capability-based access control for the internet of things. J. Internet Serv. Inf. Secur. (JISIS) **3**(3/4), 1–16 (2013)
7. Chainalyis. https://www.chainalysis.com/
8. Debreceny, R.S., Gray, G.L.: Data mining journal entries for fraud detection: an exploratory study. Int. J. Account. Inf. Syst. **11**(3), 157–181 (2010)
9. Lane, T., Brodley, C.E.: An application of machine learning to anomaly detection. In: Proceedings of the 20th National Information Systems Security Conference, vol. 377, pp. 366–380, Baltimore, USA (1997)
10. Valdes, A., Skinner, K.: Adaptive, model-based monitoring for cyber attack detection. In: Debar, H., Mé, L., Wu, S.F. (eds.) RAID 2000. LNCS, vol. 1907, pp. 80–93. Springer, Heidelberg (2000). https://doi.org/10.1007/3-540-39945-3_6
11. Kosba, A.E., et al.: How to use SNARKs in universally composable protocols. IACR Cryptol. ePrint Arch. **2015**, 1093 (2015)
12. Christidis, K., Devetsikiotis, M.: Blockchains and smart contracts for the Internet of Things. IEEE Access **4**, 2292–2303 (2016)
13. Ouaddah, A., Abou Elkalam, A., Ait Ouahman, A.: FairAccess: a new Blockchain-based access control framework for the Internet of Things. Security and Communication Networks **9**(18), 5943–5964 (2016)
14. Ouaddah, A., Elkalam, A.A., Ouahman, A.A.: Towards a novel privacy-preserving access control model based on blockchain technology in IoT. In: Rocha, Á., Serrhini, M., Felgueiras, C. (eds.) Europe and MENA Cooperation Advances in Information and Communication Technologies. Advances in Intelligent Systems and Computing, vol. 520. Springer, Cham (2017). https://doi.org/10.1007/978-3-319-46568-5_53
15. Faisal, T., Courtois, N., Serguieva, A.: The evolution of embedding metadata in blockchain transactions. arXiv preprint arXiv:1806.06738 (2018)
16. Papadopoulos, G.A., Arbab, F.: Coordination models and languages. In: Advances in computers, vol. 46, pp. 329–400. Elsevier (1998)
17. https://github.com/ethereum/wiki/wiki/White-Paper
18. https://www.forth.com/forth/
19. https://bitcoin.org/bitcoin.pdf
20. Kephart, J.O., Chess, D.M.: The vision of autonomic computing. Computer **1**, 41–50 (2003)
21. Murch, R.: Autonomic Computing. IBM Press (2004)
22. Huebscher, M.C., McCann, J.A.: A survey of autonomic computing—degrees, models, and applications. ACM Comput. Surv. (CSUR) **40**(3), 7 (2008)

23. Nygate, Y.A.: Event correlation using rule and object based techniques. In: Sethi, A.S., Raynaud, Y., Faure-Vincent, F. (eds.) Integrated Network Management IV. Springer, Boston (1995). https://doi.org/10.1007/978-0-387-34890-2_25

24. Buchmann, A., Koldehofe, B.: Complex event processing. IT-Information Technology Methoden und innovative Anwendungen der Informatik und Informationstechnik **51**(5), 241–242 (2009)

25. Deters, R.: Case-based diagnosis of multiple faults. In: Veloso, M., Aamodt, A. (eds.) ICCBR 1995. LNCS, vol. 1010, pp. 411–420. Springer, Heidelberg (1995). https://doi.org/10.1007/3-540-60598-3_37

26. Fadhil, M., Owen, G., Adda, M.: Bitcoin network measurements for simulation validation and parameterization. In: 11th International Network Conference, INC 2016. University of Plymouth (2016)

27. Maymounkov, P., Mazières, D.: Kademlia: a peer-to-peer information system based on the XOR metric. In: Druschel, P., Kaashoek, F., Rowstron, A. (eds.) IPTPS 2002. LNCS, vol. 2429, pp. 53–65. Springer, Heidelberg (2002). https://doi.org/10.1007/3-540-45748-8_5

28. Mahalle, P.N., Anggorojati, B., Prasad, N.R., Prasad, R.: Identity authentication and capability based access control (IACAC) for the internet of things. J. Cyber Secur. Mobil. **1**(4), 309–348 (2013)

A Dynamic Scalable Blockchain Based Communication Architecture for IoT

Han Qiu[1], Meikang Qiu[2(✉)], Gerard Memmi[1], Zhong Ming[2], and Meiqin Liu[3]

[1] Telecom-ParisTech, Paris, France
{han.qiu,gerard.memmi}@telecom-paristeh.fr
[2] College of Computer Science, Shenzhen University, Shenzhen, China
{mqiu,mingz}@szu.edu.cn
[3] College of Electrical Engineering, Zhejiang University, Hangzhou, China
liumeiqin@zju.edu.cn

Abstract. The recent development of Blockchain based cryptocurrency technology has enabled a high level of trust and security for many applications in people's daily life. Traditional Blockchain architecture can provide decentralized and trustworthy systems for financial services with persistency, anonymity, and auditability guaranteed. Internet of Things (IoT), as the next promising smart system, has the similar decentralized topology with Blockchain. However, deploying Blockchain in IoT system is still unpractical in many aspects. In this paper, we first point out the practical obstacles to deploy Blockchain topology in IoT system. Then a dynamic Blockchain based trust system is proposed to provide a dynamic and scalable communication architecture for IoT networks. We also present a case study to further discuss the security issues and provide future research directions.

Keywords: Blockchain · IoT · Trust · Security · Bitcoin · Privacy

1 Introduction

Blockchain has been an important technology for building trust architecture in many aspects. Blockchain was first introduced in 2008 as the technical foundation for a cryptocurrency known as Bitcoin [10] and since then has been widely used in other cryptocurrencies [11]. As a core technique for all kinds of cryptocurrencies, blockchain is built on a distributed digital ledger of transactions that is owned across all participating entities in a peer-to-peer network. Decentralization is implemented by deploying all participating entities to verify and confirm the new transactions. Once verified, confirmed, and recorded, the transaction data cannot be altered retroactively without alteration of all subsequent blocks, which requires a consensus of the network majority. In the implementation of Bitcoin, all valid transactions records are hashed and encoded into a Merkle tree [10]. Then batches of valid transactions are formed into blocks. Each block includes the hash results of the prior block which links the two adjacent blocks. Then the

M. Qiu (Ed.): SmartBlock 2018, LNCS 11373, pp. 159–166, 2018.
https://doi.org/10.1007/978-3-030-05764-0_17

linked blocks form a chain which is called blockchain [10]. The process of building blockchain is to continuously append new blocks to the existing blockchain which is also referred to mining [11]. The basic operation of mining is to solve a math puzzle (usually *Proof of Work* (PoW) [14]) which is hard-to-solve but easy-to-verify. In order to solve this puzzle, the participating entities must provide huge computation resources which restrict the number of blocks that can be mined. Also, malicious mining of blocks can be further avoided with this mechanism. The popular puzzle used in blockchain is usually or *Proof of Stake* (PoS) [7]. POW demands high computational resources which are deployed in Bitcoin protocol as finding the specific value with specific Hash results [10]. POS will consume both computational and memory resources [7]. All message exchanged between entities are encrypted with deploying changeable Public Keys which can avoid eavesdropping.

Although blockchain can be used into many famous cryptocurrencies such as Bitcoin, there are other potential applications that can deploy blockchain as a fundamental technology. As building blockchain can allow payment done without any trusted intermediary, many financial services such as digital assets, remittance, and smart contracts are developed [17]. In fact, blockchain is becoming one of the most promising techniques for designing the next generation of communication and interaction systems such as *Internet of Things* (IoT) [3].

With the rapid growth of smart devices and bandwidth of wireless networks, the concept of IoT is becoming realized with wide acceptance and popularity [16]. Nowadays, it represents a network where smart "things" having sensors and antennas are connected. As a highly dynamic network, IoT always has the scalability to allow nodes to join and leave the network. In fact, as the IoT paradigm represents a collection of connected devices and heterogeneous networks, it also inherits the traditional security and privacy issues from the computer networks [8]. However, on the other hand, different from traditional computers, IoT devices are usually equipped with constrained resources such as limited power supply, calculation capacity, and storage space [13]. This leads to the issue that the traditional security schemes used in computer networks based blockchain are difficult to be implemented in IoT networks.

One problem in IoT networks is the identity management for the devices. As the very different connection properties of IoT devices such as connection lifetime, service requirement, and trust levels, it is difficult to assign an ID that can universally identify the "things" and to maintain this identification scheme. In fact, blockchain architecture can be deployed as the foundation for further building security and privacy in IoT. The very basic design could be to deploy every IoT node as a participating entity of blockchain which can further build a trusted digital ledger for IoT applications.

In this paper, we first point out the obstacles of building blockchain in IoT networks. Then a system design with a labeled network topology for the IoT ID management is presented to indicate one solution to use a blockchain based protocol in IoT networks.

The roadmap of this paper is given as follows. In Sect. 2, we illustrate the practical problems for using blockchain design in IoT networks. In Sect. 3, we propose the layered network design to deploy blockchain as a foundation for IoT security. In Sect. 5, a brief system evaluation is given and we discuss the future work. We conclude our work in Sect. 6.

2 Research Background

In this section, we first point out the practical obstacle of building a secure IoT system. The conflict between security schemes cost and the practical low overhead requirement for deploying IoT network is discussed. Then the new architecture of blockchain with full nodes and lightweight nodes is introduced.

2.1 One Example of IoT Security Issues

As shown in Fig. 1, the IoT networks are built up by many heterogeneous digital devices with very different hardware configurations which all rely on the communication middle layer to make them connected. Many IoT devices are equipped with two basic elements for data collection and transmission. Some devices such as smartphones are also equipped with powerful calculation chips which can also process collected data.

As pointed out in Sect. 1, although IoT is inherited from the traditional computer networks which also inherit the security and privacy issues, the traditional countermeasures are difficult to inherit. The main reason is not only due to the heterogeneous devices with totally different hardware configurations, but also due to the dynamic communications in IoT concept. One example is given in Fig. 1 that there are devices with constant and dynamic links, and also devices that are always offline or frequently join and leave the networks. In such cases, it is much easier for an attacker to manipulate a compromised node with fake ids to join the communication environment. It is more difficult to manage the id in IoT than in traditional computer networks with such dynamic networks.

A review of security threats is listed in [6]. One of the threats is about the authentication and secure communications in IoT. As shown in Fig. 1, any devices in an IoT network must be authenticated first before they can communicate. However, in practical implementations, due to constrained hardware resources, the overhead of security mechanisms must be minimized to consider the efficiency problems which will further lead to security breaches [9].

2.2 Scalable Blockchain Nodes

As explained in Sect. 1, the foundation of blockchain is that all the transaction records are verified and confirmed in previous blocks which can avoid the deniable operations. This mechanism will require all participating entities in a blockchain network to maintain and more importantly, to store the verified and confirmed transaction records. In fact, once a new entity joins the blockchain network, the

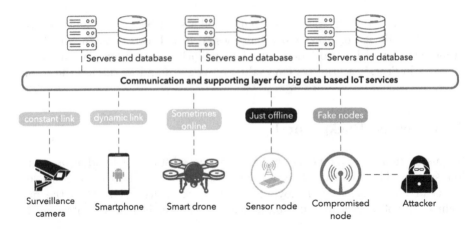

Fig. 1. IoT network with heterogeneous devices and dynamic connections.

download for all history blocks are necessary. However, this feature became the obstacle for deploying blockchain architecture in IoT network. Most devices are calculation and storage limited and the connection links between the IoT nodes are always dynamic which means either maintaining or downloading the history blocks are not practical.

Fortunately, there are new designs for blockchain nodes called full nodes and lightweight nodes in Bitcoin protocols [1]. A lightweight node only downloads the block headers to validate the authenticity of the transactions instead of all the history blocks. Then lightweight nodes are served by full nodes to connect to the blockchain network, they are easy to maintain and run without a heavy overhead.

However, the large deployment of lightweight nodes may lead to privacy issues in IoT. As lightweight nodes are served by full nodes, the malicious users hold the full node will compromise the privacy of transactions from lightweight nodes. Moreover, as the dynamic connections of IoT, once a full node leaves the network, the corresponding lightweight nodes will have problems to enjoy the blockchain network. One work proposed an IoT architecture with smart home settings shown in [4] which uses the devices such as computers in the home as full nodes to serve the lightweight nodes. However, this design fits the topology of smart home scenario which every home is assumed to have personal computers and can be seen as the connection cores for the IoT sub-networks in each smart home.

3   System Designs

In this section, we present a multi-layered blockchain based ID management topology to fit the dynamic IoT network. Different roles for nodes are defined and coordinated to maintain the whole blockchain network. More particularly, the different devices in IoT network will be assigned with different roles according to the connection life and hardware. Coordination methods are also necessary to guarantee the backup full nodes to serve the lightweight nodes when their full nodes are offline.

First, we see all IoT devices as nodes in a blockchain network. Then an unique ID will be assigned for each IoT device which will be also associated with the blockchain wallet ID. With this design, all valid IDs will be easily verified in IoT network while fake IDs are difficult to be found and refused. Moreover, any malicious actions from IoT devices will be recorded with the ID to defend attackers in the future.

In order to avoid the heavy computation or storage with existing blockchain topology, different nodes should be defined with different IoT device configurations. In this paper, we define three blockchain labels for devices in IoT: lightweight node, full node, and coordination node. Then we classified all devices by assigning different labels according to connection lifetime and hardware configurations. Lightweight node labels are corresponding to the IoT devices that have low computing capacity or have short connection lifetime. Full node labels will require the IoT devices always maintain connecting to the IoT network and have enough calculation capacity and storage space. Coordination node labels are assigned to the devices with long connection lifetime and low calculation capacity.

For example, a surveillance camera as shown in Fig. 2 is the device that has a long connection lifetime and low hardware capacity will be assigned with a coordination node. The computers which are used as the overlay layer in [4] are assigned with full node labels and the blockchain is maintained mainly on them. Then the devices which are dynamic join and leave this IoT network are assigned with lightweight node labels to allow them to participate in this blockchain system while do not need the overhead of full nodes.

By combining the decentralized blockchain topology with identity verification and recording, an IoT ID management system can be created. This system could improve security and reduce malicious behaviors in IoT networks. For any attackers with faked IDs, it will be more and more difficult to continuously maintain the connection to the IoT network as frequently faking different IDs are more difficult and costly. Moreover, considering difficult hardware configurations of the IoT devices, on one hand, the practical implementation is possible while on the othe hand, the trust system with different levels can be built further to manage the connections for different devices. One example would be there are different devices associated with different roles in IoT networks [15] such as center connection nodes or edge nodes.

4   A Brief Case Study

Once a new sensor node wants to join this blockchain network, the first thing is to send a request to the coordination nodes with its label. If it is a full node, then a high level security verification will be required until it gets permission to

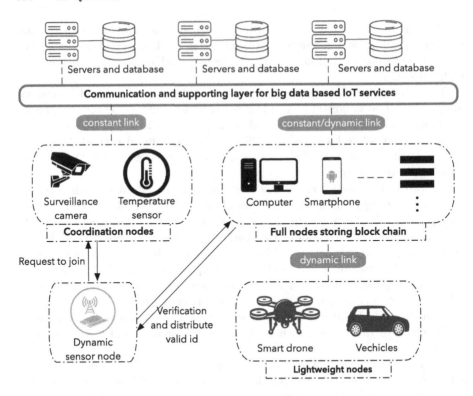

Fig. 2. IoT network with labeled devices and dynamic connections.

join the full node group. If it is a lightweight node, the coordination nodes will distribute a full node that can serve this newcomer. However, the newcomer will not get a valid id to communicate until the verification for the real id. Once a full node goes offline, the coordination nodes will then distribute new full nodes to the lightweight nodes to maintain the connections.

In this section, we assume a threat mode with a malicious user in the IoT network that may manipulate one IoT node by cracking or to fake a node ID to try to access to the IoT network. For the first case, an attacker may be able to compromise and control one IoT node in the network. Many malicious actions may be then reported by other nodes in the IoT network. In such case, the ID of the compromised node will be marked and recorded in the following blocks in the blockchain system. In the following time slots, higher security verification requirements and the lower level of trust will be modified accordingly. Thus, it will be more difficult for the attacker to compromise the same node again in future.

In the other scenario that the attacker connect into the IoT network with a faked ID. If the faked ID is owned by an IoT node that is still active, the verification process on the controller node will refuse the connection to block the attacker out. Even if the attacker manage to connect the IoT network, the report for the malicious behaviors will let this faked ID be marked as vulnerable and blocked out from this IoT network. If the ID management system is efficient, the attacker will have to frequently change the faked ID to maintain the connection. Thus higher security level will be achieved as the cost for faking IDs will be increasing.

5   Discussions and Future Work

With a blockchain based IoT network, we can record all transactions pertaining to devices in this IoT and stored locally. This information can be very useful for security purpose. For instance, once the attacker wants to fake an id to join the IoT network, the label must be assigned first. If the attacker pretends to be a full node, the high level security verification will find him or make the attack really expensive. Or if the attacker just wants to pretend as a lightweight node, it is also hard because all history is recorded and the attacker must fake everything again for each time trying to attack. However, there are still future works to do which is to define the coordination and switching protocols for lightweight nodes. Also, other situations like when full nodes cannot be trusted must be considered [5].

One further design in IoT with blockchain topology should be not only managing the ID but also protecting the information exchanged in the IoT network. For example, data sharing and verification protocols must be designed to further guarantee the IoT network security. As IoT devices have very different hardware configuration that uniform simple encryption algorithm is difficult to implement, authentication and verification are important to guanratee the security of data sharing. Lightweight encryption methods [12] should also be introduced as supplementary methods for security for some specific use cases [2]. Also, more work in future need to be done for test the system performance and practical possibility to deploy such architecture in real IoT environment.

6   Conclusion

In this paper, we presented the obstacle of deploying blockchain technology into IoT networks. We proposed an IoT system architecture with practically labeling all IoT devices which can map them to the full nodes and lightweight nodes concepts in blockchain protocol. Then we evaluated that this design could enhance the security level by managing the IDs of IoT devices while increases the difficulty for attackers to fake IoT nodes.

Acknowledgement. Dr. H. Qiu and Prof. G. Memmi are supported by BART: Blockchain Advanced Research & Technologies teamed up by Telecom-ParisTech, Inria, IRT SystemX and Telecom-SudParis. This work is also partially supported by China NSFC 61836005 and 61672358; China NSFC 61728303 and the Open Research Project of the State Key Laboratory of Industrial Control Technology, Zhejiang University, China (ICT1800417). Prof. M. Qiu is the corresponding author.

References

1. Antonopoulos, A.M.: Mastering Bitcoin: Unlocking Digital Cryptocurrencies. O'Reilly Media Inc., Newton (2014)
2. Dai, W., Qiu, L., Wu, A., Qiu, M.: Cloud infrastructure resource allocation for big data applications. IEEE Trans. Big Data **4**(3), 313–324 (2018)
3. Dorri, A., Kanhere, S.S., Jurdak, R., Gauravaram, P.: Blockchain for IoT security and privacy: the case study of a smart home. In: 2017 IEEE International Conference on Pervasive Computing and Communications Workshops (PerCom Workshops), pp. 618–623. IEEE (2017)
4. Dorri, A., Kanhere, S.S., Jurdak, R., Gauravaram, P.: LSB: a lightweight scalable blockchain for IoT security and privacy. arXiv preprint arXiv:1712.02969 (2017)
5. Gai, K., Qiu, M.: Blend arithmetic operations on tensor-based fully homomorphic encryption over real numbers. IEEE Trans. Ind. Inform. **14**(8), 3590–3598 (2018)
6. Khan, M.A., Salah, K.: IoT security: review, blockchain solutions, and open challenges. Future Gener. Comput. Syst. **82**, 395–411 (2018)
7. Kiayias, A., Russell, A., David, B., Oliynykov, R.: Ouroboros: a provably secure proof-of-stake blockchain protocol. In: Katz, J., Shacham, H. (eds.) CRYPTO 2017. LNCS, vol. 10401, pp. 357–388. Springer, Cham (2017). https://doi.org/10.1007/978-3-319-63688-7_12
8. Li, C., Qiu, M.: Reinforcement Learning for Cyber Physical Systems with Cybersecurity Case Studies. Chapman & Hall/CRC, Boca Raton (2018)
9. Mahalle, P.N., Anggorojati, B., Prasad, N.R., Prasad, R., et al.: Identity authentication and capability based access control (IACAC) for the Internet of Things. J. Cyber Secur. Mobil. **1**(4), 309–348 (2013)
10. Nakamoto, S.: Bitcoin: a peer-to-peer electronic cash system (2008)
11. Narayanan, A., Bonneau, J., Felten, E., Miller, A., Goldfeder, S.: Bitcoin and Cryptocurrency Technologies: A Comprehensive Introduction. Princeton University Press, Princeton (2016)
12. Qiu, H., Memmi, G., Noura, H.: An efficient secure storage scheme based on information fragmentation. In: 2017 IEEE 4th International Conference on Cyber Security and Cloud Computing (CSCloud), pp. 108–113. IEEE (2017)
13. Qiu, M., Gai, K., Thuraisingham, B., Tao, L., Zhao, H.: Proactive user-centric secure data scheme using attribute-based semantic access controls for mobile clouds in financial industry. Future Gener. Comput. Syst. **80**, 421–429 (2018)
14. Vukolić, M.: The quest for scalable blockchain fabric: proof-of-work vs. BFT replication. In: Camenisch, J., Kesdoğan, D. (eds.) iNetSec 2015. LNCS, vol. 9591, pp. 112–125. Springer, Cham (2016). https://doi.org/10.1007/978-3-319-39028-4_9
15. Wu, D., Arkhipov, D.I., Asmare, E., Qin, Z., McCann, J.A.: UbiFlow: mobility management in urban-scale software defined IoT. In: 2015 IEEE Conference on Computer Communications (INFOCOM), pp. 208–216. IEEE (2015)
16. Zhang, Y., Qiu, M., Tsai, C.W., Hassan, M.M., Alamri, A.: Health-CPS: healthcare cyber-physical system assisted by cloud and big data. IEEE Syst. J. **11**(1), 88–95 (2017)
17. Zheng, Z., Xie, S., Dai, H.N., Wang, H.: Blockchain challenges and opportunities: a survey. Work Pap.-2016 (2016)

The Impact of Blockchain on Food Supply Chain: The Case of Walmart

Bowen Tan[1], Jiaqi Yan[2(⊠)], Si Chen[2], and Xingchen Liu[2]

[1] Business School, Durham University, Durham DH1 3LE, UK
dlmu_tanbowen@163.com
[2] School of Information Management, Nanjing University,
Nanjing 210023, China
{jiaqiyan,si.chen}@nju.edu.cn, dorisxingchen@163.com

Abstract. Blockchain technology has become increasingly popular and attracted interests from many innovators, technologists and scholars in recent years. Beyond the financial sector, the blockchain technology is promising in addressing the current limitations in food supply chain management. As the adoption of blockchain in food supply chain is still in an early stage, it is significant to have a thematic framework for understanding the impacts of blockchain technology. This paper aims to exploring the adoption of blockchain technology in food supply chains with a thematic analysis. A desktop research is conducted and all the data is collected from online databases, including Factiva, Nexis, and Google scholar. Then we carry out a qualitative thematic analysis, according to the investigation processes suggested by Creswell. The findings illustrate four categories of impacts of the adoption of blockchain on food supply chains.

Keywords: Blockchain technology · Food supply chain · Case study

1 Introduction

Modern supply chains are becoming increasingly intricate due to globalisation and it is a normal phenomenon for organisations to outsource manufacturing, logistics and other roles. However, the length and complexity of the supply chain result in an increased likelihood of product fraud and trust shortage among the supply chain parties (Sarpong 2014). Food safety issues have become a prominent problem in the world and have aroused more attention of the public in recent years because of the endless problems in current food industry such as the 2013 horse meat scandal resulted from food labelling fraud in the Europe (Levitt 2016), a multi-state Salmonella outbreak in the US which caused by Maradol papayas in 2017 (56Menon 2018) and the contaminated egg scandal in Switzerland, Hong Kong and 15 EU states in the same year (Boffey and Connolly 2017). Therefore, traceability is an urgent requirement in supply chain industries, especially for the agri-food industry (Costa et al. 2013). Recently, some prominent organisations have worked together for the further adoption of blockchain technology in food supply chains, for instance, IBM and Walmart coupled with Chinese retailer JD.com and Tsinghua University have founded a Blockchain Food Safety

© Springer Nature Switzerland AG 2018
M. Qiu (Ed.): SmartBlock 2018, LNCS 11373, pp. 167–177, 2018.
https://doi.org/10.1007/978-3-030-05764-0_18

Alliance collaboration to deal with the product safety issues in food supply chains in China (4Aitken 2017). As the leading company in the food retail industry, Walmart has already received some great achievements in blockchain technology exploration. For example, the pork pilot project in China and the mango pilot project in America and have filed some patents based on the blockchain. Although the pilot projects have reached great success in the current stage, the mass adoption in the food supply chain may not be straightforward and might encounter a variety of challenges. Moreover, most actors in the food supply chain such as manufacturers and logistics operators, especially SMEs have little knowledge about the blockchain and have not started to take action on this new technology (Kersten et al. 2017). Therefore, although block-chain technology is considered as a promising technology and an ideal solution of increasing the trust among multiple actors in the supply chain and enhancing efficiency of the flow of finance, products and information, it is still in the infant stage with gaps between the hype and reality of blockchain technology adoption and no academic consensus on whether the technology will change the world dramatically as people hope (Busby 2018).

2 Literature Review

2.1 Definition of Traceability and Traceability System

There are many definitions on "traceability", which have been defined in ISO 8402, ISO 9000, ISO 22005, the EU General Food Law and the dictionaries but most of them present weaknesses. Therefore, Olsen and Broit (2013) redefined traceability by hiding the two terms "trace" and "track", but matched the definition with traceability systems and recorded identifications as providing products information (for example, origi-nality, components and locations) to the parties in the supply chain. Looking at the problems on traceability and collaboration in the supply chain, Sarpong (2014) suggested that collaborative ventures should pursue appropriate long-term goals and provide the correct information to the traceability system so that the collaboration can gain a good achievement. Traceability system plays the significant role in tracing products in the supply chain. ISO defined the system as the "totality of data and operations that is capable of maintaining desired information about a product and its components through all or part of its production and utilization chain" (ISO 22005:2007, 2007: 3 cited in Epelbaum et al. 2014).

2.2 Traceability in Food Supply Chain

Food supply chain is a complex chain including financial flow, goods flow and information flow, which involves all collaborative enterprises from raw material sup-pliers, manufacturers, logistics parties, wholesalers, retailers, and consumers. The requirement of traceability has become increasingly urgent in supply chain industries such as the agri-food industry (Costa et al. 2013) and traditional Chinese medicine industry (Cai et al. 2016). The food traceability system is considered as a record-keeping system (Golan et al. 2004 cited in Epelbaum et al. 2014), which makes contributions to identify the source of all food inputs such as raw materials, additives and packaging. Therefore, the supply chain members can target the products impacted by a food safety issue and implement a product recall quickly. Researchers all agree that a third party is necessary in supply chain for ensuring information accuracy and security. However, the motivation for the supply chain parties to improve traceability in food supply chain is different. Lu and Xu (2017) provide their views on traceability services from suppliers and retailers' perspective while Hobbs et al. (2005) focused on retailers' motivation and consumers' willingness on food traceability. Hobbs et al. (2005) discussed that the primary motivation for retailers to improve traceability in the food supply chain is usually because this can help them reduce the transaction costs resulted from monitoring product quality rather than to increase trust among consumers. Meanwhile, they indicated that Canadian consumers are willing to pay more when the traceability system provides additional quality and safety assurances. According to Bosona and Gebresenbet (2013), lack of coordination among the actors in food supply chain cause information delay, information asymmetry and then affect the quality of shared information, which cause inefficiency. Furthermore, Bosona and Gebresenbet (2013) suggested that although some innovations that applied for product traceability purposes have already been used such as bar code, RFID tags, and EDI, further development of technological applications on traceability in food supply chain are required.

3 Methodology

3.1 Case Study

Wal-Mart is famous for its efficient supply chain management through large distribution centres and advanced information systems such as Vendor Managed Inventory (VMI), Electronic Data Interchange (EDI) and Radio Frequency IDentification (RFID). In addition, Wal-Mart has been an initiator in technology adoption since it set up the first store in 1962. For instance, almost all Wal-Mart stores adopted the Universal Product Code (UPC) system in the mid-1980s, which dramatically improve checkout productivity and inventory management, leading to retail expansion (Lichtenstein 2010). Furthermore, Wal-Mart was an early adopter of RFID tags since 2003 and required its top 100 suppliers to use the technology on shipping crates and pallets by January 2005 to help manage their inventory (Balocco 2011; Patti and Narsing 2008). Additionally, Wal-Mart is known for its proactive stance towards blockchain technology adoption and is paving the way to a blockchain-based food supply chain. For instance, Wal-Mart opened the Wal-Mart Food Safety Collaboration Centre (WFSCC) in Beijing in 2016 and teamed with IBM and Tsinghua University to enhance food safety in China (Loria 2017). Moreover, the most advanced blockchain movement was the two pilot projects (pork in China and mangos from South America to the US) to improve traceability in the food supply chain, of which the aim was to ensure food safety, improve recall speed, maintain good reputation among consumers and also reduce cost (Castillo 2016). Recently, Wal-Mart has filed several patents for blockchain-based systems, including a medical records system, a marketplace for reselling purchased products, a "Smart Package" system to track detailed information of parcels such as package contents, environmental conditions, and location, and an electrical grid that will be powered by Bitcoin or other digital currencies (Alexandre 2018a).

3.2   Data Collection

This study uses the desktop research method to collect secondary data from different databases (Jiang et al. 2017). In terms of the research by Williams (2015), Coca-Cola company documents were collected to identify how "Big Foods" have influence on governments and key organizations in China and India. This paper adopts a similar data collection method by analyzing documentary data that focuses on the activities of Wal-Mart in order to identify the current status of blockchain adoption in its food supply chain. Wal-Mart is such a large company, rich published data news reports are readily available, so there is no need to collect primary data. Additionally, this avoids researcher issues with in ethical problems in interviews and low response rates in questionnaires (Cowton 1998). Data collection for this thesis includes three phases.

At the first stage, the researcher attempted to retrieve the databases that are directly related to the current status of Wal-Mart food supply chain from two databases (Factiva and Nexis). Factiva provides worldwide full-text coverage of international newspapers, business newswires etc., which helps the researcher get into the real business world. To supplement the articles that retrieved from Factiva, Nexis was conducted for finding more news. Nexis is a large database that covers 4000+ business information sources, including Financial Times and other global news sources. Therefore, searching these two databases provides all the up-to-date news of Wal-Mart food supply chain which meet the research goal of identifying the processes, benefits and challenges of blockchain adoption in Wal-Mart's current food supply chain. Considering blockchain technology was first invented in 2008, the searched news covers the past 10 years (from 2009 to 2018). A total of 455 newspapers articles were searched and 207 were reviewed and identified after deleting duplicated articles (Table 1).

Table 1. Summary of data collection at stage one

Database searched	Keywords	Amount
Factiva & Nexis	'Wal-Mart' and 'food' and 'supply chain' and 'blockchain'	207

At the second stage, instead of looking for the news directly about Wal-Mart supply chain, this search focused on blockchain applications in food supply chain, which may include some other companies, not only Wal-Mart. The aim is to gain more useful knowledge on technology adoption that may guide the future of Wal-Mart (Table 2). Although the same set of databases were searched, the key word were changed to 'food industry', supply chain' and 'blockchain' to reflect the broader coverage of this round of news search. After deleting duplicate articles, a total of 186 newspaper articles were identified and reviewed at this stage.

Table 2. Summary of data collection at stage two

Database searched	For database search (searched within: title, abstract and/or full text)	Amount
Factiva	'Food industry' and 'supply chain' and 'blockchain'	99
Nexis	'Food industry' and 'supply chain' and 'blockchain'	87

Furthermore, some other databases were searched for academic studies and new stories at the third stage, as seen in Table 3. A total of 35 articles were selected through reading titles, abstracts and also full text in order to select the articles most related to the research questions, including 5 academic articles and 30 news articles. "Wal-Mart" was the keyword in 21 out of 35 articles include.

Table 3. Summary of data collection at stage three

For database search (searched within: title, abstract and/or full text)	Database searched	Amount
'Food industry' and 'supply chain'	ABI/Inform Complete/ProQuest; EBSCO; Web of Science; Google Scholar; IEEE Xplore etc.	35
'Food industry' and 'blockchain'		
'Walmart' and 'blockchain'		
'Walmart' and 'food supply chain'		

With much effort, the researcher successfully retrieved and reviewed a good amount of valuable literatures. These retrieved articles and materials were systematically analyzed and synthesized, and then used as raw materials to find the processes, benefits and challenges of blockchain adoption in Wal-Mart supply chain. Through the existing research of blockchain, suggestions about how to better apply blockchain to the supply chain of Wal-Mart can be proposed in this paper. These suggestions are presented and discussed in Sect. 4.

4 Findings

Through thematic analysis of the secondary data, the results identified a range of interrelated processes, about how blockchain is applied in the supply chain and the benefits and challenges of adoption.

4.1 Reducing Food Safety Risks

The first benefit of blockchain adoption in Wal-Mart's food supply chain is to mitigate food safety issues. For example, China is the most populous country in the world and is considered as a large potential market by the world's largest retailer Wal-Mart. However, food contamination scandals, such as the 2011 pork mislabelling issues and 2014 tainted donkey meat scandals exerted great negative influence on the Wal-Mart brand (Kaye 2016). According to World Health Organisation (WHO 2017), unsafe food contains "harmful bacteria, viruses, parasites or chemical substances" and almost 1 in 10 people fall ill because of contaminated food. However, blockchain is expected to exert positive impact on food traceability in Wal-Mart food supply chain. Traceability 'tracks" and "traces" both directions of the supply chain. With digitalised traceability, food can be tracked from the origin to the store (e.g. Edmund 2018; Nicolaou 2017), which means the life journey of one specific item can be drawn transparently. Moreover, the food can be traced from the shelves to the farm so that in case of an outbreak, Wal-Mart can find sources of foodborne illnesses (Schwarzbaum 2018; Alexandre 2018b) and facilitate food tracing from days to seconds (e.g. Germano 2017; Rosenbush 2018). Therefore, this enhances contamination management and to some extent, this helps Wal-Mart evaluate the health risks (Sayer 2017) at every stage in its operations and save lives at the beginning of an outbreak (Kharif 2016). Moreover, there is no need for Wal-Mart to remove all the same kind of suspected contaminated products from the shelves, the only need is to recall the specific batch of tainted food (Cooper 2017; CQ FD Disclosure 2016). Therefore, the economic impact of food recalls on Wal-Mart can be greatly reduced.

Blockchain technology enhances information sharing in the secured situation through the entire supply chain. The data stored on the public blockchain is accessible to everyone and cannot be tampered with. Therefore, it increases the trust, security and transparency in Wal-Mart's food supply chain (e.g. Loop 2016; Creasey 2017). From the perspective of consumers, they are able to know more accurate tracking details of food from their smart phones, which enhances their confidence (Zhou 2017). As for organisations, Yiannas, who is Wal-Mart's food safety chief, claims that although paper records have the risk of being changed, they still dominate in food industry (MH & L 2017). However, through digitization of documents and recording the data of parties who input it on the blockchain, the demand for manual data management declines. In light of this, human errors can be limited and the chance of corruption can be reduced because no one can change the data history (Miranda 2018) so that food fraud is expected to be prevented (Creasey 2017; MH & L 2017; Springer 2017, Nash 2018b). Furthermore, blockchain technology is also a powerful tool for regulators to help Wal-Mart examine its food supply chain and the responsibilities of all the parties clearer according to the immutable records (Sayer 2017; iCrowdNewswire 2017).

4.2   Enhancing Efficiency in the Supply Chain

Blockchain technology can increase Wal-Mart's food supply chain efficiencies in either food flow, information flow or financial flow. Blockchain realises real-time accessibility so that Wal-Mart can capture real-time data in order to supervise the processes of food from growing, producing, processing and selling (BMI research 2018a; Lucas 2018). Therefore, the source and quality of food can be verified at any point (Schwarzbaum 2018). For instance, when any food is expired or mishandled, Wal-Mart can identify it before it reaches consumers, whether it is still in logistics or already on the shelves (Bluegrace Logistics 2018; Miranda 2018). Wal-Mart 2018 Global Responsibility Report (Wal-Mart 2018) stated their goal of reducing and even eliminating food waste in their operations and planning to achieve "Zero Waste" in Canada, Japan, the UK and the US by 2025. Currently, food waste still occurs at all levels from distribution centres to logistics process and then to the store (Wal-Mart 2018). Blockchain technology will reduce food spoilage problem in Wal-Mart by planning the best delivery routine and lessening delivery time for perishable food, thus reducing food waste and cost (e.g. Germano 2017; Shaffer 2017; EJ Insight 2018; Abrar 2018). Finally, IBM Global Finance provides Wal-Mart with blockchain and smart contracts solutions to help manage the inventory and price dynamically (Limsamarnphun 2018).

4.3   Accelerating Collaboration

Wal-Mart's food supply chain crosses multiple national borders, and includes hundreds of thousands of suppliers globally. However, blockchain technology is expected to handle the complex relationships in the supply chain through the shared ledger (Mearian 2018; Business Wire 2017a; Nash 2018b). Furthermore, considering food system as a holistic system for every single person in the world, Wal-Mart and IBM attempt to solve food safety problems under collaborative situation rather than competition through implementing the blockchain-based trials (SEC Wire 2018; IBM 2017; Armonk 2017). For example, IBM Food Trust solutions are trying to collaborate and seamlessly connect Wal-Mart with other participants, which this shows the stakeholders' positive attitude towards working together and achieves a community of interests. (IBM 2018). Therefore, adopting blockchain technology is an ideal way for Wal-Mart to gain strategic alliance cooperative effects by deepening cooperation in the food industry.

4.4   Reducing Carbon Footprint

In terms of the above discussions, food waste is a waste of resources; moreover, Scholz et al. (2015) argued that greenhouse gases are produced because of waste as well. "According to FAO (2013), the global carbon footprint of annual food wastage is 3.3 Gt CO2 equivalents (CO2e)" (Schola et al. 2015, p. 56; DiGregorio 2018). Thus, it is likely for Wal-Mart to meet its sustainable goal of reducing carbon dioxide in its global supply chain through adopting blockchain as reported in its 2018 Global Responsibility report (Krupp 2018; Loop 2016).

4.5   Potential Benefits of Blockchain Adoption in Food Supply Chain

Besides the visible benefits of ensuring food safety, improving efficiency in supply chain and accelerating collaboration that have already been discussed, more benefits may result from blockchain adoption.

Choosing More Suitable Partners. Blockchain technology helps in expanding business because when all the parties put their information on the chain, they are free to choose which partner to do business with (Mathew 2018). Therefore, Wal-Mart may no longer need to invest as much money in investigating the actual situation of food sources. Moreover, because all the trading history will be stored on the chain, (Tieman and Darun 2017) suggested that the supply chain participants can be rated in terms of their performance. Learning from this, Wal-Mart can choose the suppliers that meet its requirements.

Benefiting Farmers. In the food industry, especially agri-food, there are many companies playing the role of intermediaries that link the transactions b time they also charge a huge intermediary fee. According to a pilot project for IFPRI and Asian Development Bank pilot in Uttarakhand (2009) cited in United News of India (2018), if farmers sell products directly to organised retailers, 25%–35% of transaction costs can be saved. Moreover, United News of India (2018) reported that the presence of multiple intermediaries is one of the reasons that Indian farmer's income is 30% lower than the consumer price. So considering the automatic action of smart contracts and immutable records on the chain, there is no need for banks and agencies to provide a verified service, which means that retailers can implement direct procurement from farmers to reduce transaction costs and increase both farmers and retailers profits (e.g. Charlebois 2017; Loop 2016). Furthermore, farmers are often the group of people who are struggling in price coercion and retroactive payments but blockchain provides a legitimate option for them to sell products under a reasonable price and receive payments in time (Charlebois 2017).

Facilitating Direct-to-Consumer Sales. Since retailers may be able to buy food directly from farmers, consumers may also enjoy direct shopping experience with manufacturers through bypassing retailers (Creasey 2017). This will help consumers get lower prices but may exert negative impact on retailers' sales.

5   Discussions

Blockchain adoption in the food supply chain seems to be in a substitution stage (Iansiti and Lakhani 2017) because the technological processes are based on existing technology such as RFID and sensors but face high barriers in coordination. Since Wal-Mart has used blockchain technology in its food supply chain, it is reasonable to suppose that Wal-Mart is taking the first-move strategy based on the strategic framework proposed by Shi and Chan (2014). Wal-Mart could consolidate its dominant position in the food supply chain through technology adoption. However, high investment on blockchain adoption is a big obstacle the organization may face. Moreover, there are only substantial benefits when all parties participate in the supply chain (Shi and Chan 2014). Therefore, collaboration is a solution for the stakeholders to achieve win-win situation in the foreseeable future. However, Günter et al. (2006) suggested that coordination and collaborative planning in supply networks are the main challenges in dealing with partnership in supply chain management. Furthermore, Holma and Salo (2014) believed that collaboration is the highest level of integration, which requires trust among partners at a very high level. Therefore, considering that complete trust is still hard to realize at the current status, in order to avoid the dilemma that the technology is only accepted by focal company, Wal-Mart may have to "force" its unwilling supply chain partners to accept and use blockchain technology. However, a truly wide adoption of Wal-Mart's blockchain solution would happen when all participants in the ecosystem have a strong value proposition to join (Kamath 2018). Therefore, Wal-Mart should conduct broader trails in the food supply chain to determine the actual contribution of the blockchain, and educate stakeholders on the knowledge of blockchain technology and inform them of the benefits they can earn.

6 Conclusions

In conclusion, this paper investigates the processes of blockchain adoption in food supply chains, in the case of Wal-Mart. Furthermore, the challenges and benefits of adoption are identified. Case study and thematic analysis are used as the research methods and data analysis tools. From the analysis of findings, although Wal-Mart has initiated blockchain adoption, further improvement is required to optimize the supply chain management. The benefits of blockchain adoption in the supply chain are obvious such as reducing food safety risks, enhancing supply chain efficiency, accelerating collaboration and reducing carbon footprint. The study has possible limitations. Only Wal-Mart is selected as the case for investigation and secondary data was collected for analysing technology adoption in food supply chains. More cases and various data collection tools may be chosen for a further study on the adoption of blockchain in food supply chain in future research. Future research can conduct through interviewing the supply chain managers in Walmart and the experts in the blockchain industry to explore more factors that may influence blockchain adoption and its potential consequences.

Acknowledgement. This work was supported by Natural Science Foundation of China (NSFC No. 71701091) and the Chinese Ministry of Education Project of Humanities and Social Science (No. 17YJC870020).

References

Abrar, P.: India labs are key to IBM's AI efforts'. The Hindu, 30 April 2018. https://www.thehindu.com/business/Industry/india-labs-are-key-to-ibms-ai-efforts/article23721214.ece

Alexandre, A.: Walmart Awarded Patent for Blockchain-Based Medical Records System (2018a). https://cointelegraph.com/news/walmart-awarded-patent-for-blockchain-based-medical-records-system

Armonk: Global food supply chain leaders in blockchain collaboration with IBM. Food & Beverage News, 26 August 2017. http://www.fnbnews.com/Top-News/global-food-supply-chain-leaders-in-blockchain-collaboration-with-ibm-41038

Business Wire: Press Release: Walmart, JD.com, IBM and Tsinghua University Launch a Blockchain Food Safety in China, 14 December 2017a http://www.businesswire.com/news/home/20171213006244/en/

Aitken, R.: IBM & Walmart launching blockchain food safety alliance in China with Fortune 500's JD.com. Forbes, 14 December 2017. https://www.forbes.com/sites/rogeraitken/2017/12/14/ibm-walmart-launching-blockchain-food-safety-alliance-in-china-with-fortune-500s-jd-com/#4fb843f77d9c

Balocco, R.: RFID adoption in the FMCG supply chain: an interpretative framework. Supply Chain Manag.: Int. J. **16**(5), 299–315 (2011)

Boffey, D., Connolly, K.: Egg contamination scandal widens as 15 EU states, Switzerland and Hong Kong affected', The Guardian (2017). https://www.theguardian.com/world/2017/aug/11/tainted-eggs-found-in-hong-kong-switzerland-and-15-eu-countries

Bosona, T., Gebresenbet, G.: Food traceability as an integral part of logistics management in food and agricultural supply chain. Food Control **33**(1), 32–48 (2013)

Busby, M.: Blockchain is this year's buzzword-but can it outlive the hype?. The Guadian (2018). https://www.theguardian.com/technology/2018/jan/30/blockchain-buzzword-hype-open-source-ledger-bitcoin

Castillo, M.D.: Walmart blockchain pilot aims to make China's pork market safer (2016). https://www.coindesk.com/walmart-blockchain-pilot-china-pork-market/

Cai, Y., Li, X., Wang, R., Yang, Q., Li, P., Hu, H.: Quality traceability system of traditional Chinese medicine based on two dimensional barcode using mobile intelligent technology. PLoS ONE **11**(10), e0165263 (2016)

Charlebois, S.: How blockchain technology could transform the food industry. The conversation, 20 December (2017). http://theconversation.com/how-blockchain-technology-could-transform-the-food-industry-89348

Cooper, B.: Blockchain innovation: what's on the horizon?. Blockchain Tech-News, 26 June 2017. https://www.blockchaintechnews.com/articles/blockchain-innovation-whats-on-the-horizon/

Costa, C., Antonucci, F., Pallottino, F., Aguzzi, J., Sarriá, D., Menesatti, P.: A review on agri-food supply chain traceability by means of RFID technology. Food Bioprocess Technol. **6**(2), 353–366 (2013)

Cowton, C.: The use of secondary data in business ethics research. J. Bus. Ethics **17**(4), 423–434 (1998)

Edmund, M.: On the fast track? Qual. Prog. **51**(2), 10–12 (2018)

Epelbaum, B., Moises, F., Martinez, M.G.: The technological evolution of food traceability systems and their impact on firm sustainable performance: a RBV approach. Int. J. Prod. Econ. **150**, 215–224 (2014)

Hobbs, J.E., Bailey, D., Dickinson, D.L., Haghiri, M.: Traceability in the Canadian red meat sector: do consumers care? Can. J. Agric. Econ. **53**(1), 47–65 (2005)

Holma, H., Salo, J.: Improving management of supply chains by information technology. In: Water, G., Rinsler, S. (eds.) Global Logistics: New Directions in Supply Chain Management, pp. 227–243. Kogan Page Limited, London (2014)

Iansiti, M., Lakhani, K.R.: The truth about blockchain: it will take years to transform business, but the journey begins now. Harv. Bus. Rev. **95**(1), 118–127 (2017)

Kamath, R.: Food traceability on blockchain: Walmart's pork and mango pilots with IBM. J. Br. Blockchain Assoc. **1**(1), 1–12 (2018)

Kaye, L.: Responding to food safety concerns, Walmart invests $25 million in China (2016). https://www.triplepundit.com/2016/10/responding-food-safety-concerns-walmart-invests-25-million-china/

Kersten, W., Seiter, M., See, B.V., Hackius, N., Maurer, T.: Trends and Strategies in Logistics and Supply Chain Management – Digital Transformation Opportunities. DVV Media Group, Hamburg (2017)

Kharif, O.: Wal-Mart Tackles Food Safety with Trial of Blockchain. The Detroit News, 20 November (2016). https://www.detroitnews.com/story/business/2016/11/19/wal-mart-tackles-food-safety-trial-blockchain/94144568/

Krupp, F.: How technology is driving a fourth wave of environmentalism. Pakistan and Gulf Economist, p. 37, 3 June 2018

Levitt, T.: Three years on from the horsemeat scandal: 3 lessons we have learned. The Guardian (2016). https://www.theguardian.com/sustainable-business/2016/jan/07/horsemeat-scandal-food-safety-uk-criminal-networks-supermarkets

Limsamarnphun, N.: Blockchain technology seen driving advances in mobile commerce. The Nation, 10 March 2018. http://www.nationmultimedia.com/detail/Economy/30340615

Loop, P.: Blockchain: the next evolution of supply chains. Material Handling & Logistics, 06 December 2016. https://www.mhlnews.com/global-supply-chain/blockchain-next-evolution-supply-chains

Lucas, L.: From farm to plate, blockchain dishes up simple food tracking. 6 June, Financial Times, 6 June 2018. https://www.ft.com/content/225d32bc-4dfa-11e8-97e4-13afc22d86d4

Mathew, S.: Blockchain is a game changer in supply chain. Blockchain Technews, 16 July 2018. https://www.blockchaintechnews.com/blogs/blockchain-is-a-game-changer-in-supply-chain/

Mearian, L.: Delaware to test blockchain-based business filing system. Computerworld Australia, 17 July 2018. https://www.computerworld.com/article/3289484/blockchain/delaware-to-test-blockchain-based-business-filing-system.html

Menon, S.: Supply Chain: Applications of Blockchain Platform in Agri-Food Supply Chains. Bio Voice, 23 May 2018. https://www.biovoicenews.com/applications-blockchain-platform-agri-food-supply-chain/

Miranda, C.: McCombs to showcase how IT program will make business systems more efficient. U-Wire, 1 February 2018

Nicolaou, A.: Walmart uses store staff to deliver web orders. Financial Times, p. 13, 2 June 2017

Olsen, P., Broit, M.: How to define traceability. Trends Food Sci. Technol. **29**(2), 142–150 (2013)

Patti, A.L., Narsing, A.: Lean and RFID: friends or foes. J. Bus. Econ. Res. **6**(2), 83–90 (2008)

Sarpong, S.: Traceability and supply chain complexity: confronting the issues and concerns. Eur. Bus. Rev. **26**(3), 271–284 (2014)

Sayer, P.: IBM wants to make blockchain good enough to eat. ARN (Australian Reseller News), 23 August 2017. https://www.pcworld.idg.com.au/article/626323/ibm-wants-make-blockchain-good-enough-eat/

Schwarzbaum, E.: 4 Tech Companies Seeing High Demand For Blockchain Services. Benzinga.com, 18 May 2018. https://www.benzinga.com/analyst-ratings/analyst-color/18/05/11741312/4-tech-companies-seeing-high-demand-for-blockchain-serv

Shi, X., Chan, S.: Information systems and information technologies for supply chain management'. In: Water, G., Rinsler, S. (eds.) Global Logistics: New Directions in Supply Chain Management, pp. 210–226. Kogan Page Limited, London (2014)

Tieman, M., Darun, M.R.: Leveraging blockchain technology for halal supply chains. Islam Civ. Renewal **8**(4), 547–550 (2017)

Williams, S.N.: The incursion of Big Food in middle-income countries: a qualitative documentary case study analysis of the soft drinks industry in China and India. Crit. Public Health **25**(4), 455–473 (2015)

Zhou, M.: Consulate Future of food. Global Times, 1 June 2017

Author Index

Printed in the United States
By Bookmasters

Printed in the United States
By Bookmasters